THE MEANINGS OF J. ROBERT OPPENHEIMER

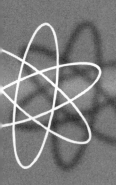

THE NEW AMERICAN CANON

The Iowa Series in Contemporary
Literature and Culture

Samuel Cohen, series editor

THE MEANINGS OF
J. ROBERT OPPENHEIMER

LINDSEY MICHAEL BANCO

UNIVERSITY OF IOWA PRESS, IOWA CITY

University of Iowa Press, Iowa City 52242

www.uiowapress.org

Printed in the United States of America

Text design by Alligator Tree Graphics

The University of Iowa Press is a member of Green Press Initiative and is committed to preserving natural resources.

Printed on acid-free paper

Library of Congress Cataloging-in-Publication Data

Names: Banco, Lindsey Michael, author.
Title: The meanings of J. Robert Oppenheimer / Lindsey Michael Banco.
Other titles: New American canon.
Description: Iowa City : University of Iowa Press, [2016] | ?2016 | Series: The new American canon | Includes bibliographical references and index.
Identifiers: LCCN 2015033641 | ISBN 978-1-60938-419-7 (pbk) | ISBN 1-60938-419-9 (pbk) | ISBN 978-1-60938-420-3 (ebk) | ISBN 1-60938-420-2 (ebk)
Subjects: LCSH: Oppenheimer, J. Robert, 1904–1967. | Physicists—United States—20th century—Biography. | Atomic bomb—United States—History. | Manhattan Project (U.S.)
Classification: LCC QC16.O62 B36 2016 | DDC 530.092—dc23
LC record available at http://lccn.loc.gov/2015033641

CONTENTS

For Sadie

ACKNOWLEDGMENTS

I have been fortunate to have many forms of help in writing this book: scholarly, financial, technical, personal, and certainly others that I will only be aware of in retrospect. I offer my thanks to an industrious team of research assistants who have helped me with a variety of tasks over the past several years: Shakti Brazier-Tompkins, Joel Fonstad, Michael Horacki, Graham Jensen, Jade McDougall, and Corie Wiebe. Several anonymous reviewers, including through the University of Iowa Press and the journals *Biography* and the *Canadian Review of American Studies*, have added considerably to this project. The enormously helpful organizers and participants at several meetings of the Canadian Association for American Studies—particularly Christine Bold, Luke Bresky, Peter Brown, Christopher Elias, Michael Epp, Jennifer Harris, Jason Haslam, Nat Hurley, Christopher Lockett, Michael O'Driscoll, Art Redding, Mark Simpson, Anthony Stewart, Bryce Traister, Percy Walton, Brianna Wells, and Julia M. Wright—have worked for many years to create a welcoming scholarly association and have generously shared their expertise and expressed support for this project. I have also benefited from discussing Oppenheimer and Cold War America with Frank Fucile, Charlotte Melin, Carter Soles, Bill Toth, and Molly Wallace. Elisabeth Chretien, Sam Cohen, and Susan Hill Newton at the University of Iowa Press deserve special thanks for their hard and incredibly patient work in bringing this book to print. While errors and infelicities of course remain my own, I am also very thankful to Carolyn Brown for copyediting this manuscript and for sharing some intriguing personal stories about Edward Teller.

I also wish to thank the staff at a number of institutions: the Bradbury Science Museum (particularly Omar Juveland), the Los Alamos Historical Society, and the Los Alamos Public Library in Los Alamos, New Mexico; the National Museum of Nuclear Science and History in Albuquerque, New Mexico (particularly Sandra Fye and David Hoover); and the National Atomic Testing Museum in Las Vegas, Nevada. I am also grateful to La Cumbre Brewing Company in Albuquerque and the Pajarito Brewpub and Grill in Los Alamos for their refreshing beverages, stimulating work-spaces, and for making a stranger feel at home. At my own institution, the University of Saskatchewan, I thank the Interdisciplinary Centre for Culture and Creativity (especially Sabrina Kehoe) for generous monetary and professional support, the Interlibrary Loans office for their efficiency, archivist Patrick Hayes for finding a very old film projector and giving me a 1940s-era immersion in cinematic mediation, the graduate students in my 2015 seminar on atomic America (especially Aaron Thacker) for their thoughtful engagement with this subject, and my department colleagues for showing interest in this project and encouraging my work. Special thanks to two department heads, Doug Thorpe and Lisa Vargo, for their nonstop support and dedicated efforts in providing research time under challenging financial conditions.

Finally, I owe more than I can possibly say to my family. Thanks first and foremost to Sara Mueller, who has supported me and this project with unfathomable patience. Thanks also to Kelly Banco, for helping me locate some hard-to-find material and for helping me understand some challenging physics principles; to my parents, Marcella and Gordon; and to Sadie, to whom this book is dedicated and who arrived about halfway through its completion and changed everything.

INTRODUCTION

Following the detonation of the world's first atomic bomb in New Mexico and the use of the weapon on Hiroshima and Nagasaki in 1945, J. Robert Oppenheimer, the scientific director of the Manhattan Project and the oft-proclaimed father of the atomic bomb, became an American hero. As the nature and scale of the destruction in Japan became clear, however, Oppenheimer's heroic questing after a particular kind of knowledge—and with it the bright fame of midcentury theoretical physics, of science more generally, and of a new phase in technoculture—became tinged with regret, guilt, fear, acrimony, and death. This was not the first time such a narrative came to be attached to a scientist, but among the unique characteristics of Hiroshima and Nagasaki, those killed by this technology left shadows behind on the walls of buildings and along the ground. These dark imprints, created by the intense light and heat of the bomb that killed them and vaporized their bodies, are the indelibly inscribed presence of their absence. Their shadows, immaterial yet permanent, both commemorate the vaporized victims of the bomb and anticipate the invisible, yet still alive, future victims (see Gusterson 198). Encapsulating presence and absence, past and future, remembering and forgetting, shattered and preserved, dispersed and converged, these shadows represent the complex legacy of the technology firmly attached to Oppenheimer's name. These binary oppositions have also become part of how the controversial man himself is represented. The bomb casts a long shadow, but its entanglement with Oppenheimer means he himself becomes a shadowy figure in the landscape of nuclear culture. His shadowiness is not, however, simply villainy. Hero and "destroyer of worlds,"[1] there and not there, bringer of both the light and the dark, he becomes the paradoxical, symbolic creator of the bomb in the historical and cultural imagination. *The Meanings of J. Robert Oppenheimer* sets out to examine those representations and to explore how they affect our knowledge of a technology possessed by what one scholar has called "the spectre of omnicide" (Gerster, "Hiroshima No More" 64).

Rather than providing another biography of Oppenheimer or another history of the Manhattan Project, the book explores the workings of Oppenheimer as a "principal metaphor"[2] in a wide range of cultural productions that depict the ambivalences and paradoxes of the nuclear age. It will ask why he has been used in these ways and what the effects of doing so have been. It will analyze him as a force anchoring, since midcentury, knowledge of nuclear culture in specific places and to specific sets of tropes and representational strategies. It will regard him as a crucial and defining facet of nuclear culture, as an index to understanding and transmitting the meaning of nuclear culture, as a lens formed in (and necessarily flawed by) World War II and through which we examine nuclear culture. It will position him as a central representational figure—a rhetorical, visual, and symbolic tool—in understanding atomic science and in the proliferation of a highly ambivalent nuclear culture. It will exhibit a desire to unify what C. P. Snow famously called "the two cultures," referring to the supposed antipathy between the sciences and the humanities, by tracing links between science and the forms of representation in which it appears. To do so, it will examine a series of different forms and genres, from those appearing immediately after Oppenheimer's rise to fame to contemporary examples, and analyze how they depict him. This analysis will reveal how such cultural productions understand the process of acquiring certain kinds of scientific knowledge, how such knowledge both reflects and produces the history of the twentieth century, and how contemporary culture wrestles with the potentially apocalyptic power such knowledge carries in the nuclear age.

Nuclear Knowledge

Developed as a weapon, the atomic bomb reaches far beyond combat and well into the cultural consciousness. As the technology credited with ending World War II and beginning the Cold War, it has helped define the second half of the twentieth century. The culmination of decades of Enlightenment thinking (that in its utopian formulations sought to banish violence altogether from human society), the bomb reveals that science has been in fact a chief instrument of violence. A device that inspired in the postwar period the possibility of boundless intervention into the natural world and of previously unthinkable human progress, the bomb also stands for limitless destruction (see Poole 4). It reorganized a great deal of modern society and inspired many hyperbolic ways of talking about such reorganization in a number of different disciplines.[3] Although obviously removed from the physical destruction in Japan, U.S. society was deeply affected by the existence of the weapon, by the military's ability and willingness to use it, and by the future ramifications—calculated, predicted, imagined—that the weapon might have. The cascade of events that followed 1945—the development of the even more powerful hydrogen bomb, an extensive aboveground testing program, and a Cold War buildup of nuclear weapons that would define the decades to come—constituted a mass of political and cultural fallout from Oppenheimer's bomb. Such fallout was, according to many historians of the era (e.g., Boyer 141), key to understanding what many now call postindustrial society.

After the first atomic bomb, code-named "Little Boy," devastated Hiroshima on August 6, 1945, the news of the secret development and use of an unprecedented weapon constituted not only a cultural but a conceptual bombshell for the American public. Scientific, military, and cultural forces began competing among themselves for knowledge of the bomb and to negotiate its ambivalent meanings. Part of the significance of the Manhattan Project to twentieth-century American society lies in the often harrowing novelty it generated. Writer E. B. White's contemporaneous response to the bomb, for instance, calls attention to no less than "the disturbing vibrations of complete human readjustment" (qtd. in Boyer 133). More recently, Rey Chow describes the dropping of the atomic bomb as "a fundamental change in the organization, production, and circulation of knowledge" (33). Such readjustments would encompass realms as diverse as science and technology, the military, art and literature, and the ethical frameworks of how nations engage with one another. Historian Jon Hunner's summary of this novelty envisions a weapon that transformed everyday experience itself: "The success of the scientists at Los Alamos ushered in a new age. They created new weapons, new sources of electricity, new diagnostic tools for medicine, new treatments for cancer, new machines to compute and process information, new relationships between science and government, and new fears about living in the twentieth century" (*J. Robert Oppenheimer* 9).

Such novelty and transformative powers produced massive epistemological shifts in postwar American culture, changes in how knowledge itself was acquired, perceived, and constructed.[4] Such changes in twentieth-century knowledge stem in significant part from the secrecy under which the bomb was developed. That a massive project like the race for the atomic bomb could be kept from political figures as senior as Vice President Harry Truman and situated in "unofficial" physical spaces indicates the power of secrecy to alter U.S. political and geographical landscapes, and it generated an immediate increase in secrecy in American political culture. As a covert laboratory on a New Mexico mesa, Los Alamos anticipated some of the ways in which secret science obscures the American landscape, even as it characterizes its origins as the quest for unprecedented knowledge and the illumination of nature. Today, secret CIA prisons, classified military bases, and other covert places and activities can be traced back to the atomic bomb. Its development has altered not only the geography of the United States but also the democratic principles on which the nation was founded and is apparently governed, as well as the very means by which it can be known.[5] And as Manhattan Project sites are poised, with the signing of the National Defense Authorization Act of 2015, to become national parks, their origins in secrecy enter into intriguing conversation with the kinds of knowledge produced by public spaces. In a larger sense, the Manhattan Project accelerates a moment of shifting opinion about authoritative bureaucracy, a movement toward distrust, suspicion, and paranoia that, in the age of Internet-spread conspiracy theory, has reached epidemic proportions.[6] Science itself, as another mode of knowing, underwent significant postwar changes in how it was practiced and funded. The Manhattan Project contributed to a new way of doing science that has come to be called Big Science, the kind of work done through huge (often multinational) institutions, costing vast sums of money, and producing very different kinds of knowledge than science of previous generations.[7] The atomic bomb forged new relationships between science and the state, particularly in the question of national security (Hughes 9). In the process, it redefined how scientists worked together, worked with the government, and sometimes worked with, but just as often against, public opinion. Secret research came to trump scientific knowledge as a public good. Its political entanglements complicated science's purported objectivity and neutrality.[8] And at the center of these changes in ways of knowing stands J. Robert Oppenheimer.

THE OPPENHEIMER PARADOXES

The "responsibility" for these historical and intellectual changes and for the cultural paradoxes introduced by the bomb (and indeed for the bomb itself) is difficult to pin down. Oppenheimer did not *invent* the technology, nor did he discover its scientific principles (the idea for the nuclear chain reaction is usually attributed to Hungarian physicist Leo Szilard). And although he was the scientific director of the Manhattan Project, the project's leadership can obviously be traced further up the administrative chain (to General Leslie Groves, the military director of the Manhattan Project; to James B. Conant, president of Harvard University and chairman of the National Defense Research Committee, which oversaw the Manhattan Project; to Vannevar Bush, head of the U.S. Office of Scientific Research and Development during the war; and, ultimately, to President Franklin D. Roosevelt). Nevertheless, Oppenheimer is often located at the center of the Manhattan Project and its consequences. Fairly or not, he functions as a touchstone, a multifaceted sign that invokes, inflects, and contests nuclear culture. For a number of provocative and often mysterious reasons, he has come to represent many of the shifting and diverse meanings of the nuclear, which is why this project focuses on him as a means of understanding that culture.

As the many biographies maintain, the man himself was extraordinarily complex. He was an absentminded professor in some accounts, but in others (and sometimes in the same ones), a charming, charismatic sophisticate. A dedicated family man in some impressions, he also maintained an adulterous relationship with a former member of the American Communist Party. A cultured, cosmopolitan reader of John Donne and Hindu theology, he was also a central figure in the creation of a new technology so massively destructive it threatened the very historical order that gave his cosmopolitanism form (see Beck 121). The leader of the project that developed the bomb, he also lobbied loudly and repeatedly *against* the dissemination of nuclear weaponry. In what Eric Schlosser calls "the days of hand-made nuclear weapons" (100)—before the industrialization of nuclear weapons, before the Atomic Energy Commission was formed to regulate the technology, before the Pantex Plant would consume 16,000 acres in Texas and begin assembling a nuclear stockpile, before Strategic Air Command was established to control the military use of these weapons—Oppenheimer was an artisanal bomb-maker. He had lasting influences on the production of physics knowledge at places such as the California Institute of Technology, the University of California at Berkeley, and the Los Alamos National Laboratory, influences Hunner characterizes as partly responsible for the westward tilt in the United States of money and scientific prestige (*J. Robert Oppenheimer* 229). With a finger on the pulse of twentieth-century science, he began his career working on quantum mechanics and the astrophysics phenomenon that would eventually be known as black holes, two new, deeply strange and important ideas for understanding the universe in the twentieth century. Born in 1904, just after the dawning of the twentieth century, he would become a key figure in the widespread changes that would soon be characteristic of that century. He appeared on the cover of *Time* in 1948, at the century's midpoint, and his death in 1967 came during a remarkably tumultuous decade of cultural change. In between, he was brought before an Atomic Energy Commission hearing, stripped of his security clearance, and denied access to a body of knowledge about atomic weapons he himself was instrumental in creating. He was construed as a threat to American power after directing a massive scientific enterprise designed to generate and secure that power. The leader of a cadre or "priesthood" of scientific experts, he presided over the paradoxical "magic" of high technology at the same time that he assumed Satanic dimensions as a technocratic warlord. He indelibly marked and was marked by Los Alamos, a place where, for some, myth and modernity are conjoined.[9] His legacy, enigmatic yet influential, can be found in both the culture of nonproliferation and in a world in which many nations still aim nuclear weapons at one another while other nations persist in acquiring them. Oppenheimer continues to play a conflicted role in postwar and Cold War history and culture, in decades of U.S. foreign relations, and in emerging discourses concerning terrorism, environmentalism, and other global concerns.

Crucial to his impact, then, is that Oppenheimer is a cultural cipher with many, often contradictory, meanings. He figures prominently in one of the most important U.S. military "triumphs" and helped usher in the nuclear age, yet his life, persona, and presence—whether rendered in textual, visual, or material forms—often *subvert* his own centrality when they depict his absence or envision him as embedded within things much larger than himself. The potency of his personal mythology in his own time made him a bona fide celebrity after the war. His celebrity has continued in the nearly seven decades that followed despite his persistent marginalization as a result of a number of factors, including his Jewishness, his Communist affiliations, his identity as a scientist (especially as a theoretical physicist), and his intellectualism, which have excluded him to a certain degree from the American mainstream. He is frequently conceived of in supernatural or transcendent terms, yet he presides over the rise of a technocratic society. He is "both noble and naïve, luminous and tragic" (Taylor, "Politics of the Nuclear Text" 442). Like the wave-particle duality at the center of quantum mechanics that says elementary particles are also comprehensible as waves, he is often depicted as a series of dualities: there and not there, godlike and machinelike, humanistic and coldly positivist.[10] His ambiguity serves to cast in multiple and often conflicting lights the end of World War II, postwar and later twentieth-century thinking about nuclear weapons, and the very processes and results of producing scientific knowledge about the physical world.

His contradictory nature is, thus, closely connected to the contradictions of nuclear culture.[11] Nuclear historian Spencer Weart calls the bomb "the atomic genie that could be either menace or servant" (88), a technology of enormous possibility for revolutionizing society as well of enormous possibility for destroying it. The bomb is the ultimate example of the twentieth century's Enlightenment-inspired positing, a scientific "putting forth" that nevertheless evokes the possibility of what political scientist William Chaloupka terms "profound, cultural negation" (7). In political form, the bomb operates according to the paradoxical logic of deterrence wherein nuclear weapons are produced and stockpiled in order to prevent their use. Collectively, nuclear images "gain their potency from a creative tension" that Weart claims is characteristic of "great images": "the endless and impossible effort of reconciling opposites" (250). Such efforts produce various results, including fear and anxiety, patriotic victory culture that celebrates the geopolitical power of the United States, and surreal or insidious reminders of the destructive potential of nuclear weapons. Understanding the ambiguity of Oppenheimer is thus an attempt to understand the paradoxes of nuclearism. His equivocal meanings, as they have been represented in a number of media forms and genres and particularly as they manifest in narratives of seeking knowledge through nuclear technology, can reveal a great deal about how his quest for knowledge is connected to the world-changing—and potentially world-destroying—technology of nuclear weapons. With this book, I hope to contribute to the diverse body of nuclear scholarship a wide-ranging critical assessment of how Oppenheimer has been represented and how his multiple meanings become a way of understanding a technology so fraught with paradox.

REPRESENTING OPPENHEIMER

A number of book-length discussions of nuclear culture in general, many of which I cite in this study, have provided valuable overviews and syntheses of the field.[12] My approach to Oppenheimer is influenced by cultural studies theory and practices and is inspired by interdisciplinary work on nuclear culture, including psychological approaches and political analysis.[13]

The first part of the book builds on nuclear criticism oriented around language and rhetoric as representational tools and on a body of work on specifically literary representations of nuclear culture.[14] The second part, focused on visual and material representations of Oppenheimer, is informed by analyses of nuclear culture in the media, photography and visual culture, film, and museums.[15] Critical work specifically on Oppenheimer (that is, other than biographical or historical treatments) exists as well, although this body of scholarship is relatively small.[16] As important a public symbol for the bomb and for science in general as Oppenheimer has become, this body of scholarship only rarely engages with the question of *how* he has been represented. Communications scholar Bryan C. Taylor's work, for instance, helpful as it is in characterizing Oppenheimer as a sign within complex systems of signification, only examines in depth one relatively limited facet of his persona: his identity as a letter writer. Religious scholar Ira Chernus mentions him only once in a book whose title seems to promise a certain prominence for him: *Dr. Strangegod: On the Symbolic Meaning of Nuclear Weapons*. Physicist Michael Day's work is, as he himself concedes, "more historical, focusing on such issues as [Oppenheimer's] development, motivation, reception, and influence" ("Nature of Science" 74) rather than on the representational strategies through which he has come to be known. Historian David K. Hecht's work perhaps comes closest to the approach I take in this book of critically exploring representational strategies. His recent book, *Science and Storytelling: Rewriting Oppenheimer in the Nuclear Age*, in addition to contributing to a robustly renewed interest in the physicist, traces important patterns in how stories about Oppenheimer's life and work are told. Hecht's focus on historiographic representation makes a considerable contribution to Cold War history, but the variety of forms of representation I will explore extends the discussion of Oppenheimer representation across several disciplines.[17] The range of forms—biographies, fiction, histories, comics, photography, film, television, museums, and others—is unique in its breadth and allows for an accumulation of analysis not available in a work of conventional literary criticism or history. This assemblage will reveal how the quest for nuclear knowledge, a quest informed by representations of Robert Oppenheimer, has become a highly contradictory platform for the multiple voices and mediating technologies competing to be heard in an age of technoscience, environmental and geopolitical precariousness, and evolving notions of community.

There are, of course, risks in producing a study of a single figure. Important as he was to the Manhattan Project, he was by no means its sole actor. In fact, the endeavor embodied multiple institutional forces from the outset: political, military, academic, and scientific structures, committees, and communities functioning collectively. Administrators came from many walks of American public life, and the organizational configurations they produced are more complicated than narratives of individual scientific heroism or villainy would allow. The scientists performed an enormously varied range of work and came to the project from many disciplines and many countries. The Manhattan Project—with roots in New York and Chicago, with imported as well as domestic scientific labor, with raw materials from Canada and the Belgian Congo, with production plants in Washington and Tennessee, and with its broad geopolitical consequences—was a national and transnational endeavor that affected nothing less than the entire world. Focusing on one man risks losing sight of all that.

At the same time, Oppenheimer is a force to be reckoned with. Several dozen biographies have been written—a remarkable number for a twentieth-century scientist—and even the more broadly contextualized historical accounts usually focus intensely on him. Phrases such as "brilliant and eccentric" (Taylor, "*Reminiscences*" 400) or "brilliant yet tormented" (Taylor, "Register" 269) signal qualities that apparently appeal, especially in those juxtapositions, to broad public interest. From children's books to documentary and fictional movies and television programs, he is, for better or for worse, a central organizing principle in thinking about atomic bombs and postwar nuclear culture. His centrality and the representational methods used to make him central deserve critical examination because they are often responsible for encouraging us to think about science in terms of lone actors and scientists in terms of disembodied intellects. I try to ensure that this book does not simply reproduce Great Men of Science adulation, in part by keeping in mind Peter C. Reynolds's admonition that "when all is said and done, [Oppenheimer's] claim to fame is a quantum leap in the technology of violence" (180). Instead, examining critically the strategies that generate his centrality while avoiding simple reiterations of that centrality or one-sided celebrations or vilifications of his legacy is crucial to understanding how lone actor narratives and narratives about the production of knowledge structure the understanding of history, science, and technology—and how they obscure other narratives.

My approach to tackling the bomb's resonances is to focus on a series of conceptual oscillations, arguing that such oscillations are both integral to understanding the moral, political, and cultural status of the bomb and reflective of the constant historical oscillations between support for and apprehension about nuclear weapons, between a spirited activism and a curious apathy concerning these devices. These oscillations—between destruction and creation, life and death, illumination and obliteration, the concrete and the ephemeral, science and theology—embed themselves throughout nuclear culture and in nearly every manifestation of Robert Oppenheimer. Such manifestations often contain visions of the scientist in the nuclear age as committed to harnessing nature's power for peace and social betterment on the one hand and as an amoral, misanthropic technocrat on the other.[18] In my analysis, these diverse manifestations mirror the contradictions of the bomb, both immediately after its revelation and in the decades that followed, as well as the complexities of the search for knowledge in the nuclear age. Like the simultaneous presence and absence of the shadows of those killed at Hiroshima and Nagasaki, Oppenheimer is paradoxically there and not there in the representations I explore. Seen at once as godlike yet corporeal, untouchable yet material, he circulates in the cultural consciousness in much the same way nuclear weapons, radiation, and other emanations of nuclear culture do: hanging over all our heads with graphic (in several senses of the word) potential yet highly secret and virtually invisible. Many of the representational strategies used to depict him—textual, visual, material—function by paradox and, among other things, assert his absence and negate his presence. In their contributions to the simultaneous invisibility and omnipresence of nuclear weapons, to the potential in atomic science for energy revolution and for global destruction, these representations animate nuclear culture itself. His presence, so often evoked through representations of his physicality, helps conjoin scientific and mystical ideas. Yet his potential absence, frequently reiterated right alongside his presence, works in many instances to dehumanize nuclear culture, to remove the human behind the creation of the bomb and thus the imperative to engage ethically with those affected by it.[19] This process both emerges from and helps construct public perceptions of a conflicted scientist, simultaneously a creator and a destroyer. A diverse body of cultural representations thus reveals the many different facets of seeking knowledge in the nuclear age. Representing Oppenheimer, and representing the particular quest for knowledge that resulted in the atomic bomb, profoundly influences the roles science and technology play in the contemporary. To depict him as seeking enlightenment about the bomb is to frame science and technology as instrumentalist yet mystical, hyper-rational yet imaginative, and ultimately present in its absence, yet absent in its presence. This type of meaning, the bomb's flexible capacity to signify, ensures its omnipresence in political, social, and artistic discourse.

Reflective of the broad range of forms and genres in which Oppenheimer appears, my methodology is interdisciplinary. The Manhattan Project itself, where responsibility for the creation of this destructive technology could be found "between the fractures" (Thorpe, "Violence" 79) of the various specialized scientific disciplines that it incorporated, compels an integrative approach. Studying nuclear culture more generally involves rhetorical investigation, literary analysis, and media scholarship as much as it involves history, political science, and nuclear physics.[20] My title—*The Meanings of J. Robert Oppenheimer*—uses the plural noun quite deliberately because representations of Oppenheimer tend to produce a constellation of meanings in both individual cultural texts and across a range of them. Often divergent and contradictory, but sometimes convergent and complementary, such a plethora of meanings prevent this (or likely any) book from being a singular or definitive explanation of a complex, multivalent cultural figure. Such meanings are also often at odds with perceptions of "the true Oppenheimer" or "the historical Oppenheimer." Generally speaking then, this study of Oppenheimer is one among many, but it is also one that builds on decades' worth of work by other scholars in its various attempts to provide new ruminations on and further starting points for discussion and analysis of this important, influential, and often mysterious scientific figure.

Many of the arguments I will make about representing Oppenheimer involve seeing him as rooted in or dependent on particular conceptions of place and particular ways of seeing (or not seeing) him as a visual or material construct. Each chapter bases its analysis on a particular trope found in the genre or type of cultural production being analyzed. Each trope, I argue, serves as an index to how that genre or type of material represents him and his relationship with nuclear knowledge. Each trope helps ascertain how he is imagined as a force for good or a destroyer of worlds, a coldly rational bureaucrat or a mystically intuitive sage, as mechanical or ethereal, embodied or disembodied. And each chapter attempts to position these shifting and contradictory representations within some of the larger categories through which nuclear culture might be understood: science, history, responsibility, knowledge, imagination, and subjectivity. His "discursivity," the ways he is created through various cultural discourses, is a basic premise of my argument and permits an exploration of many different kinds of text. The first part takes the word "text" in its more conventional sense and focuses on iterations of Oppenheimer in print. Inspired by a growing critical interest in life writing, the first chapter examines several Oppenheimer biographies and their creation of the "life-text" through a discussion of the representational strategies they use, particularly their depiction of the desert as the place where the bomb was assembled and a place with evocative symbolic meaning. Chapter 2 explores the rhetorical strategies, as revealed in the use of the sun as a metaphor, that histories of the Manhattan Project use to depict the atomic bomb and to frame its creators in their search for this "forbidden" knowledge that is both earth-shattering and otherworldly. Chapter 3 explores fictional representations of Oppenheimer, particularly the kinds of knowledge he embodies or can access, and how they are used to try to reimagine the past, the present, and the future. The second part of the book explores visual and material culture. Chapter 4 begins with some brief analyses of several "transitional" forms—comic book depictions, both historical and fictional, of Oppenheimer, as well as photographs—followed by more extended studies of film and television representations. These analyses focus on how television and cinematic texts use mechanical and technological metaphors visually to represent Oppenheimer's often mystical knowledge. In chapter 5, I explore Oppenheimer's positioning within a number of nuclear museums with the aim of analyzing material representations and ways in which his embodiment and disembodiment in physical space is related to the knowledge museums create. The final part of the book consists of a single chapter: an analysis of Oppenheimer's own writing. That chapter examines his speeches and essays as acts of self-fashioning within public textual spaces. Although it does not privilege his own public self-representations over representations in other forms and by other people, the last chapter does approach Oppenheimer's texts as something of a response to the representations discussed in earlier chapters. Consistent with this book's focus on presence and absence, its final chapter traces Oppenheimer's use of self-negation and synecdoche in his public articulations of scientific and cultural knowledge.

My analysis of representations that span the better part of the seventy years since the Trinity test is an attempt to address, through the illumination of many different facets of Oppenheimer representation, the powerful claims staked by nuclear culture. From the utopian visions of plentiful and revolutionary power in the 1950s to massive antinuclear demonstrations in the 1980s, from Mutually Assured Destruction to terrorist dirty bombs, and from Three Mile Island and Chernobyl to Fukushima, nuclear ideas and technologies have shaped the world. The degree to which Oppenheimer figures directly or indirectly in these manifestations is, of course, open to debate, but those cultural productions in which he does appear hold an important key to understanding one of the most equivocal, and certainly the most destructive, technologies the world has ever known.

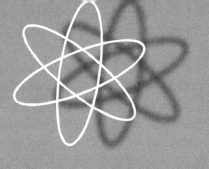

PART I

READING
OPPENHEIMER

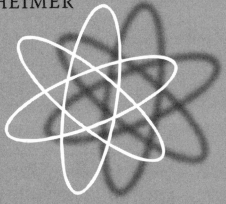

In a well-known piece of nuclear criticism, the philosopher Jacques Derrida asserts that, because Hiroshima and Nagasaki represented the end of a conventional war rather than the beginning of a nuclear one, nuclear war has not yet occurred and remains "fabulously textual." As a (thus far) purely rhetorical event, nuclear war is wholly encoded in linguistic and visual representation and is only comprehensible through interpretation and decoding ("No Apocalypse" 23). Despite the realities of Hiroshima and Nagasaki, and despite the fabulously expensive materiality of subsequent weapons proliferation, the bomb exists largely as a discursive construction for most who live in its shadow. As a "nonevent," nuclear war remains hypothetical. It is an underlying foundation of geopolitical relations, a supposition or possibility in warfare. It is also a fantasy, dwelling at least partly beneath rational thought, that structures narratives and discourses. The nuclear event occurs as fabulation, but its material consequences, manifested through those bomb-structured narratives and discourses, are nonetheless real. In a book of postmodern philosophy provocatively titled *Letter Bomb*, Peter Schwenger writes: "Nuclear strategy mingles science with beliefs about others' beliefs, and of course about others' science, and one's own, in a proliferating and paradoxical network of speculation which yet constitutes our reality" (v). The ways in which texts signify, and how their significations interact, inform understandings of the bomb, but as Schwenger points out, the reality of the bomb also tells us as much about literature as our textual fantasies tell us about the bomb.

I am not the first to note that Oppenheimer functions as an important "text" for discussing the ideological assumptions, material operations, and cultural effects of nuclear weapons—or broader issues such as national defense and even science and technology themselves—but he remains a vital node in the web of nuclear signification.[1] As a sign circulating throughout nuclear culture and lending meaning to many of its facets, he becomes a discursive construction that can be read in a variety of ways.[2] Oppenheimer's circulation and the many acts of reading and rereading Oppenheimer constitute an example of Schwenger's "letter bomb," a productive explosion of language and textual production that counteracts the annihilating, supremely negating qualities of the nuclear explosion. Whether this kind of textual fabulation counts as hope in the nuclear age is open to debate, but a reading of its outlines and trajectories can, at the very least, help produce knowledge about one of the central figures in the development of this vexing technology.

Part 1 will read Oppenheimer in a series of textual formations. It will assume that texts have material relations with the world and thus exceed their putative status as mere language games. First, I begin with the assumption that the facticity of the life of a historical figure is in part constructed through the genre of biography. The word "biography," signaling "life writing," renders one of the most powerful signifiers of a historical figure (his or her life, as "actually" lived) into textual form. The word reinforces the fact that the historical events in a life make sense *as* a life when imparted "graphically," when written into existence as narrative. Such texts are thus a crucial starting point for this project because, in positing *a* life—the life of Oppenheimer—and in offering ways it can be known, they posit life itself and the ethics of how life is valued as an ante in the nuclear gamble. Next, I examine historical texts, those (highly privileged) textual iterations that situate Oppenheimer within the truth of history at the same time that they constitute constructions *of* history. Again, the assumption that history is a text positions history itself—the archive that comprises it, the subject positions from which it can be ascertained—as another wager to be won or lost at the technomilitary table. And third, the fictional text, in which imagination is the primary discursive mode for understanding Oppenheimer, both supplements the facticity of biography and history and complicates the kinds of knowledge they produce. Once again, imagination is both a portal through which nuclear weapons and war may be understood and one of the crucial human endeavors put at risk by the bomb. Each of these kinds of text and the interpretations I supply are part of a broad, multidisciplinary discussion of the meaning of Oppenheimer and his relation to nuclear weapons.

Within these textual forms, Oppenheimer assumes a variety of meanings and—as I argue by focusing on the way these texts depict his search for knowledge—lends an equally varied range of meanings to atomic weapons. In some instances, the rhetoric presents him as an intellectual hero and thus justifies and celebrates the construction of atomic weapons. In other instances, he is inscribed as more maleficent, which brings into question not only atomic bombs but nuclear science in general as a knowledge-production endeavor. Both of those discursive strategies rely upon an unambiguous subject—a hero or a villain—at odds with Robert Oppenheimer's complexity. Other textual Oppenheimers exist as nearly illegible traces, shadows or gaps in the text that function as complex and shifting contradictions of the strategies just described. In any case, he becomes both a textual object to be interpreted and a lens through which nuclear culture can be interpreted.

CHAPTER 1

DESERT SAINT OR DESTROYER OF WORLDS: OPPENHEIMER BIOGRAPHIES

THE LIFE-TEXT

The life of J. Robert Oppenheimer—and how his life has been represented in textual and other forms—is important to understanding his cultural meaning. For this reason, this chapter opens with a short biographical sketch. Born April 22, 1904, in New York to wealthy German-Jewish immigrant parents, Oppenheimer attended the Ethical Culture School as a boy and showed early proclivities for both science and the arts. He earned a bachelor's degree in chemistry from Harvard in 1925 and a doctorate in physics from the University of Göttingen in Germany in 1927. He moved to California, where he married Katherine (Kitty) Puening, a former member of the Communist Party, and taught physics for several years at the University of California at Berkeley and the California Institute of Technology. He also developed interests in Buddhism and Hinduism and taught himself to read Sanskrit. Robert and Kitty's first child was born in 1941. In November 1942, with fears that Germany was about to acquire atomic weapons, the U.S. government selected him to head an intense, crash-course project. With Oppenheimer's firsthand input based on childhood trips to the Southwest, a secret assembly site was selected for the bomb: Los Alamos, an isolated mesa twenty miles west of Santa Fe, New

Mexico. To this site came an international team of science luminaries to do the theoretical and experimental work, a team that included Enrico Fermi, Hans Bethe, Edward Teller, and, of course, Oppenheimer himself. His second child was born in Los Alamos in 1944. Most biographies provide harrowing accounts of the six-foot-tall scientist working himself down to a skeletal 110 pounds in a feverish attempt to complete the job before the Nazis did. Following the successful test in July 1945, in the desert near Alamogordo, New Mexico, two hundred miles south of Los Alamos, two bombs were dropped on Japan in August (after, it should be noted, Germany had surrendered), bringing World War II to an end and making Oppenheimer—at least briefly—the most famous and influential scientific hero in the world. With the scope of the bomb's destructive power now in evidence, he started publicly to express misgivings about his work. After he famously said to President Truman, "I feel I have blood on my hands," Truman told Dean Acheson that he was a "cry-baby scientist" and called him a "son-of-a-bitch" (qtd. in Bird and Sherwin 332). Following these misgivings, as well as more overt statements opposing the proliferation of nuclear weapons, Oppenheimer was no longer in the good graces of the U.S. government. In 1953, at the height of McCarthyism and the same year the Rosenbergs were executed, his security clearance was revoked, and in 1954 he was brought before an Atomic Energy Commission security hearing on what many believe were trumped-up charges of Communist affiliation and spurious accusations of selling secrets to the Russians. Following the hearing, he spent several years in quasi exile before President Lyndon Johnson presented him with the Enrico Fermi Award in 1963 for his contributions to science. Oppenheimer died in 1967.

I begin with a discussion of his life because it constitutes one of the narrative foundations of the Oppenheimer mythology, a life-text upon which so many of the other Oppenheimer texts depend at least in part.[1] Asserting the primacy of the life-text in this way is perhaps a "conservative" activity, one that reiterates some dimensions of an avowed past, but at the same time his life-text (and perhaps the life-texts of nearly any biographical figure) breaks from biography's conservative impulses when it primes the subsequent and always evolving Oppenheimer mythology.[2] As biography scholar Richard Holmes asserts, certain subjects come up again and again for biographical treatment because "each generation sees itself anew in its chosen subjects" (19). The aesthetics of renewal involved in this process helps ensure that biography is not a wholly conservative genre and that it has broad powers in shaping the cultural imagination. The biography of Oppenheimer is itself an important recurring trope in the narrative of nuclear weapons. The narrative's many dualities—creation and destruction, heroism and villainy, beauty and horror, among others—ensure that the quest for knowledge at the center of that narrative both supports and complicates the twentieth century's legacy of Enlightenment thinking.

The narrative, as I have suggested, is a fraught one. It presents a figure who, in some ways, embodies the American dream: entrepreneurial initiative, forging a new world of "progress" and "enlightenment" in the wilderness in the tradition of the frontier, and achieving spectacular success through the practical application of science. In other ways, however, his life reveals some of the most deep-seated strains of paranoia and cynicism in the American character. Like many scientists, he was dogged by skepticism over his supposed "overreaching," his meddling with forbidden knowledge and eerie manipulations of nature, his self-fashioning as a mystical artist in the Romantic tradition, and his alleged Communist ties. Such skepticism resulted, for Oppenheimer, in disgrace. The ambiguity of this narrative, the seemingly irresolvable contradictions suffusing Oppenheimer, makes for a provocative and compelling life story.

With more than thirty biographical works published between 1953 and 2014, Oppenheimer rivals Albert Einstein and Isaac Newton for his attractiveness to biographers.[3] His life story is persistent and has a tendency to revitalize itself during historical moments of particular resonance. In 2005, for example, sixty years after he looked out over the New Mexico desert and witnessed the result of eighteen months of work on what was then the world's largest and most expensive scientific endeavor, there appeared no fewer than four biographies of the man. That moment in 2005 marked, among other things, an important reassessment of the life, the legacies, and the meanings of both Oppenheimer and the nuclear culture that emerged following the world's first atomic explosion on July 16, 1945. For that reason, this chapter focuses on the biographies published on the sixtieth anniversary of the bomb. These biographies, like many cultural

productions in which Oppenheimer appears, offer detailed representations of a man who redefined theoretical physics in the United States and,
through his role in the Manhattan Project, forever altered not only the
relationship between science and what President Dwight D. Eisenhower
would later call the military-industrial complex but the very unfolding of
twentieth- and twenty-first-century global history.

That such reassessment could manifest itself in a spate of biographies
points to the importance of the genre to understanding postwar nuclear
culture and other changing aspects of American science during that time.
As a product of the Enlightenment, an age that also produced the scientific
method, the genre of biography and the practice of modern science share
affinities.[4] That such an age, with its insistence on empirical evidence,
could provide both a new way of inquiring into the natural world and a
professed means of understanding the life story of a prominent individual
suggests one such affinity: the life of the scientist, "as it really happened,"
becomes relevant to science itself. Furthermore, the persistent retelling of
the lives of some scientists echoes the importance of repeatability to the
scientific method (rarely does a new biography alter dramatically the life
narrative of its subject) while also calling attention to the seeming fragility
of the life narrative (why *must* it be drawn and redrawn so many times?).
Simultaneously, biographies must necessarily fill in gaps with speculation
and conjecture.[5] In the twentieth century, likely since Lytton Strachey's
Eminent Victorians (1918) and Virginia Woolf's *Orlando* (1928), biographies have come to question both the purported objectivity of the genre
and to satirize the adulation biography is often assumed to provide. They
foreground the perspective of the individual biographer, the relativistic
standpoint from which the life-text is constructed and which will influence
a reader's understanding of the narrative.

The existence of so many Oppenheimer biographies likewise invokes
these issues while simultaneously speaking to the importance of the scientific activities with which he was associated in the middle of the twentieth
century. Retelling his life raises a number of questions that help form the
organizing principle of this chapter: How are readers to make their way
through the different narratives? What do the biographies suggest about
the role of Oppenheimer's life in understanding the atomic age? How do

we manage the cultural similarities between the literary form of the biography and the scientific content of a scientist's biography?[6] What recurring tropes might shed light on the relationships between the construction of Oppenheimer biographies and the biographers' governing assumptions?

Most textual iterations of Oppenheimer dramatize that early morning in 1945 when he watched from a bunker ten miles away as a surreal, multicolored ball of fire erupted out of the desert floor, bloomed into the now familiar mushroom shape, and rose, accompanied by an unearthly roar, seven-and-a-half miles into the air. The trope in the biographies that this chapter focuses on is the desert landscape in which that moment occurred, because this trope seems to indicate ways in which biographical depictions contribute to Oppenheimer's meaning in the nuclear age. The analysis in this chapter reveals how the desert functions as an index to the ideological, conceptual, and rhetorical understandings of Oppenheimer in three of the four 2005 biographies.[7] For many reasons, the physical landscape is important in conceptualizing the atomic bomb. Environmental historian Mark Fiege, for example, discusses the "sense of wonder," the powerfully emotional and intellectually expansive sense of curiosity inspired in Manhattan Project physicists by their presence in the New Mexico landscape. Fiege asserts the importance of landscape—"peaks, slopes, rocks, and the sunlight and shadow that played across them" (579)—in understanding how the sense of wonder and mystery evoked by the countryside complicates the view that Manhattan Project physicists (supposedly like all scientists) were "reductive, abstract, and mechanistic" (580) and thus had no qualms about the morality of the atomic bomb.[8] The landscape is also important because its striking and vexed status as nature bears heavily on how the Manhattan Project—and how science in general—purports to be about the manipulation of nature. Although the practical reasons for conducting a large-scale atomic test in the desert are evident, less obvious—yet highly pertinent to an examination of these biographies—are the aesthetic and affective consequences; the literary tropes and figural terrains evoked by the physical landscape leave their mark on the story of Oppenheimer and, consequently, on how the bomb project and its legacy are conceived. In other words, the presence of the desert in these texts offers ways of negotiating the contradictions Oppenheimer embodies. Charming yet arrogant, patriotic yet friendly with Communists, he could be a coldly calculating scientist or a Donne-quoting esthete. Such contradictions constitute a stumbling block if biographies are assumed to provide "unified" portraits of their subjects, but if other assumptions about biography are at play—if, for instance, that biography is supposed to represent the partial and contradictory multiplicity of its subject—then these contradictions become productive sites for the construction of subjects with complex ideological meanings. The desert constitutes an important and revealing map of the meaning of Oppenheimer—a map as unpredictable and challenging, however, as the desert itself.

The primary opposition with which these biographies engage is the supposed antipathy between the hyperrational quest for knowledge attached to the scientist and the many not unproblematic signals encouraging us to read Oppenheimer as an American version of the Romantic artist tapping emotionally into sublime, incomprehensible knowledge—Immanuel Kant's intuition versus John Stuart Mill's empiricism.[9] The scientific portrait of Oppenheimer often turns on the idea that the rational process of acquiring knowledge arises from a scientist's privileged position and unquestionable presence surveying a stretch of landscape with a penetrating gaze. The second, more Romantic portrait of Oppenheimer relies on emphasizing emotional responses to the landscape and eliding his presence or making it increasingly ephemeral. Such a process often uses metaphors of gnosticism, knowledge that emerges from contact with the impalpable world of gods and the spiritual, to render him as a mysterious, godlike, determinative, or shaping force. The first portrait relies on positing a physical presence and evoking the rationality of science, while the second depends on the aesthetics of absence, immateriality, and mysticism. The biographies under examination in this chapter, although sometimes favoring one type of portrait over the other, nevertheless often posit a shifting and contradictory relationship between both portraits. The scientist-as-artist is an influential figure in American culture, yet the privileged access to secret knowledge implicit in such a figure resembles the often threatening omniscience found in images of the hyperrational scientist, the artist's purported opposite. How the biographies see Oppenheimer's own multiplicity in light of these conflicting images reveals much about what those biographies take to be the primary identity of mid-twentieth-century American scientists—their roles, their obligations, the contributions they make, the dangers they pose. I also assert that how the biographies depict the desert landscape where he acquires these various identities illuminates (to use an unquestionably loaded Enlightenment metaphor) the paths the biographers take through the various meanings Oppenheimer assumes. In echoing his role as an almost magical creator of a previously unimaginable new thing *and* as an uncanny destroyer, the desert thus serves heuristically in the examination of these biographies.

The Desert

As the focal trope in this chapter, deserts are conceptually ambiguous. Despite their complex, subtle ecologies, they are often relegated to the status of wasteland. Despite their prominence in the westward orientation of Manifest Destiny and the American Dream, they have often proven to be hallucinatory nightmares to unwary travelers. With daunting and fantastic temperature extremes and vast, often monotonous open expanses, they are marked by both excess and lack.[10] The stark objectivity they suggest sits in juxtaposition with the mysticism the place demands from the Romanticized figure of the desert dweller. Their heat and aridity force an inhabitant to concentrate on bodily presence and self-reliance, yet their minimalism reinforces the stripped-down meaning suggested in the absence, abandonment, or denial of the *deserta* that constitutes their etymological root. The desert's tendency to define by negation rather than assertion, the duality of its light as simultaneously all-revealing and blinding, and even its inescapable physicality all echo many of the strategies used to represent Oppenheimer. As the writer Edward Abbey suggests, the desert's negation is apparent in its "indifference...to our presence, our absence, our coming, our staying or our going." Yet Abbey contends that from this indifference "living things will emerge" (334). The desert contains the potential for strange creation or unexpected provision despite its apparent emptiness. This focus on the corporeal, occurring on an apparent tabula rasa, makes the desert an ideal catalyst for the genre of biography and its mandate to write a life into existence. Theorists have noted the ways in which the desert combines the materially real with the dreamlike to produce new orders of reality, what Jean Baudrillard calls "hyperreality" (63) or what Gaston Bachelard calls "a space that is psychically innovating" (206). Of the Southwest, in particular, Robert Kaplan claims similar characteristics: "the dimensions of the sky and desert here are fantastic to behold. At 7,000 feet the air loses a quarter of its density, which explains the dreamy combination of sharp, prismlike sunlight and deadly dark shadows—the mark of high-altitude deserts—giving every image, whether a bare yellow escarpment or a lonely gas station, a one-dimensional dioramic quality" (184). Stark and clear, Kaplan's desert likewise evokes the purported illuminating objectivity of the scientific enterprise, but it also induces the nonrational realm of dreams. Peter Goin, who has frequently written about and photographed deserts and the interior West of the United States, identifies many of the paradoxes of those places: "this arid, often inhospitable, and unforgiving landscape possesses a character both spiritual and sublime. This is a land of contradictions that often defy description. The sound of quiet can be deafening.... The rocks are sharp and rough, yet in the soft evening light the distant hills appear covered with velvet. At any moment, there may not be one person within ten square miles; still, every step reveals human history. Mirages are commonplace, and nothing really is what it seems. This is a landscape defined by the image and absence of water" ("Magical Realism" 254).

Other scholars have also noted the twofold quality of deserts. The apparent passivity of the desert, for example, becomes a screen on which human fantasies can be projected and perhaps become reality.[11] Speaking more politically, the desert as a mythological space makes it an ideal backdrop for the mushroom cloud to enter the cultural iconography and thus to serve certain ideological ends.[12] Because the mushroom cloud represents military ideologies related to threat and deterrence, the natural setting in which they appear allows nuclear weapons to be depicted as the ultimate instrument for manipulating nature, for transforming it into a "national sacrifice zone."[13] Doing so thus manipulates geopolitical relations to U.S. advantage.[14] Similarly, the apparent hostility of the desert environment—its preclusionary characteristics that have long kept people out—can appear transformed by the mushroom cloud into a "fruitful" display of "spectator democracy," another important national ideology.[15]

The duality of the desert, apparent in all these conceptualizations, powerfully informs biographical portraits of Oppenheimer and, consequently, the multiple meanings of his mythology. The desert's forbidding qualities, its potential, its transformative powers, its dualisms and contradictions, and its haunting aesthetics make it an unstable space whose meaning is never secure and where the knowledge it produces is itself ambiguous. Although representations of the desert in Oppenheimer biographies do not wholly determine the nature or the scope of the text, their sometimes surreal or dreamlike qualities, and at other times their emphasis on materiality, can offer a map of the conceptual terrain of the atomic bomb, the historical construction of Oppenheimer as scientific persona, and the twin fascinations of technoscience with the incredible and the pragmatic.

THE ARTIST AND THE SCIENTIST: *AMERICAN PROMETHEUS* (2005) AND *J. ROBERT OPPENHEIMER AND THE AMERICAN CENTURY* (2004)

The first two of the three biographies I wish to examine position Oppenheimer, in different but related ways, as something of a representative of his nation. In contrast, the third biography interrogates—often at the level of form—many of the assumptions the genre itself sometimes makes. The first two understand him as a synecdoche, a part representing the whole, for national characteristics. One of the two, Kai Bird and Martin J. Sherwin's *American Prometheus: The Triumph and Tragedy of J. Robert Oppenheimer*, is likely the most well known. Published in the sixtieth anniversary year of the first atomic bomb test and the end of World War II, the book was a culmination of twenty-five years of research and was widely acclaimed and extensively and positively reviewed. It received the 2006 Pulitzer Prize for Biography or Autobiography. In their construction of Oppenheimer, Bird and Sherwin focus on the physicist's sensitivity, his aesthetic faculties, and his role as shaper of the physical and scientific landscapes around him, but they also highlight his brusqueness, his arrogance, and his mean streak, qualities not always as prominent in public understandings of the "father of the atomic bomb." Their version of Oppenheimer becomes a complex figure of the American sublime, endowed with an awful (in the doubled sense of awe-inspiring and horrifying) power to influence his nation and to be defined by his nation.

The landscape is clearly important in Bird and Sherwin's understanding of the emotional dimensions of his life. They offer a "primal scene" of sorts in which an eighteen-year-old Oppenheimer encounters the deserts of the Southwest for the first time and comes away "love-struck" (28) with the landscape and, in his own words, which Bird and Sherwin quote from a letter, "insanely jealous" (28) of a friend's upcoming trip to the region. Bird and Sherwin also quote another well-known letter in which he declares: "My two great loves are physics and New Mexico" (81). In recounting his arrival in Santa Fe in 1943, Bird and Sherwin conclude that he "had fallen in love with the stark beauty of the place" (213). For the authors of *American Prometheus*, Oppenheimer's entanglement with the landscape is a deeply emotional one, a relationship governed by sublime insanity and overpowering love, not cool reason. Although not their only way of characterizing him, emphasizing this emotional connection to New Mexico has, in Bird and Sherwin's biography, the rhetorical effect of constructing an emotional scientist, one whose feelings are as important as his intellect. Such a configuration reveals the investment *American Prometheus* makes, by the language its authors deploy, in framing Oppenheimer in part as an aesthete, a Romantic with an intangible, suggestive, and mythologized— more so than objective or definitive—relationship to the landscape and to the knowledge that will be produced there.

The strategies Bird and Sherwin use to describe the landscape in and around Los Alamos help characterize Oppenheimer as an artist or creator. For instance, the landscape often becomes a blank canvas, emptied out by adjectives such as "pristine," "spartan," "stark," or "desolate." Such voiding of the landscape, which in some readings elides the indigenous presence in the U.S. Southwest and masks ecological complexities under the guise of "wilderness," helps present him as a shaper extraordinaire, as a resourceful scientist who transformed an "empty" mesa into an intricate weapons laboratory and the primary tool for winning the war. Clearing the landscape before his arrival is part of the process that allows conceptions of innocence and purity to support narratives of the hardworking, efficient American creator generating power and wealth from (supposedly) nothing and then reestablishing his heroic status after a great fall. What is more, such status means that the American political system that produced it, after sufficient trials and tribulations, is confirmed as one in which such difficulties are worth it.[16] The Oppenheimer who appears in Bird and Sherwin's biography participates significantly in this mythology.

The Romantic overtones of this narrative of creation, this image of an author building ex nihilo something talismanic, and this American mythology find echoes in many of Bird and Sherwin's other landscape descriptions. The lyricism and the often exuberant detail that appear in their accounts, while running somewhat contrary to the "spartan" and "stripped-down" landscape, are nevertheless consistent with the Romantic notions of authorship and artistry the biographers draw on in constructing Oppenheimer. For instance, setting him on the mesa in 1942 for the selection of the site, Bird and Sherwin write: "To the west, the snow-capped Jemez Mountains rose to 11,000 feet. From the spacious porch of the Fuller Lodge, one could look forty miles east across the Rio Grande Valley to Oppenheimer's beloved Sangre de Cristo mountain range, rising to a height of 13,000 feet" (206). In this warm, spectacular locale, "dramatic thunderstorms rolled in over the mountains for an hour or two in the late afternoon, cooling the terrain. Flocks of bluebirds, juncos and towhees perched in the spring-green cottonwoods" (255). Such a lush, picturesque setting points to a fundamental reality of the desert, although one generally thought to be paradoxical: the desert is "about" not merely stark absence but also lush presence. The mythology of frontiersmanship, which owes at least some of its texture to the deserts of the American West, similarly tempers the notion that deserts are wastelands with the notion that they are places of democratic possibility, places where seers and seekers can find whatever kinds of knowledge they want.

The enchanting and expansive visual spaces and soaring heights in the preceding passages produce, in addition to emotional responses on the part of the scientist, a medium for divine inspiration and knowledge that, consistent with the Promethean myth alluded to in Bird and Sherwin's title, comes from on high. In characterizing Oppenheimer as lovestruck, Bird and Sherwin emphasize, along with the great depths of emotion and aesthetic sensitivity that feed his identity as Romantic genius, an affinity for divine knowledge. The mesa is a "strange new mystical landscape" (255), a "magical dominion" (256) the vastness of which has been implicated in American identity from the time of the Puritans; it is a place where emotional resonances gain primacy over, say, the nuclear magnetic resonances at play in the work being done at Los Alamos. In this landscape, genius stems from the heavenly (yet ultimately dangerous) touch invoked in the myth of Prometheus. Representing Oppenheimer this way helps align *American Prometheus* with a longstanding biographical practice in which the power of the pastoral landscape produces personal revelation and, with it, the story of a life.[17] This Romantic vision complicates the often implicit idea that Oppenheimer's nationalist orientation was deeply rational and pragmatic, gauging the Nazi threat and, later, the hazards of a land invasion of Japan as real and present dangers that could be avoided by deploying atomic bombs.

Bird and Sherwin's Romantic vision of the Manhattan Project also informs the motif of destruction that runs through the Oppenheimer narrative. Their biography, like the myth of Prometheus, focuses as much on his downfall as on his heroics, but it does so by highlighting his emotional dimensions. One of the first glimpses of the role of destruction in the narrative occurs when Bird and Sherwin quote Oppenheimer's expressing regret over his participation in the construction of an atomic bomb at Los Alamos; "I am responsible for ruining a beautiful place" (207), he reportedly said, which again links his aesthetically inclined perception of landscape to his identity as a potentially destructive scientist. Interestingly, though, the narrative strategy Bird and Sherwin employ when introducing this quotation itself evokes some of the mystical connotations attached to the figure of the Romantic genius. Bird and Sherwin present this quotation early in the narrative, when Oppenheimer is choosing Los Alamos as the site for the Manhattan Project, even though he spoke those words in 1955, ten years after the war ended. This brief disruption in chronology offers a proleptic peek into the future from their narrative vantage point in

1943. Such a technique—common to, say, omniscient narrators in fiction—allows Bird and Sherwin to "foresee," a decade before it happens, the shift in public perception of American science once the scope and the nature of the destruction at Hiroshima and Nagasaki became clear and once the Cold War was underway. Bird and Sherwin's "visionary" abilities as authors reveal their own investment in the figure of the self-fashioning Romantic artist and thus come to influence their understanding of Oppenheimer. Quoting a statement he made in 1955 in the 1943 portion of the account aligns their visionary powers as authors with Oppenheimer himself. In this biography, the Oppenheimer of 1943 knows—if only for a moment—what the Oppenheimer of 1955 will know; his persona as desert visionary reinforces the remarkable powers he possesses in their narrative.

Bird and Sherwin also recount the well-known moment when Oppenheimer, on first seeing the mushroom cloud, quotes the *Bhagavad Gita*: "I am become Death, the destroyer of worlds" (309). The importance of allusion and quotation to this moment has been analyzed elsewhere (see, for instance, Canaday 183–187), but the moment—especially with its focus on sublime destruction—remains for Bird and Sherwin a prime tool in fashioning him as a Romantic genius. In these instances Bird and Sherwin reassert both the Romantic sensitivities of Oppenheimer in particular and the superhuman dimensions of the twentieth-century American scientist in general. They also suggest, in characterizing this destruction specifically as the destruction of beauty, that the annihilating potential of this Romantic artist stems from his emotional sensitivities and, paradoxically, from the imperative to lay those sensitivities aside in the quest to win the war.

This narrative of destruction—and the accompanying focus on Oppenheimer's emotional landscape—reaches a climax later in *American Prometheus* when Bird and Sherwin discuss the Atomic Energy Commission's investigation and eventual public humiliation of the physicist. They argue that the AEC stripped him of his security clearance because it felt his objection to developing even more powerful hydrogen bombs was "disloyal" and because the chair of the AEC, Lewis Strauss, despised Oppenheimer's literary pretensions and newfound role as public intellectual and ethical compass.[18] Bird and Sherwin stress that Oppenheimer's reluctance to develop the hydrogen bomb derived from his fear that the United States would be perceived as a wanton killer. This argument is again supported by a focus on his "love," the seemingly ungovernable emotion that rational scientists are supposed to be able to suppress. Bird and Sherwin highlight, for instance, the interchange in which Oppenheimer's friend, diplomat George Kennan, tells the disgraced scientist he would be welcome in countless research institutes around the world. Oppenheimer's response: "Damn it, I happen to love this country" (5).

Like his love for the desert, his love for the country as a whole and his adamant rejection of the possibility of leaving reveal his emotional tendencies. In Bird and Sherwin's construction, Oppenheimer's complex emotional makeup was at least as significant a factor in the AEC affair as was his rational objection to what he saw as irresponsible weapons proliferation. The complications his literary and emotional inclinations brought to his role as hyperrational scientist—and, particularly, his failure on occasion to overrule his emotions with his intellect—clearly inform Bird and Sherwin's characterization of his disgrace. For them, those emotions augmented and helped shape the AEC's doubts about his role as a scientist. And as some critics and historians have pointed out, such feelings may in fact have inhibited his scientific career (see, for instance, Fiege 594). His Romantic sensibilities likely posed trouble for his public persona in general in a nation that expects cool rationality from its scientists even at the expense of their destructive disconnection from humanity. Bird and Sherwin's biography thus highlights the lack of space within popular conceptions of the midcentury scientist for emotional attachment, for metaphysical speculation, and for nonrational mysticism. Oppenheimer's love of the desert, part of popular perception of his "charm" and his "humanity," ultimately becomes a liability in a nation invested in the idea of a scientific brain trust devoted unquestioningly and instrumentally to technomilitary supremacy.

Oppenheimer's supposed ability to embody (or fail to embody) national characteristics also forms a conceptual foundation in David C. Cassidy's *J. Robert Oppenheimer and the American Century*. From its title on, Cassidy's book commits itself less to an individual portrait of Oppenheimer and more to positioning him within social structures and institutions. Like Bird and Sherwin, Cassidy equates Oppenheimer with the nation, claiming in the first sentence of his introduction that "the story of J. Robert Oppenheimer is the story of twentieth-century America" (xi), but he also implicates him in "The American Century," the phenomenon *Time* magazine publisher Henry Luce coined in 1941 to describe the ostensible obligation of the United States to spread democracy. In other words, Cassidy charts the lines of influence between a heroic Oppenheimer and a country eager to produce heroes at the same time that he maps Oppenheimer's role in the American exceptionalism and imperialism that has sometimes so disastrously colored recent history. Consistent with the revelatory possibilities of the desert, Cassidy's representation of the landscape that so enamored Oppenheimer reflects both conceptions of the scientist.

Cassidy's desert is interesting—perhaps perversely, perhaps consistently with the desert's own evocation of lack—because it is mostly absent from his book. He touches briefly on Oppenheimer's early obsession with the Southwest and on a trip he took to New Mexico to select the site, but the lyrical descriptions of *American Prometheus* are largely absent. Rather than using adjectives such as "spartan" and "pristine" in paradoxically lush passages, Cassidy's descriptions of the desert are themselves sparse and spare, enacting (rather than describing) an austere, minimalist setting. The passages are short, with for example, less than fifteen lines devoted to Oppenheimer's first trip to New Mexico as a teenager and only two adjectives—"rugged" and "lonely" (63)—adorning Cassidy's description of the landscape in that instance. The absence of even the desert allows Cassidy to position Oppenheimer inside a thoroughly evacuated space and thus to augment the Romantic vision of the artist as a solitary genius working on a blank canvas.

Cassidy's narration of the bomb test, a crucial moment in any account of Oppenheimer's life, is similarly spare and is left behind quickly for more abstract discussions of science and ethics. But I nonetheless wish to argue for the scene's importance—and for its function in casting Oppenheimer as artistic landscape manipulator—in light of the anthropomorphic imagery Cassidy uses to describe the scene. To anthropomorphize the landscape, to grant it human characteristics, Cassidy depicts Oppenheimer watching "in awe while the world's first atomic blast stretched its fiery hand into the heavens from the New Mexico desert" (211). The hand, which represents human intervention, crucially replaces the more familiar image—drawn from nature—of the mushroom cloud.[19] The shaping power the hand possesses represents cultural interventions *into* the natural world.[20] Furthermore, this hand originating "from" the desert (an effect confirmed by some of the photographs of the Trinity test that depict the blast as roughly hand-shaped) imparts humanness to the landscape through the use of the atomic bomb (fig. 1). The desert, more or less absent from Cassidy's account until now, roars dramatically (if briefly) to life in this scene. The desert reaching up suddenly in a quasi-blasphemous grab for the heavens deprives the scientists of their supposed job of making visible that which has hitherto been hidden away inside the atom and claims it for itself. The possessive pronoun "its," attributing the hand to "the atomic blast," reminds readers that the blast is Oppenheimer's handiwork. The hand allows Cassidy to anticipate the powerful interventions Oppenheimer's work will make on the physical landscapes of Hiroshima and Nagasaki, on the deserts of Nevada and the Pacific islands where subsequent tests would be held, and on the psychic and cultural landscape of Cold War America. The hand is in this instance a reflection of instrumentalist technology that seeks to master the purported chaos of the natural world, so it functions as a chief metaphor for the kind of interventionary knowledge production that atomic science engaged in during this time.

As a synecdoche for Oppenheimer (the powerful shaper, the guilt-ridden scientist), the hand also, however, represents an incomplete self. Like other synecdochic representations of Oppenheimer, this partial self undermines the notions of complete truth and transparency at the core of scientific inquiry. The expurgated self suggested by the photographs of the test from which Cassidy draws his descriptions likewise questions, by its incompleteness and thus its openness to interpretation and change, the claims to scientific objectivity of those particular images. The incomplete scientist wringing his hands in the empty desert forms an apocalyptic image that further transforms scientific discovery into destruction. "Opening up the atom" and "revealing its secrets," common scientific formulations fraught with violent implications, leave devastation in their wakes. It is worth remembering that the hand also becomes a central symbol for

FIG. 1. *Trinity test explosion. Digital Photo Archive, Department of Energy (DOE).*
Courtesy AIP Emilio Segrè Visual Archives.

Oppenheimer through which he expresses his guilt to Harry Truman
when, like Lady Macbeth, he complains of having blood on his hands. Such
repeated interrogations of the essence of science reflect a postwar shift in
public consciousness toward viewing the scientist with skepticism. This
shift, coinciding with the AEC's 1953–1954 investigation of Oppenheimer,

"was to culminate," as Roslynn Haynes asserts, "in a witch hunt for atom spies" (256). The cultural transformation of the scientist from hero to villain, which lurched ahead with Oppenheimer's disgrace at the hands of the AEC, is deeply indebted to the logic and even the aesthetics of absence and synecdoche that run through these images.

This interpretive oscillation—between the hand indicating Oppenheimer's manipulation of the desert and the desert itself roaring to life and reaching for the sky—sheds light on the dualities that Cassidy traces. Evoking his handling of the natural landscape, the cloud represents Oppenheimer's dedication to science as a means of discovering almost unimaginable new energies, of asserting his power in making those energies visible and controlling them, of winning the war, and of leaving an indelible handprint on history as an American hero. Evoking the desert itself stirring to life, though, the cloud embodies the fear—which became rampant as nuclear weapons proliferation began in earnest—of the scientist's failing to see beyond science to his social responsibilities, of losing control of his creation, of being knocked from his privileged position by the uncontrollable nature of the discovery itself. An important theme since Mary Shelley's *Frankenstein* (1818) and apparent in countless subsequent sci-fi novels and films, scientific technology's spiraling out of control thanks to the reckless questing after secrets of nature scientists should not possess belies an even older anxiety over certain kinds of knowledge. The notion of an ungovernable scientific discovery, from the earliest alchemists to Cassidy's hand-cloud reaching for the heavens to contemporary biotechnical dilemmas, echoes Adam and Eve's punishment for eating from the forbidden tree or Prometheus's gruesome penalty for raiding knowledge from the gods. With this evocative image of the desert come to life, Cassidy implicates Oppenheimer in the long-proscribed act of unleashing powers beyond one's control. Like Bird and Sherwin, he complicates the purely heroic portraits of Oppenheimer often found in other biographies. Like Bird and Sherwin, Cassidy holds him at least partly responsible for the subsequent corporatization and militarization of post-1950s science. Unlike Bird and Sherwin, however, Cassidy locates Oppenheimer's downfall in his single-minded, Faustian dedication, at least from 1942 to 1945, to developing this new technology, to overreaching scientific and epistemological limitations, and to contributing rather devastatingly to the belief in American global supremacy.

Together, *American Prometheus* and *J. Robert Oppenheimer and the American Century* depict the Manhattan Project leader by drawing simultaneously on Romantic portraits of the emotionally driven artist and pragmatic portraits of the hyperrational scientist. Such portraits are vital to American conceptions of what scientists are supposed to be. The scientist's dedication to rational knowledge about the natural world is readily exploitable and, in the American tradition since at least World War II, capable of being monetized and disciplined by regimes of efficiency and instrumentality. At the same time, the Romantic inclinations of scientists, their "madness" in the face of forbidden knowledge and the surprise of discovery, allows them to function as a repository for lingering anxieties over where knowledge comes from and the mysteries of what lies beyond its limits. Neither Bird and Sherwin nor Cassidy entirely embraces either the portrait of the hyperrational scientist or the Romantic artist, of course; rather, they attempt to account for elements of the Oppenheimer narrative—"early genius" or "tragic downfall"—using understandings, drawn from both portraits, of how knowledge is acquired and what such acquisition means. For all their value as texts, however, neither biography pushes the boundaries of the form in ways that question the link between science's pursuit of knowledge and the biography's implicit task of representing an individual's comprehensive life story.

LOOKING ASKANCE: PRIVILEGE AND POSITION IN *109 EAST PALACE* (2005)

The third biography I wish to discuss, Jennet Conant's *109 East Palace: Robert Oppenheimer and the Secret City of Los Alamos*, is a fascinating study in indirectness, one that navigates a middle ground between Bird and Sherwin's and Cassidy's books.[21] Conant's title refers to an address in Santa Fe for what appeared to be a nondescript "housing office" but which was, as Conant describes it, "actually a front for a classified laboratory under construction on a sparsely populated mountaintop thirty-five miles outside of town" (Conant 59), a vital entry point to the Manhattan Project where all newcomers to Los Alamos first had to check in, receive credentials, and prepare to go up the treacherous mountain road to the mesa. Conant's biography is remarkable for focusing the Oppenheimer narrative primarily through the perspective of Dorothy McKibbin, the stalwart and much-beloved secretary of the office at 109 East Palace (though, as Conant reveals, McKibbin's role was much more than "merely" secretarial). This strategy allows Conant's book to function as something of a corrective to the ways in which most biographies are, as the scholar Laura Marcus puts it, "ineradicably masculinist" (153). Through such a strategy, Conant creates a portrait of McKibbin that necessarily also becomes a portrait of Oppenheimer. Conant's biography fashions itself, from its title onward, as an oblique portal or gateway into the Oppenheimer narrative rather than a vast, quasi-omniscient, mythological or national vista of the sorts found in Bird and Sherwin's or Cassidy's biographies. Conant's approach to the multiple meanings of the Oppenheimer narrative involves deliberately looking at it obliquely and displacing it from the center of her text in acknowledgment of the impossibility of resolving it. Such an approach, relatively rare in other Oppenheimer biographies, questions the conception of biography as a genre with the potential to make known, in a full and "definitive" manner, an individual life. Such an approach fully embraces the logic and aesthetics of synecdoche. The size and majesty of Bird and Sherwin's biography, for instance, or the comprehensive historical and cultural context Cassidy evokes suggest the genre's investment in comprehensiveness and in the fullness of a life textually resurrected. Their approaches have long been suited to scientific biography in particular because science tends to assume similar epistemological positions in which knowledge can (eventually) be understood in its totality. However, Conant's version of Oppenheimer, achieved through McKibbin, is less a portrait (a metaphor reliant on the presumed omniscience of visuality) than a nod toward the scientist (a metaphor of gesture replete with subtlety, uncertainty, and interpretability) or a reconstruction (a metaphor that foregrounds metaphoricity). Part of that reconstruction involves implicating Oppenheimer in several of the political and ideological consequences of presuming scientific omniscience. Conant's nodding toward Oppenheimer is a gesture toward the problems inherent in trying to construct "definitive" biography, and again the desert landscape serves as an indexical trope to the biographer's way of managing indeterminacy.

One example of Conant's landscape functioning in this way occurs in a description of the view from McKibbin's house just outside Santa Fe: "On clear days, even Mt. Taylor, the legendary 'Sentinel of the Navajo Land,' was visible, its snowcapped peak glittering in the winter sun" (18). The concept of a sentinel overlooking the landscape from above is appropriate because it conveys the sense of privileged knowledge and possible omniscience that undergirds many scientific biographies. The sentinel in this description symbolizes the presence of the scientists, particularly Oppenheimer on the mesa at Los Alamos, operating like a Cartesian subject at the center of all he surveys, unlocking miraculous physical knowledge, and protecting the United States in the process.[22] But unlike many biographies, which focalize their narrative through this watchful, knowledgeable position and thus ask readers to identify with it, Conant's biography asks readers to read through McKibbin, not Oppenheimer, and thus to assume a very different position in relation to the sentinel. It is McKibbin (and thus the reader) who is being watched over by the sentinel, who is subject to the privileged knowledge that resides elsewhere. As a woman, as a nonscientist, and as a gatekeeper but not a prime mover, McKibbin reveals that there are always others—outsiders, strangers—who are subject to the often overwhelming and subordinating will to knowledge embodied in both the scientific process and the biographical enterprise. Such "outsiders"—whether the wives of Manhattan Project scientists, manual laborers at Los Alamos, or indigenous inhabitants of New Mexico—were integral to the project yet were marginalized for their supposed proximity to nature and their distance from the rarefied world of theoretical physics. Despite the vital role they played in this massive scientific endeavor, they were disempowered by masculinist science. It would be overstating the case somewhat to call McKibbin a "victim" of scientific epistemologies, but her position constitutes an important reminder of what they can sometimes (and sometimes literally) overlook.[23]

A more specific example of how landscape indexes Conant's Oppenheimer will further illustrate these points. At an early moment in the narrative of the Manhattan Project, six months into the construction of Los Alamos, Conant describes some of the vistas the scientists were seeing and speculates on what their appeal might be to Oppenheimer: "From their vantage point at Los Alamos, raised high above the world, even something as simple as the sunset behind the Jemez peaks became terrifyingly beautiful in its great sweep of color and sky. When they considered the scale of the towering dark mountains and limitless heavens, all their problems were reduced in importance to that of any of the earth's tiny creatures. Perhaps [Oppenheimer], who had known what a perilous journey awaited them, had hoped they would look down with wonder at the world and feel uplifted and inspired even in their darkest hour" (166). Again, the landscape derives power partly from how it elevates Manhattan Project participants into privileged spaces above the terrain. Such positions, however, become uncertain in Conant's prose, when familiar and supposedly joyous sights such as sunsets become "terrifyingly" beautiful. The jarring adjective reminds readers of the destabilizing sublimity of the elevated vantage point. For Conant, Oppenheimer supposedly experiences humility while occupying that vantage point, a decidedly human feeling of insignificance in the face of magnificent scale and the wonders of sky-sized spaces. The next sentence, however, suggests that he draws power from being up in a privileged position, that bringing the other scientists up to the mesa with him allows them simultaneously to "look down" on the world and to look up to the mountaintop for divine inspiration. Conant is, in the last sentence of that passage, equating Oppenheimer with the massive scale, heavenly infinitude, and supreme power that, in the preceding sentence, was supposed to humble all those who experienced it with a sense of their own diminished scale. The historical Oppenheimer likely felt both ways in these landscapes, and to her credit, Conant does not try to resolve this ambivalence. Instead, she offers a desert that is consistent with many views of the desert as full of surprising and productive juxtapositions.

Conant's descriptions of the desert exemplify the deft oscillations her biography makes as it both reinforces and questions the privilege, the penetrative powers of rational inquiry, the near omniscience of possessing an all-encompassing vantage point, and the characteristics and consequences of ways of knowing that are obscured by technology's domination of nature. Conant also supplies a somewhat more limited version of Cassidy's collective biography, a reminder that scientific knowledge and practices do not arise solely in the presence of "great men" but in fact develop in interpersonal social spaces. Her biography reminds readers that biography as a genre extends well beyond the life of the individual and reveals the intricate contexts in which individuals live—frameworks fraught with the contingencies of history, class, race, and gender.[24] Conant's biography emphasizes the Manhattan Project as a shared experience; Oppenheimer and McKibbin, from different vantage points and accompanied by different historical narratives about them as individuals, nevertheless participate in the same historical moment. Linking the historical with the personal in this way illustrates the difficulty of ignoring one category of knowledge while trying to understand the other.

As this chapter suggests, representations of the life story of Oppenheimer are, in a wider sense, representations of twentieth-century scientists, particularly in their newly minted, mid-twentieth-century prominence on the global stage. In *American Prometheus*, Bird and Sherwin measure him against the seemingly common expectation that the American scientist must be both an artist and an intellectual, and they imply that his love for his country was too powerful—that his fall from grace was the result of his failure to play the part of the steadfast, unemotional scientist. Similarly, Cassidy's *J. Robert Oppenheimer and the American Century* locates the tragic flaw in Oppenheimer's inability to live up to one side of this paradoxical image. For Cassidy, the flaw is in the scientist himself—too much science and too little concern for what it can unleash—a characterization that allows him to be critical of orthodox representations of scientists who privilege intellectual inquiry and a seemingly inhuman hyperrationality over social and moral responsibility. He is critical of this portrait precisely because it has, in the twentieth century, so often been harnessed for the sake of furthering militarist imperialism. Both Bird and Sherwin's and Cassidy's versions of the scientist emerge, it seems, out of a vision of the desert as a place of "disincarnation, of the separation of the body from the spirit" (Baudrillard 71), whereas Conant's version attempts to convey a fuller range of the meanings of the American physicist at mid-century: heroic, all-knowing, and all-powerful, yet enigmatic, conflicted, and potentially dangerous. He is both artist and scientist, heart and mind, and known and unknowable. As biographers, Bird and Sherwin are more interested in him as an individual persona, while Cassidy questions the notion of individual genius when he focuses on extensive cultural context. Conant, meanwhile, blends the two approaches, evincing keen interest in Oppenheimer as an influential individual but presenting him obliquely, through the eyes of another (though differently) influential individual.

This chapter takes the desert as a point of entry not only because of its practical importance to the development of U.S. nuclear weapons but because it has long been an evocative landscape, one loaded with exotic and threatening connotations, tabula rasa assumptions, and deceptively complex ecologies and aesthetics that lend themselves to multiple readings. Such multiplicity compels readers to (among other things) focus on the role of performance in the creation of self instead of trying to get at the "essential" self. During those frantic months near the end of the war, the desert was, to the people working there, one of the organizing principles in making sense of a deeply unsettling, contradictory, unprecedented, and surreal project. The same goes for contemporary biographers. In the case of Bird and Sherwin the desert reflects Oppenheimer's complex and ultimately detrimental feelings of nationalism, and in Cassidy's biography it points the way (quite literally) to the disturbing consequences of emotionally detached scientific militarism. In Conant's work, the desert is a fluid, kaleidoscopic space where Oppenheimer wrestles with his identity as a scientist and with the consequences that that identity has on others. In any case, the desert is very much part of the portrait of the scientist his biographers strive to produce.

This conflicted terrain of the life-text, as I have suggested, helps generate other understandings and representations of Oppenheimer that I discuss in subsequent chapters and that are, in turn, connected to popular understandings of the twentieth century. For instance, the biographies of Oppenheimer—and the other representations they produce and with which they form links—reflect a persistent dialogue between the hyper-rationalism of science and the irrationality of Cold War doctrines such as Mutually Assured Destruction (MAD). In negotiating such contradictions, these biographies reflect the paradoxical terms of life during the

Cold War: scientific rationalism and militarism are supposed to protect us, but they do so by endangering the entire globe. The biographies also reflect embodied notions of science and history—the idea that science and history are materially real and graspable—but also the ways in which science and history depend on notions of "nothingness" and "purity": the "blank canvas" of the desert landscape in the biographies themselves but also the purported objective detachment of science and history in general.

Putting these three biographies into conversation with one another (and with the texts discussed in subsequent chapters) emphasizes the relationship between cultural context and the individual at the center of the text. Constructing biography, like constructing atomic bombs, is both a vexing and illuminating activity because the form itself encourages repeated attempts; after all, as the scholar Andrew Sinclair notes, a biography "exists only to be rewritten" (128). This complex portrait of Oppenheimer, with both its multiple dimensions and its intense focus on the individuality of its subject, infuses scientific biography with a humanness and multiplicity that sits in fascinating tension with the purported objectivity of science.[25] The ambiguity inherent in this sort of biographical practice, the speculation and conjecture biographers use to hold their often conflicting and incomplete narratives together, means that, as in physics, probability and uncertainty rule the day. In the biographies of a man so intimately connected to probabilistic physics and the uncertainty principle underlying the quantum world, pinpointing either his Romantic, conflicted humanity or his scientific objectivity necessarily alters the other. Embracing uncertainty and simultaneity seems especially crucial when reading scientific biography in a post-Einstein age.[26]

CHAPTER 2

UNDER THE SUN:
OPPENHEIMER IN HISTORY

Readers often judge the "accuracy" of a biography (or, for that matter, a novel or a film) on the basis of its resemblance to the "truth" of the historical record. Despite a given text's acknowledgment of the gaps in the record and the textual strategies used to account for such gaps, biographies are frequently read with the assumption that history is an objective referent for texts. Similarly, many readers try to understand the Manhattan Project and its legacies through a genre sometimes assumed to be the most transparent of conveyors: the history books. Critics sometimes make these assumptions as well. Sociologist Matt Wray, for instance, writes: "Behind all of these questions and conflicts [that nuclear weapons engender] stand the complicated and intricate histories that produced them, histories that until recently have been shrouded in secrecy" (467). Now that secrecy has been dispelled, this rhetoric suggests, the truth of history can transcend representation. Such a fantasy is appealing in the face of nuclear weapons because the destruction they promise, in which no one might be left to remember the past and no texts might remain to record it, is potentially so complete that it threatens history itself.[1] Historical accounts thus attain prominence in those attempts—large and small, popular and academic—to dispel the secrecy and make sense of the Manhattan Project and the meaning of the atomic bomb. Thanks to the supposedly objective knowledge they contain, history books constitute privileged sites of representation for Oppenheimer. But objectivity, that logical guarantor of transparency, neutrality, and truth, also must come into question.

The relationship between history and the texts that impart it has long been a problematic one. As historian Peter Munz writes, the "distinction between the past as it is in itself and as it is narrated is old enough—we find it even in ancient times as the distinction between *res gestae* and *historia rerum gestarum* (854), terms that translate as "past events" and "history of past events." Twentieth-century shifts in how history is written echo this concern. Philosopher Walter Benjamin, partly inspired by the surrealist movement, resisted the idea of history as teleology, as moving toward a clearly defined purpose, and emphasized noncausal relationships between temporal moments. Later, the so-called linguistic turn sought to ensure that textual representations of history are not conflated with the historical referents they seek to denote.[2] Like twentieth-century revolutions in physics (including the relativistic turn that drove the work that led to the bomb), recent understandings of historiography complicate the notion of a single, stable perspective from which facts can be indisputably seen. The discursive nature of history warns against treating texts as straightforward "copies" of a reality outside of discourse (see Barthes, "The Discourse of History" 138). In a review essay of four important books from the late 1980s on the postmodern turn in the philosophy of history, Kenneth Cmiel states (perhaps a little too confidently): "Objectivity, that dull-witted monarch who despotically ruled the discipline of history since the late nineteenth century, lies dethroned" (170).[3]

Dethroning the monarch of objectivity does not, however, mean killing it completely. History books still refer to actual events and people. A text's "reflection" of the actuality of history is a colored and active one (rather than a transparent and passive one), but it does not obviate the reality of past events. Studying history's narrative structures and tropes reveals, in part, how the past acquires meaning.[4] Accordingly, my approach is to assume the reality of the history of the Manhattan Project while examining the textual, rhetorical, narrative, and symbolic dimensions of its historical accounts. I am not claiming any dramatic revision of historical reality but instead reflecting on how the historical reality of the Manhattan

Project comes filtered through representations of Robert Oppenheimer in the history books. As an analysis of how histories of the Manhattan Project envision Oppenheimer, this chapter will examine how his quest for knowledge of the natural world, within the context of trying to produce a weapon, has been depicted. At the same time, it will examine how the histories themselves manage the competing impulses to seek objective knowledge of the Manhattan Project and to acknowledge the subjectivity of that textual endeavor.

In the way the first chapter looks to depictions of the desert as an index of biographical representations of Oppenheimer, this chapter focuses on a particular trope in a number of important and popular historical accounts. Each of these accounts, in one way or another, uses the sun as a rhetorical device. The bomb itself, the new age that supposedly dawned with its detonation, the knowledge produced by the Manhattan Project, and the responsibility borne by the scientists unfold in the glare of a rhetorical device Elizabeth DeLoughrey calls the heliotrope. The sun as an explanatory image—and, as DeLoughrey argues, as a dangerously naturalizing metaphor—helps to make visible Oppenheimer's role in historical accounts of the bomb.[5] As with my discussion of the desert, this analysis of the heliotrope is not intended to suggest that the linguistic device in question is the only or even the most important way of understanding a particular type of historical account. Rather, I take this trope to be significant in framing the knowledge of nuclear weapons as well as the knowledge of Oppenheimer's moral stance toward and responsibility for such weapons.[6] In addition to making nuclear knowledge seem familiar and harmless, as DeLoughrey notes, the heliotrope also has the opposite effect: it defamiliarizes the bomb. The strangeness solar metaphors provide, the sense of the unknown into which they cast readers, also colors the representations of Oppenheimer found in these texts. And like the paradoxical union of presence and absence often apparent in these representations, such strangeness frequently serves to diminish, occlude, or even efface him from the text. This kind of transparency, rather than the supposed transparency of the historical record, appears in many Oppenheimer representations and frequently extends from Oppenheimer to countless other facets of the Manhattan Project. Depending, it seems, on his relationship with the heliotrope within a given text, such effacement complicates a text's depiction of the sense of responsibility with which Oppenheimer wrestled. Despite his famous lament to President Truman about having blood on his hands, Oppenheimer's moral anxiety sometimes fades from these accounts under the influence—traceable through the heliotrope—of a knowledge of history as inevitable or inescapable.[7] In other words, the heliotrope both makes him seem familiar—it brings him "down to earth"— and distances him to make him more ethereal or otherworldly. The dual function of this trope becomes central to understanding Oppenheimer in history. The knowledge he produces is esoteric and counterintuitive, yet it needs to be domesticated—made as familiar and benign as the morning sunrise—if it is to be weaponized and made an accepted and practically invisible part of the nuclear age.

HELIOTROPES

The splitting or fusing of atoms produces colossal amounts of energy, and much of the spectacular release of that energy at the moment of an nuclear bomb's detonation is in the form of brilliant light. It is thus unsurprising that images of light, including the sun as a literally unearthly source of tremendous illumination, figure prominently in representations of the atomic bomb and of Oppenheimer. In a pair of articles on the nuclear tropes used to recount hydrogen bomb testing in the Pacific Islands, DeLoughrey asserts the importance of solar imagery to understanding nuclear weapons, ecology, and globalization. Specifically, she locates in these heliotropes a defusing or acclimatizing effect: "In American Cold War propaganda, these weapons of mass destruction were naturalized by likening them to harnessing the power of the sun, and their radioactive by-products were depicted as no less dangerous than our daily sunshine" ("Heliotropes" 236). In that sense, heliotropes help domesticate the resulting planetary nuclear fallout and even turn it into an index of the "progressive" power of "inevitable global modernity" ("Radiation Ecologies" 472). DeLoughrey locates heliotropes in some early examples of nuclear culture: in the first report on the Manhattan Project, journalist William L. Laurence (discussed in detail in the next section of this chapter) characterizes the development of the atomic bomb as a project that would "bring the sun down to earth as its gift to man" ("Heliotropes" 236); President Harry Truman announced the bombing of Hiroshima by saying, "the force from which the sun draws its power has been loosed against those who brought war to the Far East" (252 n. 4); and the first chair of the Atomic Energy Commission, David E. Lilienthal, compared atomic energy to the rays of the sun as "the magic stuff of life itself" (237). Such rhetoric, which DeLoughrey calls "nuclear heliocentrism" (241), left the sun as a central metaphor for the nuclear age, a metaphor that has come to characterize modernity as one in which nuclear weapons and the global irradiation they have produced are, even if not natural, clearly inevitable.

Although this sort of domestication undoubtedly occurs, the sun is in fact a double-edged metaphor. It is indeed the familiar life-giving light in the sky, the foundation for so many cultural tropes and the basis of so much of our understanding of the universe, yet it is literally otherworldly. DeLoughrey does not much discuss this second set of connotations. This chapter, however, extends DeLoughrey's work and explores the duality of the heliotrope through readings of five historical accounts of the Manhattan Project. These readings focus on the relationship between heliotropes and the texts' depiction of Robert Oppenheimer. In the first section, I examine William L. Laurence's *Dawn over Zero* (1946) and Robert Jungk's *Brighter than a Thousand Suns* (1958), two of the earliest popular accounts of the development of the atomic bomb. In the second section, I discuss Lansing Lamont's *Day of Trinity* (1965) and Ferenc Morton Szasz's *The Day the Sun Rose Twice* (1984) as texts grappling with increasingly loaded solar metaphors. I dedicate the third section to an analysis of Richard Rhodes's *The Making of the Atomic Bomb* (1986), widely regarded as the definitive account. I should note that although other histories of nuclear culture also employ solar metaphors, the texts discussed in this chapter provide the most extensive depictions of Oppenheimer and thus forge provocative connections between him and the dichotomous solar metaphor.[8] How heliotropes function to illuminate his quest for knowledge and the application of such knowledge is thus the focus of this chapter.[9]

OLD AND NEW SUNS: *DAWN OVER ZERO* (1946)
AND *BRIGHTER THAN A THOUSAND SUNS* (1958)

Owing to the nearly complete secrecy within which the bomb was developed, one of the first accounts of its existence deserves special attention as a source of some of its governing metaphors and a privileged site for the discovery of nuclear knowledge. William L. Laurence, a Lithuanian-born U.S. journalist with the *New York Times*, joined the Los Alamos laboratory in 1945 to serve as official historian. He was the only journalist to attend the Trinity test and was aboard one of the aircraft that dropped the bomb on Nagasaki. After World War II, and with the veil of secrecy lifted, Laurence published widely on the bomb, winning a Pulitzer Prize in 1946 for his reporting in the *New York Times* and publishing *Dawn over Zero*, an account of the Trinity test, in the same year. As its title suggests, Laurence's book employs the solar metaphors that would later recur in many places. In some instances in his book, his use of solar metaphors aligns with the naturalizing function DeLoughrey identifies as well as with the process, common to many accounts of the Manhattan Projects, of idolizing Oppenheimer. In other instances, however, Laurence's sun metaphors complicate this function, casting the bomb in horrific, uncanny, or hyberbolic terms and working to minimize, efface, or render Oppenheimer ephemeral in the process. In negating Oppenheimer, *Dawn over Zero* and the subsequent histories it influenced underscore the negation at the conceptual center of atomic weapons. Negating Oppenheimer reveals how notions such as annihilation and its accompanying sense of the abdication of responsibility provide an important qualification to an often unqualified modern narrative of scientific progress and enlightenment in which the bomb is a centerpiece.

Laurence's title refers to the emergence of a new scientific technology, the atomic bomb, at a specific point in the New Mexico desert. Point "zero" is a site of supreme negation, but the endless circularity of the figure zero also ensures its equivocation. Laurence's dawn frames the bomb as the beginning of a new age, but this new age is potentially one of annihilation. Laurence notes: "For everyone concerned, Zero became the center of the universe. Time and space began and ended at Zero. All life centered on Zero. Everyone thought only of Zero and the zero hour, or rather the zero microsecond" (189). In its centrality and psychic prominence, and in the way "the zero microsecond" is the instant in which the new age dawns, this space is in Laurence's account a productive one where time begins and to which "all life" directs its attention. But time and space *end* at zero too, and the obvious traces of annihilation in that designation—the negation connoted by "zero" and mapped onto the desert with its already-in-place connotations of emptiness and blankness—evokes the unknown territory into which atomic physicists were heading. In this ambiguous space and time, as first evoked in Laurence's title, a new day "dawns." The dawn, however, with its suggestions of novelty and enlightenment, casts this destructive technology in the fresh light of a new day's sun.[10] Locating the dawn "over" zero continues this dialectic of enlightenment and negation (a dialectic present in many of the representations discussed in this book) when the bomb denies its own rationalized destruction and "illuminates" itself, bringing itself into the comfortable realm of "that which is known."[11]

The complexity of this initial "dawn" does not entirely eclipse the naturalizing function of the heliotrope, however. In many places in the text, consistent with the notion that Laurence was the government's official historian, *Dawn over Zero* indeed harnesses the power of the sun to naturalize and aestheticize the violence offered by the genesis of the atomic bomb.[12] In setting the scene for the Trinity test, for instance, Laurence writes: "The night was still pitch-black, save for an occasional flash of lightning in the eastern sky, outlining for a brief instant the Sierra Oscuro Range directly ahead of us" (6). Like the bolt of lightning that supposedly reveals the truth of the new science to a young Victor Frankenstein in Shelley's *Frankenstein*, the lightning presaging the Trinity test, especially in its illumination of the Oscuro (Spanish for "dark") mountains in the distance, anticipates the intense light of the bomb and its own apparent penetration into the darkness of nature. This metaphor, central to the scientific method of knowledge production, is enfranchised in this passage (as it often is elsewhere) in its evocation of a powerful natural phenomenon. In narrating General Leslie Groves's and Oppenheimer's concern over the weather, Laurence describes the men "going out of the control house into the darkness to look at the sky, constantly reassuring each other that the one or two visible stars were becoming brighter" (191). They too gaze to known, familiar, and natural analogues as they try to come to grips with the extraordinary process they are about to unleash. Laurence also compares, using generally scientific rhetoric, the detonation of the bomb to the natural processes at work in the sun—an association DeLoughrey finds integral to subsequent uses of the heliotrope: "Atomic energy, harnessed for the first time by scientists for use in atomic bombs, is the practically inexhaustible source of power that enables the sun to supply us with heat, light, and other forms of radiant energy, without which life on earth would not be possible. It is the same energy, stored in the nuclei of the atoms of the material universe, that keeps the stars, bodies much larger than our sun, radiating their enormous quantities of light and heat for billions of years" (21). Laurence draws repeatedly on the sun as a scientific touchstone for the unprecedented experiment the Los Alamos scientists were conducting: "to light an atomic fire for the first time on earth," he writes, was to build "a miniature model of the sun or a star" (72). Laurence's heliotropes emphasize the importance of the sun for human existence, drawing striking (but dubious) comparisons between the atomic energy unleashed at Trinity and the solar energy stored in plant chlorophyll and eventually consumed by humans (267–268). Laurence aestheticizes the bomb even (or perhaps especially) through the elaborate rhetorical flourishes for which he was known and which are sometimes objects of criticism.[13] Calling the tower in which the bomb rests "a cradle for the star about to be born" (72), for instance, joins the heliotrope with a biological and familial metaphor—one in which the birth of a child comes to characterize the testing of a terrifically destructive piece of technology—to naturalize or even domesticate the process.[14] Several references to the Biblical story of Genesis (with its phatic utterance, "Let there be light") also help place the strange and destructive weapon within a narrative of creation familiar to Laurence's audience.

Despite such strategies, which undoubtedly help produce the rhetorical effects DeLoughrey attributes to the heliotrope, many of Laurence's references to the sun have a rather different effect. Instead of only making the bomb seem natural, Laurence's heliotropes also help highlight the uncanny

effects produced by the bomb and anticipate the anxious, troubling knowledge that such technology would come to reveal. At the moment of the
device's detonation, writes Laurence: "there rose from the bowels of the
earth a light not of this world, the light of many suns in one. It was a sunrise such as the world had never seen, a great green super-sun climbing in
a fraction of a second to a height of more than eight thousand feet" (10).
The actual sun, the body that gives human beings life, pales in comparison
to the uncanny thing the physicists have created:

> The sun was just rising above the horizon as our caravan started on its
> way back to Albuquerque and Los Alamos. We looked at it through
> our dark lenses to compare it with what we had seen.
>   "The sun can't hold a candle to it!" one of us remarked. (12)

Returning to the process of developing the bomb, Laurence notes that in
creating plutonium scientists "took three steps beyond nature" (147)—
beyond the known limits of the periodic table—to produce "an entirely
new element not known to exist under the sun or anywhere else in the
cosmos" (147). Similarly, the bomb dropped on Hiroshima is remarkable
for generating a temperature "about three times as great as the temperature estimated for the interior of the sun, and nearly ten thousand times
the temperature of the sun's surface. To attain an internal temperature of
such magnitude would require a star with the luminosity of 400,000,000
suns" (171). All these instances of exceeding the sun or surpassing nature
to disrupt the limits of the known world begin with the known and the
familiar but in fact *de*naturalize the sun and undermine the comforting,
domesticating effects its rhetorical use has on this strange new weapon.
The bomb in *Dawn over Zero* thus becomes otherworldly and terrifying.
    Both of the heliotrope's functions are at work in Laurence's depictions
of Oppenheimer. Laurence's first mention of Oppenheimer occurs when
he places the leader of the Manhattan Project among "the vanguard of
the atomists" (8). Like the Biblical language and cadences that crop up
in *Dawn over Zero*, the archaic word "atomists" evokes ancient natural
philosophers (even as the phrase is supposed to place nuclear physicists at
science's cutting edge) to mythologize Oppenheimer—to remove him, in

effect, from modern history. It locates him simultaneously in the obscure mists of time and at the forefront of scientific theory. "Vanguard" has military connotations that secure him within the establishment project he was directing, but it is also related to the term "avant-garde," suggesting a position antithetical to the hierarchical force he was conscripted to serve and sympathetic to the more subversive artistic realm with which he frequently dabbled. A dialogue thus develops between the distance and indeterminacy of mythology and the prominence of science, between the obscurity of the avant-garde and the visibility of heading a program that would provide a climax to the first half of the twentieth century. That Oppenheimer would be the "head" of such a program again reveals that the war-making activities of the first half of the twentieth-century—activities that included development of ingenious poison gases in World War I, the assembly line massacre of Jews in World War II, and that culminated in mushroom clouds over Japan—were hyperrationalist ones, with their origins in the heads of the scientists and the heads of the heads of state.

An explicit comparison of Oppenheimer to a mythological figure, a comparison common in books subsequent to Laurence's, soon follows: "Prometheus had broken his bonds and brought a new fire down to earth" (13). Imagining Oppenheimer in some mythically elevated position, from which he brings a new fire "down," and even calling him "one of the top-flight theoretical physicists" (183), raises him to a godlike position. From that position he, like the sun, sends down a strange power. Laurence also lends Oppenheimer a prophetic ability. Being able to foresee the future, whether as a visionary making explicit pronouncements or in the subtler rhetorical clairvoyance found in some of the biographies discussed in chapter 1, contributes to the otherworldliness so prominent in depictions of Oppenheimer. Laurence's Oppenheimer has his expectations come true as a result of the Trinity test ("'Each component did exactly what it was expected to do,' Dr. Oppenheimer said to me on the morning after the New Mexico test" [185]); he creates "marvels of ingenuity and inventiveness" (185); and he makes predictions about the atomic weapons of the future (174–175). In these moments, he oscillates between conceptual categories: between myth and cutting-edge novelty, between the obscurity of the past and the hypervisibility of the present, and between embodying the bewildering nature of atomic technology in Laurence's present of 1947 and personifying uncanny knowledge of the future. Such oscillations are, in part, a process of casting the scientific manipulation of matter in supernatural terms, a process that both affirms and denies the responsibility of the people carrying it out.[15] Such oscillations, like Laurence's use of the heliotrope, also make the process of representing Oppenheimer one that uses the simultaneously familiar yet untouchable past and the simultaneously modern yet baffling novelty of the present. Using both past and present in these ways simultaneously obscures and highlights Oppenheimer and makes the bomb both familiar and inscrutable.

The paradoxical nature of this type of representation can perhaps be best understood through Peter Hales's analysis of the relationship between the atomic bomb and the American conception of the sublime. For Hales, as for Edmund Burke, the sublime is "that combination of terror and wonder that accompanied confrontation with the Infinite with a capital I" and in its "optimistic American version...served to link wild American nature to a divine covenant between God and American culture" ("The Atomic Sublime" 12). Hales locates Laurence's rhetoric within this long-standing discourse of sublimity in American culture but criticizes it, as DeLoughrey does, for how it "reinvoked the American doctrines of nature in a way that enabled this profoundly disruptive new presence to enter the language of American culture as an element of the mythic natural landscape" (13). In other words, human responsibility for the bomb diminishes when nature and the divine take over as animating forces in the inevitable construction of this device. So those moments in Laurence's text that evoke the sun or depict Oppenheimer as strange draw on the sublime. They do so to naturalize it within an American tradition that regards with reverence the technological as a mechanical expression of American ingenuity.[16] The sublime sense of awe in the face of terrible technology, exemplified by the heliotropes Laurence uses and their connection to Oppenheimer's bomb, encourages readers to view Oppenheimer and his work as part of a covenant with God and as therefore legitimized.

Robert Jungk's *Brighter than a Thousand Suns*, written less than ten years after Laurence's account, uses an even more explicit heliotrope in its title. Perhaps more than any other history examined in this chapter, it focuses on the sense of responsibility borne by the physicists who did the work. Yet also more than any other history discussed in this chapter, it has been subject to rather scathing reviews. Oscar E. Anderson calls it "a poor book" (117), and E. U. Condon, writing in *Science*, calls it "thoroughly bad" (1619). Manhattan Project participant Hans Bethe calls it "misleading" (427), and his colleague Robert R. Wilson claims it is full of "deliberate distortion" (148). One point of contention regarding Jungk's book is the overly flattering portrait he paints of German scientists. Wilson summarizes Jungk's thesis as follows: "Physicists in Germany managed, by their great diligence, *not* to build a bomb; physicists in the U.S., on the other hand, failed—they did *not* manage *not* to build a bomb" (145; emphasis in original). In fact, as Bethe points out, "ethical reasons played only a minor role in [the German] decision not to push the development of the atomic bomb" (427), with a lack of resources, understanding, and political coordination—incompetence, in other words—standing as the more likely reason the Nazis failed to produce a bomb. Anderson finds Jungk's noxiously flattering conclusions regarding German scientists unconvincing (118), and they are compounded by what the reviewers see as Jungk's simplistic view of American physics: his failure to credit American physicists for their groundbreaking work in the 1930s, for instance, or his supposedly inaccurate portrayal of how American physicists (including Arthur Compton, Ernest Lawrence, and Oppenheimer himself) gleefully went about targeting Japan. As Wilson points out, however, "*Brighter than a Thousand Suns*, like the Bhagavad-Gita, has its Krishna—Robert Oppenheimer" (146)—a figure whose presence in Jungk's book, although perhaps not "accurately" rendered, encompasses the powerfully conflicted ethics of the scientist at the center of Los Alamos. Although Oppenheimer weighed in approvingly on the bombing of Japan, he was also a contributor to the Franck Report, which was instrumental in placing the control of nuclear energy in civilian hands. Jungk's book thus offers, despite its problems, an important corrective to Laurence's naturalizing portrait of the scientist.

Such a corrective stems from Jungk's relentless focus on Oppenheimer's equivocation about the bomb and the attention paid to the difficult moral questions with which Oppenheimer wrestled. Jungk notes, for example, that Oppenheimer's "remarkable capacity for seeing the other point of view" (132) made him a formidable opponent of any simplistic assessments of atomic weapons work. Far from being the cold-blooded scientist, he "could quote Dante and Proust. He could refute objections by citing passages from the works of Indian sages which he had read in the original. And he seemed to be aflame with an inward spiritual passion" (132). Such humanism, wide-ranging erudition, and Romantic sensibility allow Jungk's Oppenheimer to seek knowledge from many places. Jungk reproduces a long quotation from Oppenheimer's own deliberation about targeting Japan, a text in which he ultimately affirms using the bomb on Hiroshima and Nagasaki but which is nevertheless full of hedging and qualification. In one section Oppenheimer claims: "We said that we didn't think that being scientists especially qualified us to know how to answer this question of how the bombs should be used or not; opinion was divided among us as it would be among other people if they knew about it" (186). Similarly, statements such as "Oppenheimer oscillated between fears that the experiment would fail and fears that it would succeed" (200) and "seldom can jubilation have made a man so sad and adulation made a man so skeptical as they did Robert Oppenheimer as he watched the frenzied delight with which his countrymen greeted the end of the Second World War" (229) ensure that Jungk's book emphasizes Oppenheimer's engagement with moral responsibility. Although such attention leads Wilson to criticize Jungk for assuming "U.S. physicists [should] bear the full responsibility for the bomb" (146) despite its internationalist origins, Oppenheimer's anguish over the consequences of Los Alamos allows *Brighter than a Thousand Suns* to denaturalize significantly the work of making nuclear weapons.

Such denaturalization begins with the heliotrope in the book's title, with the "thousand suns" evoking an otherworldly realm whose excess, signaled by the bomb's still "brighter" luminescence, cannot but make the work of nuclear weapons overwhelm the benign sunlight that falls on earth. Despite Jungk's occasionally employing the familiarity of the sun and its associated metaphors to domesticate the bomb, his title reinforces the incomprehensibility of the results of the undertaking.[17] One of the epigraphs to Jungk's book, a quotation from the *Bhagavad Gita*, is the apparent source of his title:

If the radiance of a thousand suns
were to burst into the sky,
that would be
the splendor of the Mighty One—
(vii)

This occurrence of the heliotrope, in almost as prominent a textual place
as the title of the book, reinforces the excessive, supernatural multiplicity
of the sun at the same time that it associates it with the virtually incomprehensible power of a deity. Later, when readers arrive at Jungk's account
of Oppenheimer's late-night meeting with Groves on board a train as they
plan the construction of Los Alamos, the epigraph from the *Bhagavad
Gita* reappears in Jungk's own prose (or, more accurately, in the English
translation of his prose): "The train thundered through the darkness of
the night while man envisioned a light that would be brighter than a thousand suns" (128). The devotional diction in this sentence, not to mention
its remarkably trainlike string of iambs, elevates the men in the train to
the prototypical "man" who, in this moment, is envisioning usurping the
power of God. Jungk again returns to this quotation from the *Bhagavad
Gita* in his account of the Trinity test, where readers finally discover the
purported "source" of the sacred text: "People were transfixed with fright
at the power of the explosion. Oppenheimer was clinging to one of the
uprights in the control room. A passage from the *Bhagavad-Gita*, the
sacred epic of the Hindus, flashed into his mind" (201). There follows a
requotation of the lines in Jungk's epigraph. Helpless and "clinging" before
the bomb, the language Oppenheimer has in which to cast this scientific
and technological achievement is religious, reflecting the inadequacy of
rational thought. The language he uses to describe the bomb is not the scientific language of solar energy. Rather, it is nonrational language, drawn
from the fearful uncanniness of thousands of suns bursting.

Jungk's association of the heliotrope with unfathomable divinity has the
defamiliarizing effect of distancing the bomb from mortal and technological realms and of inverting Enlightenment tropes so the "light" shed
on the physical world becomes inscrutable. It also paves the way for the
possibility in later histories of moral abdication on the part of the nuclear

scientists and of Oppenheimer in particular. When "Oppenheimer adopts the icons of exotic religious traditions, quotes from Scripture, and cultivates an air of spiritual detachment," Peter C. Reynolds asserts, he is also obscuring his role in "a quantum leap in the technology of violence" (180). Such language locates the agency necessary to construct the bomb in a wholly untouchable realm.

The tropology that links the natural world to divine knowledge appears repeatedly in *Brighter than a Thousand Suns*. Jungk explains at one point, for example, that "Oppenheimer typified for the general public the new worldly variety of scientist, with the mighty forces of Nature arrayed behind him" (240). He quotes a former student who says that after the war Oppenheimer "began to consider himself God Almighty, able to put the world to rights" (241). Such language also leads those disgruntled reviewers to complain about Jungk's portrait of American scientists—and understandably so, because Jungk is sometimes explicit in his assertion of American moral indifference concerning the bomb:

> The hopes of those who opposed the use of the bomb were revived for a moment longer when they heard that Oppenheimer was closeted with General Groves at a specially arranged meeting. In reality, however, the scientist, in seeking this interview with Groves shortly before the bomb was dropped, merely desired in the first place to convince his companion that it would soon be time to think about constructing less primitive atomic weapons. Thus the sum of a thousand individual acts of an intensely conscientious character led eventually to an act of collective abandonment of conscience, horrifying in its magnitude. (209)

In that passage, the "magnitude" of Oppenheimer's disregard arises from his position as a remote god sneering with contempt on the landscape arrayed before him as a plaything. This is, as reviewers have noted, a somewhat unfair portrait of Oppenheimer. Nonetheless, the rhetoric with which it is constructed has proven appealing for subsequent writers of Manhattan Project histories and their representations of Oppenheimer because it helps position the dangerous knowledge of the atomic realm, knowledge from which American society benefited greatly, in one conveniently remote man.

RESPONSIBILITY: *DAY OF TRINITY* (1965) AND *THE DAY THE SUN ROSE TWICE* (1984)

Subsequent histories of the Manhattan Project use various textual strategies to deify or absolve Oppenheimer. Lansing Lamont's *Day of Trinity* and Ferenc Morton Szasz's *The Day the Sun Rose Twice*, two histories focused mostly on the Trinity test itself, employ the heliotrope partly to efface Oppenheimer rhetorically and then, like Jungk's book, to attempt to remove responsibility from the hands of mortal scientists. In that both Lamont and Szasz go to some lengths to depict Oppenheimer's moral equivocations and complex relationship with guilt, it would be inaccurate to state that they deliberately or consciously try to absolve him. Rather, I focus on the effects of their language and on the consequences of using as conceptually loaded a device as the heliotrope. One of the consequences heliotropes have, I argue, is textually to separate Oppenheimer from responsibility, even if the bulk of the historical record (including the work of Lamont and Szasz) suggests his moral engagement. That such suggestions nonetheless slip in is perhaps also an unconscious effect of the tendency to frame Oppenheimer as a scientific genius whose quest for knowledge is more important than its moral consequences or else as a victim of the growing military-industrial complex. Such a tendency allows these texts to remain consistent with the hagiographic effect of many representations of Oppenheimer, representations that romanticize him as a scientist or idealize him as a public figure and avoid negotiating the fraught territory of the bomb itself. In any case, one of the consequences of this displaced responsibility is an understanding of history as an inexorable narrative, one that has Oppenheimer in its clutches and thus seems to exempt him from responsibility for his acts. History becomes, in other words, as inevitable as the sunrise.

Twenty years after the bomb was tested, journalist Lansing Lamont published *Day of Trinity*. Lamont's book was, according to the *New York Times*, the first internationally bestselling book about the Manhattan Project.[18] Its title, along with opening rhetorical moves that place the reader at "Dawn, July 16, 1945," awaiting the bomb's "first terrifying sunrise" (Lamont 3), evoke the rising sun to position the bomb as a technology that marks a new era. The disturbing novelty of the bomb is accommodated into a familiar, comfortable framework—the rising of the sun at the beginning of each day—that structures daily life and the conception of time. A closer look at Lamont's use of solar metaphors, however, reveals another meaning at the center of the heliotrope that in fact underscores the disruptive nature of the bomb. Lamont describes the moment of the test:

> A pinprick of brilliant light punctured the darkness, spurted upward in a flaming jet, then spilled into a dazzling cloche of fire that bleached the desert to a ghastly white. . . . For a fraction of a second the light in that bell-shaped fire mass was greater than any ever before produced on earth. Its intensity was such that it could have been seen on another planet. The temperature at its center was four times that at the center of the sun, and more than 10,000 times that at the sun's surface. The pressure, caving in the ground beneath, was over 100 billion atmospheres. (235–236)

Again, the presence of light in this passage emphasizes the strange rather than the commonplace, the unearthliness of the bomb rather than its sunriselike familiarity. The light unleashed is a "pinprick" popping into existence rather than a warm, gradual glow over the horizon. It "spurts" with "ghastly" results. Its excess (as a light "greater than any ever before produced on earth" and many times hotter than the sun) is so extreme that it becomes otherworldly, visible from other planets and multiplying into billions of worlds' worth of pressure.

Through this otherworldly tropology, Lamont also depicts Oppenheimer as otherworldly. In his description of Oppenheimer's Harvard years, for instance, he focuses on the future scientist's precociousness, on the "lonely, driving years" (18) he spent pursuing his education, on his ambition to be an "architect, artist or poet" (18) in addition to a scientist, on his reputation as "a rather peculiar egg" (19), on his magnetic personality that "drew others to him" (20), on the curious physicality produced by his "dancer's grace" (20), and on the way his intense "sapphire-blue eyes fram[ed] a delicately aquiline nose" (20). Lamont depicts the moment of the selection of the Los Alamos site as one predicated on a kind of divine inspiration: "Groves and Oppenheimer drove into the piney hills north of Santa Fe, New Mexico, to inspect a site for the laboratory Oppenheimer would soon head.... Suddenly Oppenheimer recalled a rustic boys' school he had often spied during pack trips from his family ranch nearby" (38–39). With this "sudden" moment of knowledge-production in a natural setting, Oppenheimer abruptly decides that the boys' school is to be the site of a physics revolution and America's grandest contribution to the war effort. His attempts to recruit other physicists to the program are characterized by "mysterious" (46) phone calls and cryptic communiqués. Once the work at Los Alamos gets underway, Lamont focuses on Oppenheimer's enigmatic combination of cold intellectualism and nurturance. "His peers," writes Lamont, "respected his ability to pick apart their brains and suggestions. The junior scientists marveled at his ability to soothe the elder prima donnas" (64). His intellect is not only a scientific one; Lamont notes that, when asked for his opinion on naming the test site, "Oppie was relaxing with a book of John Donne's poems" (70), and thus the name "Trinity," presumably inspired in Lamont's scenario by the poet's famous "three-person'd God," emerges gnomically from Oppenheimer.[19] Lamont's speculation about Oppenheimer's solitary visit to the top of the bomb's tower before the test also presents the scientist as an otherworldly figure: "Oppenheimer wanted to see for himself that nothing had been neglected in the bomb's final toilet. Perhaps, too, he wanted to feel the Gorgon's head one last time and stare it in the face with all its barbarous accouterments. Perhaps, more than anything else, he wanted to be alone where he could think, high above the busy desert with just the wind and the bomb for companions" (190–191). Consorting with mythological Gorgons, confronting the sublime techno-horror at the top of the tower, and elevating himself above everyone else "to think" as a desert visionary contribute pointedly to this ethereal portrait. We even find Lamont's physicist pausing in his ministrations to the bomb "to dip into his anthology of Baudelaire" (201).

Such rhetoric has, for Lamont, an additional (and more problematic) effect of diminishing Oppenheimer's presence. Depicting him as a learned humanist and melancholy visionary also allows Lamont to frame the director as fragile, insubstantial, and frequently absent. As the bomb test nears and obstacles crop up, Oppenheimer freezes with apprehension (173) in one instance, becomes "almost visibly ill" (178) in another, and "a wax statue" (225) in still another. As the scientists assemble the final components of the bomb, "Oppenheimer was so fidgety that [fellow physicists Robert] Bacher and [Marshall] Holloway finally had to ask him to leave the premises until the assembly was done" (171–172). His lack of bodily control undermines his presence at the site, and then he is literally "depresented" when asked to leave the room. These moments of diminishment are, for the most part, "historically accurate," but they also influence Lamont's prose, and his prose in turn influences how readers imagine these moments. For example, Lamont describes the arrival of good news for the harried director: "A telephone call from Bethe reached Oppenheimer at the mess hall as he was finishing breakfast. The news brought a smile to his haggard features" (183). In both sentences, Oppenheimer becomes a passive object, being reached by a telephone call and having a smile brought to his face—a man acted upon by other forces and thus surrendering his agency. Similarly, while waiting for the weather to clear just before the test, Groves and Oppenheimer become "a pair of shadows" standing in the rain and pausing "to hold silent communion with the bleak heavens" (211). Their lack of substance and their yielding to large, incomprehensible, uncontrollable forces reflect the diminishment they face as they contemplate technological intervention into the natural world.

Such ethereality problematically reduces Oppenheimer's responsibility for the bomb. Lamont firmly locates the Los Alamos scientists in a rarified realm and signals their detachment from the earthly consequences of their work. Referring to misgivings on the part of their colleagues working at Chicago, Lamont notes: "The Los Alamos scientists seemed detached from all this. Absorbed in their labors, swept up in the invigorating atmosphere of the mesa, they lived remote from the problems of Washington and the world at large" (83–84). Although Lamont is careful to mention the misgivings the Los Alamos scientists did have, his text ultimately endorses their work and the use of the bomb on Japan. He quotes Oppenheimer's admitting that he was "a little scared of what I had made" but then going on to say: "A scientist cannot hold back progress because of fears of what the world will do with his discoveries" (267). Emphasizing this notion of progress, Lamont quotes fellow Manhattan Project chronicler William Laurence—"The decision to use the bomb was not a human decision at all but one predetermined by historic forces" (299)—which again has the effect of absolving the scientists of responsibility. Thanks in part to its use of the heliotrope and its extended effects, Lamont's book offers a version of history as an irresistible force and the development of nuclear weapons as an inevitability.

In the midst of renewed Cold War tensions, Ferenc Morton Szasz published another historical account of Trinity, *The Day the Sun Rose Twice* (1984). Like Lamont's title, Szasz's begins with the heliotrope as a means of slotting his account of the Trinity test into what was by the mid-1980s a tradition of evoking the sun to make sense of the bomb. However, the familiarity of the sun's daily rising and setting is immediately brought into question by the strangeness suggested by Szasz's title. Evocations of the sun within the text similarly denaturalize the detonation. "It lit up the sky like the sun," writes Szasz, but he quickly adds: "throwing out a multicolored cloud that surged 38,000 feet into the atmosphere within about seven minutes.... The light created equaled almost twenty suns" (83). Szasz then quotes several observers: "At a crossroads store, an old man remarked, 'You boys must have been up to something this morning. The sun came up in the west and went on down again'" (84); a railroad engineer working a line says: "The glare lasted about three minutes and then everything was dark again, with dawn breaking in the east" (85); a highway traveler remarks: "The surrounding countryside was illuminated like daylight for about three seconds.... The experience scared me. It was just like the sun had come up and suddenly gone down again" (85); and a seismologist working in the area says the light was "not like one but a dozen brilliant suns" (87). Finally, Szasz quotes Laurence's account, reiterating his likening of the bomb to "a great green super-sun" (89). In all these instances, the sun is only a point of conceptual departure; the actual solar metaphors at work in Szasz's text point overwhelmingly to the strangeness and the surrealism of the sight. The bomb becomes a sun rising in the wrong place, rising with extraordinary intensity, or rising and setting with unnerving unpredictability.

Again like Lamont, Szasz depicts a similarly unusual and unpredictable Oppenheimer. Szasz's Oppenheimer arrives into the dreamy and sublime landscape of New Mexico—a world of "abrupt mesas, the world largest extinct volcano crater (the Valle Grande), numerous ancient Indian ruins, bustling modern Indian Pueblos, and tiny Spanish-American villages still speaking a seventeenth-century patois" that make the area "one of the most striking in the continental United States" (17). His "romantic" (27) arrival culminates at the Los Alamos laboratory, "an unreal world, part mountain resort and part military base. Locally it was often termed 'the Magic Mountain' or 'Shangri-La'" (17). Oppenheimer's "magnetic personality and brilliant mind made Los Alamos hum" (19), but this machine aesthetic sits next to his poetic and artistic inclinations in an environment in which one "could knock on any Los Alamos door and soon find himself in a stimulating conversation on poetry, science, art, or music" (21). Whether unreal, mechanical, romantic, mesmerizing, or artistic, his own strangeness and grandiosity in his quest for knowledge repeatedly echo the strangeness of the device he tested in the desert.

Szasz's Oppenheimer, like Lamont's and Laurence's, becomes insubstantial through a number of tropes and techniques. Szasz also uses passive constructions to describe Oppenheimer; for instance, at one point a "variety of emotions cascaded through the mind of the director" (89). At another point, Szasz refers to a radiation phenomenon described by scientists Joseph Hirschfelder and John Magee and says: "Copies of their memos to this effect reached Oppenheimer's desk" (63). Oppenheimer's passivity in this construction—*receiving* the memos rather than reading them or acting upon them—is underscored by its use of synecdoche, with the desk effectively replacing the man and dehumanizing him. As the test grows nearer, Oppenheimer's instability again comes to the fore in Szasz's descriptions. He seems to slip into dazed reveries and needs to be reminded of crucial technical details (117) and of his own potentially dangerous exposure to radiation (162).

Although Szasz does depict Oppenheimer wrestling with responsibility, the technique of having the scientist fade into the background or slip into insubstantiality allows him to assume the role of the apolitical scientist seeking that which is "technically sweet" without having to wrangle with its real-world consequences.[20] In a telling description of the moment in 1939 when Leo Szilard and others convinced Albert Einstein to write to President Roosevelt about the potential exploitability of nuclear fission, Szasz seems to depoliticize Oppenheimer even while arguing for his political engagement. "Up until 1938," Szasz writes, "theoretical physics ranked as one of the most esoteric of all disciplines. It was comparable, perhaps, to Medieval architecture or English Renaissance poetry. Overnight it transformed into the most political of all fields" (11). Szasz appears to be locating Oppenheimer in this now extremely political scientific field, but his comparison of science to art reveals his belief in the supposedly apolitical nature of art, an assumption that no doubt colors his depiction of Oppenheimer's artistic and romantic side. Despite being a post-1938 theoretical physicist, he is also an apolitical artist in Szasz's account. Despite its being as unusual as a dual sunrise or a colossal, miscolored sun, the atomic bomb becomes a foregone conclusion, a product of "disinterested" technological determinism, and Oppenheimer's participation becomes as inexorable as the rising and setting of the real sun, as inevitable as a normalizing heliotrope.

HISTORY UNDER THE SUN: RICHARD RHODES'S *THE MAKING OF THE ATOMIC BOMB* (1986)

The final section of this chapter examines perhaps the best-known historical account of the Manhattan Project: Richard Rhodes's *The Making of the Atomic Bomb*. Widely cited, frequently reviewed, funded by the Ford and Sloan Foundations, and awarded a Pulitzer Prize, a National Book Award, and a National Book Critics Circle Award, Rhodes's account was republished in 2012 in a "25th Anniversary Edition" with a new foreword by Rhodes and accompanied by a new round of accolades. Rhodes himself is a frequent historical consultant and interviewee on popular television programs about the bomb. Vast in scope and often technical, *The Making of the Atomic Bomb*, like Bird and Sherwin's hefty biography, situates its truth claims within a detailed and comprehensive historical context.[21] In a number of instances, Rhodes's book reinforces the normalizing power of the heliotrope. But he also uses the heliotrope in a way that underscores its potential for depicting the bomb as excessive, bizarre, and frightening— and, unlike Szasz, he does so by cross-referencing the sun quite directly with Oppenheimer himself. Ultimately, this effect has representational consequences similar to those in some of the other histories: depicting Oppenheimer through the language of passivity, effacing him through eli- sion and synecdoche, and distancing him from the consequences of his work. However, in making explicit what is often implicit in the other his- tories—Oppenheimer's relationship to the heliotrope within narratives of the atomic bomb—Rhodes highlights the rhetorical and representational importance of the heliotrope to a technology that, in so many ways, has ruptured history itself.

When Oppenheimer is not in the narrative, Rhodes's solar metaphors tend to function in the way DeLoughrey characterizes them: a means of naturalizing atomic weapons as part of, in her words, the "nuclearization" of American society in the twentieth century ("Radiation Ecologies" 472). In the early pages of his book, for example, Rhodes illustrates how the pioneering atomic work of Ernest Rutherford marked an early instance of using the sun as a governing metaphor in the conception of atomic struc- tures: "What Rutherford had visualized, making calculations and drawing diagrammatic atoms on large sheets of good paper, was exactly the sort of curving path toward and away from a compact, massive central body that a comet follows in its gravitational *pas de deux* with the sun" (50). This early example of the metaphor illustrates how conceptually important the sun would be to understanding (and hence, DeLoughrey would emphasize, to domesticating) atomic weapons. As Rhodes points out, the sun also sup- plies a vital store of inspiration for the development of nuclear science because the mysteries of how it burns so hot and for so long fueled early twentieth-century inquiries into the atomic structure of matter by British astronomer Robert Atkinson and his astrophysicist colleague Arthur Eddington (370).

In addition to laying conceptual foundations for the science itself, the comforting, reassuring sun serves an important narrative function in *The*

Making of the Atomic Bomb. In, for instance, Rhodes's account of Werner Heisenberg's breakthrough in matrix algebra while on Heligoland, a small German island in the North Sea, Rhodes first notes that "so often with deep physical discovery, the experience was elating but also psychologically disturbing" (117). But he then quotes Heisenberg himself: "I was far too excited to sleep, and so, as a new day dawned, I made for the southern tip of the island, where I had been longing to climb a rock jutting out into the sea. I now did so without too much trouble, and waited for the sun to rise" (117). Even as the disturbing "dawn" of a new mathematical era occurs in Heisenberg's head, the rising sun provides comfort and therefore functions conventionally in this part of Rhodes's narrative about the science that would eventually yield the bomb. Describing German chemist Kurt Mendelssohn's escape from the Nazis to Britain in 1933, Rhodes quotes Mendelssohn's joy at seeing the sun in London and then concludes his chapter on escaping German scientists with a lyrical invocation of the heliotrope as a central component of no less than the human experience: "Before it is science and career, before it is livelihood, before even it is family or love, freedom is sound sleep and safety to notice the play of morning sun" (197).

Rhodes's account of the Trinity test is suffused with solar metaphors that serve similar normalizing functions. Describing the assembly of the bomb at Alamogordo, Rhodes writes: "Before they opened the upper polar cap to expose the trapdoor plug they erected a white tent over the assembly area; thereafter a diffused glow of sunlight illuminated their work" (660). With its soft light in this scene, the sun allows this part of the construction of the world's most destructive weapon to resemble a pleasant camping excursion. When the bomb goes off, it is, to Edward Teller, "like opening the heavy curtains of a darkened room to a flood of sunlight," and to Ernest Lawrence, like being "enveloped with a warm brilliant yellow white light" (672). In Rhodes's account, the benignity and pleasantness of these comparisons liken the bomb and its shocking insights into the possibilities of manipulating the natural world to everyday sunshine—bright, cheery, and ordinary. Perhaps the most absurd example of normalizing the dangers of the bomb occurs when Teller, the man largely responsible for the even more dangerous hydrogen bomb, notes just before the Trinity test: "I thought the blast might be rather bigger than expected. So I put on some suntan lotion" (668).

Despite the relative consistency with which these solar metaphors work, there are several instances in Rhodes book—notably when Oppenheimer and the sun come together in a passage—where the heliotrope changes. The difference is subtle, but it marks one way *The Making of the Atomic Bomb* emphasizes the strangeness of the device by recourse to its depiction of the scientist most closely associated with it. For instance, in an early section of the book, Rhodes makes a claim—based on Oppenheimer's work, which "modeled the imploding collapse of dying suns"—that the scientist possessed "originality not so much ahead of its time as outside the frame" (150). In contrast to the longevity and immutability of our sun, the suns Oppenheimer thought about were dying suns, stars in the process of going out instead of illuminating the universe. The comparatively frightening image of an imploding star, and the connotations of violent negation it evokes, anticipates the destructive effects of the forthcoming weapon. But such imagery comes to stand as evidence in Rhodes's account for Oppenheimer's own peculiar ingenuity. His brand of originality is, as Rhodes puts it, not ahead of its time—not a perspective that can be cast knowingly backward—but rather out of sight. Outside the frame of past, present, or future, and also removed from conventional "frames of mind," his invisibility within history and his unusual intellectual bent both arise textually from a reference to strange suns.

Similarly, although through different rhetorical techniques, Rhodes's account of the arrival of the scientists at Los Alamos in early 1944 links Oppenheimer and the sun in an intriguing way. Rhodes frames the journey to Los Alamos, with an emphasis on the strange wartime lengths to which travelers and officials had to go to arrive in New Mexico, as a surreal undertaking: British scientists were brought to the pier in Liverpool in mortuary vehicles, for instance, and when Otto Frisch sees an orange in the United States for the first time after years of food shortages in England, "that sight was enough to send me into hysterical laughter" (523). Once in the United States and after a security briefing by General Groves in Washington, a "succession of trains delivered them into a fantastic landscape" (523): "There in the bright sunlight of a pine-shouldered mesa was Robert

Oppenheimer smoking a pipe and shading his close-cropped military haircut with a porkpie hat: 'Welcome to Los Alamos, and who the devil are you?'" (523). The culmination of a surreal trip, the sight of Oppenheimer standing in the sunlight functions as a strange synecdoche for the extraordinary quest for knowledge on which these scientists were about to embark. His appearance—unsettlingly "unscientific" in the rugged, outdoor setting—is highlighted by the sun's shining on him. His jocular yet penetrative question—"who the devil are you?"—reinforces the illumination, suggested again by the sun, that the sagelike or supernatural Oppenheimer was seeking according to these popular representations of history. This moment appears on the surface to be a simple rhetorical flourish used to underscore the fantastic qualities of Los Alamos in those early days, but in a book in large part about nuclear science, a discipline so rhetorically and conceptually dependent on solar metaphors, this is not an insignificant connection. It lends Oppenheimer a power to illuminate but also to unsettle; knowledge and the potentially rupturing effects of knowledge come together in this trope.

The decidedly "unscientific" characteristics that make him seem so unusual in his iconic, sunlit appearance emerge elsewhere in Rhodes's depiction of the scientist. In an early part of *The Making of the Atomic Bomb*, Rhodes recounts the eighteen-year-old Oppenheimer's first trip to New Mexico. After focusing on the toll taken on Oppenheimer's body by bouts of dysentery and colitis suffered while in Europe ("He was six feet tall, on an extremely narrow frame; he never in his life weighed more than 125 pounds and at times of illness or stress could waste to 115" [121]), Rhodes portrays the trip west as a movement into mysticism: "Like Eastern semi-invalids in frontier days, Oppenheimer's encounter with wilderness, freeing him from overcivilized restraints, was decisive, a healing of faith" (121). This metaphor, in addition to emphasizing mystical knowledge, contains two crucial components of the Oppenheimer narrative: his bodily presence and his affinity for the sunlit region of the United States, both of which would become inextricably bound up with the Manhattan Project and nuclear weapons. An object of fascination for biographers, novelists, and historians, his body is repeatedly depicted in terms drawn from stories of emaciated desert mystics. Leaving the body behind for more religious, intellectual, or otherwise ephemeral pursuits, such figures influence depictions of Oppenheimer by conjoining science with mysticism, but often by displacing science entirely. The profuse scientific detail of *The Making of the Atomic Bomb* ensures Rhodes does *not* displace science in this way, but the language of mysticism nonetheless functions as a strong undercurrent in the book. Likewise, his connection to New Mexico depends on, in Rhodes's construction, Oppenheimer's freedom from excessive civility, his liberty to indulge in "uncivilized" pursuits out in the sunny desert.

Although the historical reality of Oppenheimer's body or his artistic inclinations are not in question, the narrative effects of such representation bear scrutiny because they affect how the Manhattan Project as a historical reality is understood. For instance, in discussing Oppenheimer's Harvard years, Rhodes mentions Oppenheimer's youthful tendencies toward histrionics.[22] Oppenheimer "was prone to baroque exaggeration" (122), Rhodes writes. The floridity suggested by the term "baroque," to say nothing of the artistic tradition from which the word comes, clearly reinforces Oppenheimer's stereotypically humanistic qualities. But immediately after invoking such qualities, the text makes a remarkable formal move, one that connects the ways in which this historical narrative is sometimes told with Oppenheimer's humanistic qualities. Explaining his lengthy treatment of Oppenheimer's tendency to exaggerate, Rhodes writes: "Since that tendency would eventually ruin his life, it deserves to be examined" (122). Like Bird and Sherwin quoting the 1955 Oppenheimer in the 1943 portion of their biography, Rhodes anticipates the future. This brief proleptic moment, an allusion to Oppenheimer's eventual fall from grace at the hands of the AEC, reminds readers of Rhodes's omniscient position over the historical narrative. Like Bird and Sherwin, Rhodes as "visionary" historian discloses the importance of the Romantic artist figure in not only his portrait of Oppenheimer but in his own self-presentation as historian. This is not to criticize Rhodes's impressive text; rather, it is to discern some of the ways in which the intuitive, artistic components of Rhodes's portrait influence how knowledge is sought in a historical account of the Manhattan Project.

Working, it seems, hand in hand with Rhodes's focus on Oppenheimer's humanistic qualities is a subtle language of critique directed at the Manhattan Project leader. The author refers early on, for instance, to "Oppenheimer's youthful preciosity" (149), the overrefinement of his humanistic proclivities. Such preciosity does not necessarily dissipate as Oppenheimer ages, as seen in moments in Rhodes's account where Oppenheimer assumes the role of absentminded professor. In Rhodes's depictions, he frequently appears scattered or haphazard in his behavior; a phrase such as "Oppenheimer turned up in Chicago and dropped by to see Seaborg" (41) depicts the scientist as governed by chance and whimsy, turning up and dropping by seemingly at random. More significantly, however, Rhodes focuses on instances in which Oppenheimer fails in his humanism. Recounting Oppenheimer and Fermi's dispassionate 1943 discussion of poisoning the German food supply with strontium-90, Rhodes laments the way Oppenheimer, "a man who professed at various times in his life to be dedicated to *Ahimsa* ('the Sanscrit word that means doing no harm or hurt,' he explains) could write with enthusiasm of preparations for the mass poisoning of as many as five hundred thousand human beings" (511). This example of "the increasing bloody-mindedness of the Second World War" (511), appearing as it does in Oppenheimer, lodges Rhodes's critique of Oppenheimer in the scientist's failed cosmopolitanism and ethical standards. Oppenheimer later reveals a similarly cold attitude toward using the bomb itself (649), an attitude that undermines the careful philosophical image he cultivated elsewhere and that Rhodes reiterates in so many ways.

The mystical tropes discussed earlier and the veiled and not-so-veiled criticisms of Oppenheimer that Rhodes levels are important parts of a broader process of effacing Oppenheimer—of participating, in other words, in a rhetorical practice seemingly common to Oppenheimer representation: rendering his presence in large part through absence. Rhetorical examples of such effacement proliferate in Rhodes's text as the scientist gets Los Alamos up and running. Rhodes quotes Oppenheimer's own troubling self-erasure, for example, in a passage in which he talks about the difficulty of recruiting others to the project: "The notion of disappearing into the New Mexico desert for an indeterminate period...disturbed a good many scientists" (452). When those scientists then tried to work together, their conflicts "forced Oppenheimer to intervene" (545), and in cataloguing Oppenheimer's difficulties, Rhodes writes: "chain-smoking as much as meditative poetry drove him through his days" (663). In both cases, Rhodes uses passive constructions, which reflects his diminishment of Oppenheimer. The climax of this section of *The Making of the Atomic Bomb*—and probably the climax of the book as a whole—is the Trinity test. Rhodes's account of the test quotes General Thomas Farrell's observations about Oppenheimer's unruly body: "Dr. Oppenheimer, on whom had rested a very heavy burden, grew tenser as the last seconds ticked off. He scarcely breathed. He held on to a post to steady himself. For the last few seconds, he stared directly ahead" (669).[23] These minimizations, immobilizations, and enfoldings within the landscape and the technologies of the bomb itself no doubt reflect the difficult science being practiced under difficult conditions and the difficult administrative position Oppenheimer filled: seemingly only nominally in charge of a vast, ever-expanding, and ultimately unpredictable venture. He could not help but feel ineffectual, and Rhodes's language reflects that. These small examples of effacement, however, contribute to a broader effect.

Rhodes's critique of Oppenheimer extends to the "self-destructiveness" (444) etched even into Oppenheimer's body. Rhodes points to "the chain-smoking, the persistent cough persistently ignored, the ravaged teeth, the usually empty stomach assaulted by highly praised martinis and highly spiced food" (444) as small examples of a self-effacement with broader conceptual implications for the depiction of Oppenheimer; "Oppenheimer's emaciation," Rhodes writes, "suggests he had an aversion to incorporating the world" (444). Such an aversion connotes his "otherworldliness," his tendency to dwell in intellectual and artistic realms above and beyond mortal concern, but it also suggests a disconnection. The enchanting effects of the heliotrope on that early depiction of Oppenheimer serve eventually to reconfigure his "otherworldliness" as an "unworldliness"—a naiveté about the affairs of ordinary people that Rhodes claims was a youthful affectation (445) but that nonetheless permeates his depiction of Oppenheimer throughout the book. The literal otherworldliness of the sun eventually becomes the emaciated body "at a remove," as it were, from the world whose incorporation he strove to avoid. The production of nuclear knowledge under these conditions thus becomes a dispassionate, disembodied process seemingly with no connections to Oppenheimer personally or to the world at large.

To depict his presence in the Manhattan Project narrative by absenting him also contributes significantly to the process of absolving him rhetorically from the fraught morality of the bomb. When, for instance, Rhodes describes Oppenheimer's climbing the tower "to perform a final ritual inspection" (664) of the bomb, he casts him as a magician, an alchemist of old, carrying out a sacrament rather than science. "There before him crouched his handiwork" (664), writes Rhodes, as if to emphasize the bomb's independent menace. He becomes Victor Frankenstein as he looks at the bomb one last time, cognizant of his hubris and its hideous results but ultimately not responsible for what the creature does: "Its bandages had been removed and it was hung now with insulated wires that looped from junction boxes to the detonator plugs that studded its dark bulk" (664). Rhodes's concluding gesture in this scene makes clear Oppenheimer's disengagement from what is to come: "His duty was almost done" (664). Again, it is not my intention to accuse Rhodes of deliberately trying to absolve Oppenheimer. Rather, that sense of disconnection from the bomb is a consequence of depicting his quest for knowledge as an otherworldly one, a strategy that ultimately comes from the important role the sun— literally an otherworldly object—plays in understanding the bomb.

Like the inevitability of the rising sun, history in these texts becomes an ungovernable force to which one can only surrender and that, like the bomb, quickly becomes habitual and unnoticed. But because the sun is also a prime cultural source of otherness, its metaphoric function in these books dehumanizes Oppenheimer and the Los Alamos scientists and places them in the realm of mythology and ethereality.[24] Just as our distance from the sun and the sun's own vast immutability strip us of any sense of responsibility to it or for it (at the same time that we remain utterly dependent on it), history and the moves it makes on us seemingly cannot be altered but also define us. The history of the Manhattan Project, in this sense, thus becomes definitive of contemporary culture: from the postwar paranoia that resulted in Oppenheimer's disgrace at the hands of the AEC, through the weapons proliferation of the Cold War, to anxieties over the multifaceted nuclear future. And at the core of the historiographic process of definition and redefinition are representations of Oppenheimer as metaphysically inclined, artistically detached, and frequently supernatural or superhuman. Interrogating these types of representations, which frequently involves examining the heliotrope's function, ensures that the histories of the Manhattan Project are not taken as transparent representations of the inevitability of historical "progress." Under this analysis, the knowledge Oppenheimer is said to embody is not pure enlightenment but in fact, in the words of philosophers Max Horkheimer and Theodor W. Adorno, a dialectic of enlightenment.

CHAPTER 3

HISTORY IMAGINED:
OPPENHEIMER IN FICTION

To conclude the first part, on textual iterations of Robert Oppenheimer, I turn to fiction. Biographies, which I discuss in the first chapter, show an indebtedness to fiction when they speculate about the psychological states of their subjects, recreate conversations between individuals, or even simply when their literary qualities challenge conventional understandings of truth.[1] Histories too, as "remembrances" of the past, necessarily engage in reconstruction, fictionalization, and other overtly rhetorical strategies.[2] Discerning the textual meaning of Oppenheimer can thus be sharpened by an analysis of fiction. As a very large body of literary scholarship assumes, fiction changed following World War II.[3] Postmodern literature is, first, a historical construct that assumes the war deeply altered twentieth-century culture. Part of that alteration occurs through technology: mass production techniques revolutionize American society domestically at the same time they are adopted by the Nazi killing machine; astonishing discoveries in the realm of atomic physics alter the very perception of reality at the same time they are implemented in the technology that would kill thousands of Japanese and prompt philosophers Horkheimer and Adorno to remark that twentieth-century enlightenment "radiates disaster triumphant" (3). Postmodern literature is also aesthetically distinct. Its self-reflexivity, to name one of its most prominent features, indicates a profound suspicion

of language, literary and otherwise, and its attempt to refer meaningfully or transparently to the world. Such suspicion arises in part from the
"unspeakable" possibility of nuclear holocaust and the bomb's ability to
destroy all meaning. In both of these instances—the historical and the
aesthetic alterations characteristic of postmodernism—the bomb figures
prominently.[4] For those reasons, many postwar novelists who depict the
bomb take the Manhattan Project as a primal scene and its scientists as
chief actors in the creation of the postmodern. Nuclear culture, its participants, its imagery, and its legacies form a rich matrix that feeds the
postmodern aesthetic. Oppenheimer, therefore, also figures both prominently and obliquely. Novels in which he appears or in which Manhattan
Project scientists are depicted are imaginative contributions to his cultural
significance but also interventions into the historical narrative in which he
is embedded. Fictionalizing him—giving voice to his thoughts, imagining
alternative histories in which he figures—contributes to the imaginative
labor that helps create, disseminate, and understand the knowledge of the
natural world and of the nuclear technologies he helped engender as well
to the imaginative labor that makes up his cultural legacy.

For many of the observers, victims, beneficiaries, and ultimately,
inheritors of its legacy, the atomic bomb is both unimaginable and hyper-
stimulating. The physical properties of nuclear weapons, as well as the
protocols in place to produce, store, maintain, and finally deploy them, are
largely impenetrable to most, and the destruction they have wrought—in
Hiroshima, Nagasaki, the Marshall Islands, the Nevada proving grounds—
frequently verges on the incomprehensible. As Paul Boyer indicates, many
literary responses to the bomb, especially early ones, are characterized
by elision, omission, and the insufficiency of language that become the
primary mode through which to (not) discuss the bomb (247). Such silence
often comes across as a reluctance to transcend orthodox views of the
bomb as a product of ingenious American innovation, institutional power,
and military prowess.[5] This failure to discuss the bomb, however, also
seems to have more heterodox effects on received wisdom about nuclear
weapons. Boyer writes: "Silence may have signaled not a failure of imagination, but intensity of imagination" (250). Because nuclear weaponry
quickly came to provide fertile imaginative ground for countless novelists

and filmmakers, there seems to be a productively stimulating influence to be found in the nihilism, the gaps, and the silences of nuclear culture. We see such an influence in some of the major characteristics of Oppenheimer representation discussed in this book: the synecdochic and minimalist aesthetic often used to depict him. This chapter will locate ways in which some of these texts explode nuclear truisms and thus modify knowledge about the histories and futures of the bomb.

One obvious place to look for such challenges is in, for instance, fictional representations of nuclear war, with all-out apocalyptic global conflicts, nuclear holocausts, and nuclear winters reaping broad swaths of human and ecological destruction.[6] All such attempts—even the most future-oriented of science-fiction texts—have deeply entangled relationships with the past. Imagining the bomb requires articulating a stance on the conflicted history of its development and meaning. What constitutes an accurate, ethical, or critical way of imagining a weapon that at once broadened scientific knowledge and unleashed colossal devastation, that simultaneously represented a superhuman reckoning with a technical puzzle and the spectacular production of more than a generation of fear? Furthermore, how does one engage aesthetically, ethically, or historically with a scientific invention that, without too much of an imaginative leap, could destroy humankind and human history? Attempts to answer such questions and to confront such species-wide oblivion emerge often in fictional representations of the bomb and of its creators, particularly in some of the ways these texts engage with history and historical knowledge.

Because the bomb represents, alongside massive ruptures in the relationship between science and technology and within the practice of warfare, the possibility of destroying history itself, literary art that appears in its wake is frequently preoccupied with the question of history.[7] As critics have argued, literature distinctly self-reflexive about its relationship with history—the famous term in this context is "historiographic metafiction" (Hutcheon 5)—has become central to postmodern literature. This form of literature, in the wake of the history-threatening capacity of the atomic bomb, calls into question the very possibility of history as a knowable entity and of the rational subject who can perceive it objectively.[8] Even historical fiction more generally, although not often as explicit in its questioning of history as historiographic metafiction, becomes a prominent form in the postwar era for the ways it foregrounds history. Fictionalizing Oppenheimer in particular is thus an important attempt to engage imaginatively with the historical, epistemological, and aesthetic problems created by those bursts of unearthly light in the desert and over Japan. The fictional texts explored in this chapter position him with and against certain forms of knowledge—scientific and rational in some cases and intuitive and mystical in others—in their exploration of history and historiography. In some instances, novelists position him in relation to knowledge in an attempt to restore history through objectivity and rationality, positing an Oppenheimer who counteracts the bomb's unruly effects on history. That such novels frequently and intriguingly fail to do so is at once a reflection of Oppenheimer's personal and historical contradictions and yet another means of creating such contradictions in the popular imagination. Conversely, other novelists embrace the problematic nature of history and, in negating Oppenheimer as the "objective correlative" (Eliot 100) of history, foreground the disruptive nature of the bomb. Together, these fictionalizations constitute part of the postmodern nuclear imagination.

TRENDS

Oppenheimer began appearing as a fictional character shortly after the war ended, and since then, depicting him generally takes one of two approaches. In this section, I will briefly discuss examples of novels that help form these patterns of Oppenheimer representation before undertaking in the rest of the chapter more detailed analyses of two novels I take to be representative of these patterns. Some of the earliest examples of fictionalizing the Manhattan Project include Michael Amrine's *Secret* (1950), Dexter Masters's *The Accident* (1955), and Pearl S. Buck's *Command the Morning* (1959). Published before Oppenheimer's death in 1967 and thus needing to negotiate libel laws, these novels do not depict him by name (or even at all). Masters, for instance, fictionalizes the fate of Louis Slotin, a Canadian physicist who worked on the Manhattan Project until a lab accident caused his death from radiation poisoning. Masters is clearly dedicated to scientific accuracy, and in using the flashback to attempt to access history authoritatively, *The Accident* is firmly based on the known historical narrative. The novel figures Louis Saxl (Masters's fictionalized Slotin) in heroic terms for using his own body to shield the other scientists in the room from deadly radiation during the accident. Masters's novel thus joins the cultural desire to document history carefully, even or especially in fiction, with the understanding of the scientist as one who provides heroic, superhuman access to truth and knowledge. Similarly, both Buck's *Command the Morning* and Amrine's *Secret* are marked by a fascination with science and by Oppenheimer-like protagonists with single-minded commitments to science. Buck's protagonist, Burton Hall, and Amrine's, Benjamin Franklin Halverson, evince a devotion to science and an excitement over the bomb project in particular that make them Faustian figures—like Louis Saxl, they are scientists whose commitment to absolute knowledge no matter the cost makes them at once tragic and heroic.[9] Representing Oppenheimer (or Oppenheimer-like scientists) in this way goes hand in hand with how these novels invest in scientific detail, immerse themselves in the realist mode, and strive for a sense of historical authenticity by linking themselves firmly to the known historical record. In their attempts to underscore the import of the Manhattan Project and its scientists, these novels aim to align as closely as possible their imagined versions of the Project and its actors with midcentury's version of historical truth. In the process, though, the version of Oppenheimer that emerges is often single-minded and unproblematically in possession of the full scientific truth.

Such commitment to a high level of historical accuracy and its accompanying representations of Oppenheimer's scientific power is not confined to early examples of Manhattan Project fiction. In John Lawton's recent thriller *A Lily of the Field* (2010), for instance, Oppenheimer plays a minor but important role in framing the first atomic test for Karel Szabo, a fictional Hungarian physicist working on the Manhattan Project. Szabo eventually joins Lawton's intelligence officer protagonist Frederick Troy and contributes to Troy's murder investigations and espionage. Oppenheimer's influence on Szabo drives home for Szabo—and thus for the detective Troy—that the scientific method is essential to the kind of knowledge

discovery Troy makes as investigator and spy and, presumably, to the kind
of knowledge discovery at the core of large-scale technomilitary endeavors
such as the Manhattan Project. Oppenheimer's role in *A Lily of the Field*,
also consistent with the type of fiction to which I am suggesting this novel
belongs, is primarily an instrumental one; he functions as a fount of factual
knowledge, as a historical touchstone on which a fictional protagonist can
draw in his Enlightenment-inspired quest for truth. Lawton includes an
appendix, wryly titled "Notes, Anachronisms, Explanations…and stuff,"
which confirms his investment in historical accuracy, in the explanatory
power of text, and in maintaining the boundary between truth and fiction.
Other novels using a realist aesthetic in which Oppenheimer appears as
a more or less "accurate" fictional character include Larry Bogard's *Los
Alamos Light* (1983), James Thackara's *America's Children* (1984), Frank
Waters's *The Woman at Otowi Crossing* (1966/1987), Roberta Silman's
Beginning the World Again (1990), Bradford Morrow's *Trinity Fields* (1997),
and Dennis Bock's *The Ash Garden* (2001). Similar novels for children or
young adults include Paul Zindel's *The Gadget* (2001), Carolyn Reeder's
The Secret Project Notebook (2005), and Ellen Klages's *The Green Glass Sea*
(2006). As my analysis of Joseph Kanon's *Los Alamos* (1997) in the next
section will show, however, the attempts such novels make to solidify history or to gloss over Oppenheimer's mysticism are not always successful,
and they can write against themselves in intriguing ways.

A second general trend in Oppenheimer fictionalization is one that,
although certainly not denying the historical import of the Manhattan
Project, seeks to question the very processes of constructing and understanding history. Robert Olen Butler's *Countrymen of Bones* (1983), for
example, is about a fictional archaeologist who, while in the midst of a love
triangle, discovers the bones of an Aztec king in the Jornada del Meurto
desert at the same time Oppenheimer and company are testing the bomb.
Partly through a focus on Oppenheimer's own bony physicality, Butler
aligns him with the skeleton of the Aztec king, and thus allows him to
become more metaphorical than factual, more a divine figure than a scientific one. Such metaphors reveal a novel powered by, on the one hand,
the hard boniness of physical embodiment and concrete presence and,
on the other hand, by the complete unknowability evoked by death and

the ephemerality of the rarified world of ancient kings. The bones, which contain this contradictory tropology, serve as a metaphor for the equivocal effects on history Oppenheimer has had as well as the oscillating conceptual understandings of Oppenheimer himself. One possible bone of contention, so to speak, with Butler might be his treatment of gender roles, which, like his style, he seems to borrow from Ernest Hemingway. Nevertheless, his engagement with history highlights poetics as much as it does science in the construction of history. In addition, the notion of the "collision," which the scholar of historical fiction György Lukács identifies as the driving revolutionary power of historical fiction (53), emerges as a central component in Butler's novel. Conjoining Oppenheimer with ancient Aztecs in a novel written (though not set) in 1983 (and being read—or not—in the present) effects the dramatic impact between different actors and different social forces across a broad swath of time, which Lukács suggests is a potent creative force.

Another novel exemplifying this second broad trend is Martin Cruz Smith's *Stallion Gate* (1986).[10] Focalized through Joe Peña, a fictional Native American serviceman on the Manhattan Project, *Stallion Gate* adopts a generally fluid approach to knowledge and identity. Neither Peña nor Oppenheimer inhabits coherent racial identities. As a Native American "half-breed" with interests in a predominantly African American music scene and a predominantly white military culture, Peña's identity is troubled territory. Similarly, garbed in the clothing of the American West and the religious trappings of Far Eastern Hinduism, Oppenheimer is at odds with both the expected racial identity attached to his German-Jewish name and Eastern U. S. establishment background and with the scientific rationalism expected of his secular identity as a scientist (see Williams 190). Smith in fact goes to some lengths to qualify Oppenheimer as a fount of scientific knowledge by highlighting the value of doubt within his epistemology. Smith's Oppenheimer demonstrates many of the physicist's usual characteristics: his knowledge is impeccable, his will is ironclad, and he "inspires everyone to work so hard" (Smith 183). At the same time, however, he is enigmatic. His appearance is strange (in one moment, for instance, as "he spread his arms, turning, holding flags, he seemed, in his ungainly way, to be dancing in the snow" [49]), often self-contradictory ("his head

seemed gaunt and swollen at the same time" [255]), and frequently at odds
with his identity as a scientist ("he looked like a poet dictating" [77]). His
trademark tendency to elicit hard work from others, which is often represented as hypnotic, makes him more of a mystic than a bureaucrat. When
Joe encounters a blind, mad Native American visionary who reveals prescient knowledge about the top secret bomb tests in the desert and who
possesses the telling name Roberto, one character is prompted to remark,
"medicine men, physicists, they're all the same to me" (312). The novel
ends abruptly with a countdown to the Trinity test and Joe's diving for
cover in the desert. Consistent with the novel's uncertainty over history
and historiography, *Stallion Gate* leaves unclear what Joe's future holds
or even if he survives the explosion. The uncertain conclusion of *Stallion
Gate* reflects the novel's multivalent assessment of the bomb's historical
import to those who have been (and continue to be) affected by it (see
Williams 194).

Like Butler's poetic novel or Smith's exploration of the fluidity of identity,
other fictional treatments place Oppenheimer within alternate histories or
fantasy worlds or, if they employ a more realistic frame, otherwise invoke
him through remembered reconstructions and dreamlike scenarios that
also foreground the role of fantasy in fictionalizing historical characters.
As such, they bring the notion of transparent historiography into question. Robert Mayer's spy thriller *The Search* (1986), for example, depicts
Oppenheimer as a figure in one character's childhood memories. Similarly, he makes brief, oblique appearances in flashbacks in Robert Cohen's
The Organ Builder (1988). James Kunetka's *Parting Shot* (1991) imagines an
alternate history of the Manhattan Project and includes Oppenheimer as
a character. Gore Vidal's *The Smithsonian Institution* (1998), although set
when Oppenheimer was alive in 1939, also challenges the straightforward
fictionalization of historical figures through its use of time travel, animate
wax figures, and other extravagant conceits. Peter Millar's *Stealing Thunder*
(1999) reimagines some of the history of the espionage that occurred during
the Manhattan Project. Tom Carson's *Gilligan's Wake* (2003), an imaginative reweaving of James Joyce, *Gilligan's Island*, and various pop culture
allusions, freely intermingles fictional characters, such as Daisy Buch-
annan and Ginger and Mary-Ann, with historical figures, such as Sammy

Davis Jr. and Oppenheimer. John L. Casti's *The One True Platonic Heaven* (2004) speculates inventively on conversations about the moral dimensions of science that Oppenheimer may have had with Kurt Gödel, Albert Einstein, and T. S. Eliot at the Institute for Advanced Study. Marc Estrin's *Insect Dreams: The Half Life of Gregor Samsa* (2005) borrows Franz Kafka's most famous character and introduces him to a number of historical figures, including Oppenheimer. In a similarly farcical vein, Swedish writer Jonas Jonasson's hit debut novel *The 100-Year-Old Man Who Climbed Out the Window and Disappeared* (2009; published in English in 2012) depicts Oppenheimer as one of a series of famous historical figures whom the novel's Forrest Gump–like protagonist blunders into over the course of his long life. And Larry Niven and Jerry Pournelle's *Escape from Hell* (2009) is a science-fiction novel that, like Carson's, includes Oppenheimer among a diverse cast of historical figures, including Sylvia Plath, Pontius Pilate, and Anna Nicole Smith.

This general approach to fictionalizing Oppenheimer in relation to the contingencies of knowledge, and its resulting perspective on history, can trouble some critics. For example, in a review essay of more than twenty generically diverse books about the bomb, Robert Seidel devotes a paragraph to *Stallion Gate*. Although he acknowledges that historical fiction can be "an exercise in disciplined imagination," he criticizes Smith's novel because "it so deviates from reality" (528). Seidel's objections take troubling form when he reveals an investment in authoritative master narratives about "reality." One of his complaints, that "Smith has introduced as protagonist not a scientist, but...a Native American soldier" (528), emerges from the presumption that only a scientist can offer access to "reality." Seidel also calls Joe Peña a "not-so-noble savage," which discloses Seidel's not-so-subtle assumptions about what kinds of characters make "proper" protagonists and what a Native American character in fiction should be like. In criticizing Smith for "taking liberties," Seidel in fact denies the imaginative component in his earlier approving characterization of historical fiction as "disciplined imagination." This gambit perhaps reflects the way Enlightenment ideals of rationality persist even in the face of a technology as imaginatively disruptive as the atomic bomb.

"The Oppenheimer Principle": *Los Alamos* (1997)

To reiterate: there thus seem to be two general approaches to fictionalizing Oppenheimer. In the first, he functions largely (though not always
consistently) as an impeccable source of scientific knowledge and factual
detail that aligns with the novel's realism and that attempts to satisfy a
presumed authorial or a perceived readerly desire for the "historically
accurate." Novels in this first category tend toward historical verisimilitude, the first of four categories of historical fiction David Cowart outlines
in his study of that genre, a category he calls "The Way It Was." In the
second approach, Oppenheimer fills a more conflicted, often contradictory, conceptual purpose that seems to question the very foundations
of historical knowledge. The rest of this chapter discusses in detail two
fictionalizations, one exemplifying the first trend and one representing
the second. Joseph Kanon's *Los Alamos*, a historical murder mystery that,
perhaps thanks to its appearance shortly after the fiftieth anniversary com-
memorations in 1995 of the development of the atomic bomb, spent six
weeks on the *New York Times* paperback bestseller list in 1998. Consistent
with the epistemological assumptions of many mystery novels, *Los Alamos*
privileges logical inquiry as the means of acquiring knowledge and to that
end presents history as a linear construct that builds inexorably toward
the revelation of truth. Kanon's Oppenheimer largely helps serve that
purpose, although the inevitable paradoxes that suffuse depictions of him
also bring that purpose into question. Lydia Millet's *Oh Pure and Radiant
Heart* (2005) will serve as an example of the second type of Oppenheimer
fictionalization. Millet's novel presents history as considerably more malleable, uncertain, and unstable. Millet does not simply depict 1945 in 2005
(as Kanon does in 1997); her novel, evoking the uncertainty at the core of
the post-Einsteinian scientific method that led to the development of the
atomic bomb, questions the very historiographic principles by which the
past informs present understandings of truth and knowledge. By asking
readers to look at Oppenheimer's inquiry into the natural world through
some highly disruptive fabulation, Millet is able to highlight the mediating
power of the devices—historical, but also more generally textual as well as
more dislocatingly cinematic—used to comprehend him and the bomb.[11]

Such a process ensures Oppenheimer's inseparability from the media in which he is expressed and thus situates the process of acquiring knowledge about him firmly in its contextual texts. In putting these two novels into conversation, I do not wish to hierarchize them (i.e., to offer Kanon's novel as an example of "bad" historiography and Millet's as an example of "good") but rather to point out two things: one, that the novels exhibit differing degrees of historiographic metafictionality and are thus both emblematic of postmodern/postbomb literature; and two, Oppenheimer seems to function in both as a destabilizing presence with disruptive effects on historical narrative.

Kanon's *Los Alamos* is, first, characterized by a depiction of Oppenheimer as an all-knowing mandarin with privileged access to knowledge and a potent ability to disseminate it. The novel, set in 1945 and stocked with about equal numbers of historical figures and fictional characters, opens with the fictional Michael Connolly, an Army Intelligence agent, investigating the mysterious death of a Manhattan Project security officer in Santa Fe. One of his first stops upon arrival in Los Alamos is to see General Leslie Groves. Groves meets briefly with Connolly, and they discuss, among other things, Robert Oppenheimer. Groves, who in most historical accounts respected Oppenheimer but had a prickly relationship with the civilian physicists at work on the atomic bomb, comes across as perhaps more accommodating in Kanon's novel than in the historical records. He says, in response to a question Connolly has about the scientific director, "Dr. Oppenheimer knows everything. If for any reason I'm unavailable, consider him me" (24). This magnanimous statement constitutes one of the novel's early attempts to create an all-knowing Oppenheimer, to establish the physicist's process of acquiring knowledge as one characterized by virtual omniscience. Tellingly in Groves's statement, such omniscience also suggests omnipotence. The injunction to "consider him me" makes Oppenheimer a powerful force capable of assuming the identity and embodying the expertise of others. Although it contributes to imagining Oppenheimer as a supreme historical force, Groves's statement also imparts preternatural connotations. The mistaken assumption that a scientist "knows everything" helps sow the distrust and even the fear often attached to the image of the scientist as an all-powerful master of domains usually out of reach of other people, and Oppenheimer's potential "shape-shifting" ability makes him ominously mercurial.

Groves also calls Oppenheimer "a hero" (24), which shapes Connolly's perception of the scientist. Connolly's first meeting with Oppenheimer is accompanied by a revealing description:

> Connolly had seen photographs, but he was unprepared for the focus of Oppenheimer's gaze, eyes that took him in so quickly that he was enveloped in an intimacy even before he spoke. Oppenheimer was thin, even frail, so that the hollow face offered no distraction from the eyes... [that] were quick and curious. Behind them was a tiredness so profound that their shine seemed almost feverish. He had a cigarette in one hand and a drink in the other, so he had to bow his head in greeting, which he managed with an ironic oriental grace. His voice was low but as quick as his eyes. (44)

This passage discloses much about Kanon's fictionalized Oppenheimer. It reveals, first, the importance of visual technologies of mediation in representing him. To make known by making visible is a powerful Enlightenment trope and one decisively of the scientific method; in this passage, it provides advanced knowledge for Connolly that constitutes the truth of Oppenheimer for him. The photographic mediation of Oppenheimer underscores his importance to the development of technology in general in the second half of the twentieth century. The passage's focus on the scientist's eyes, similarly indebted to Enlightenment metaphors of visuality, offers readers an Oppenheimer with a penetrative, knowing gaze. At the same time, however, as soon as Kanon establishes the visionary qualities of the highly rational scientist—an Oppenheimer-as-seer—shades of the supernatural, of the nonrational, start to modulate his portrait. The effect of Oppenheimer's eyes on Connolly—their ability to "take him in," to "envelope" him, to presage a loss of self or an absorption into a greater power—owes much to conceptions of the captivating, transporting, artistic genius. Oppenheimer's hollow face resembles the evacuated desert in which he works and from which he draws his power; his frail, tired, even diseased ("feverish") body hints at a neo-Romantic altered state; and even the cigarette and the drink in his hands reinforce his affinity with Romantic notions of otherworldly knowledge imparted by mood- and mind-altering experiences. The exoticism of such tropes, reinforced by the "ironic oriental grace" with which he greets Connolly, is part of the colonialist gaze Kanon's protagonist employs elsewhere, but it is also a crucial component of the figure of the sage Kanon invokes.[12]

Oppenheimer's heroic, superhuman characteristics, his ability to transcend his surroundings, crop up frequently despite the novel's realism. "He sat there smoking," Kanon writes, "so animated and intense that the rest receded to the flatness of a still life" (55). In the hot desert sun, "Oppenheimer seemed unnaturally cool" (158) because everywhere he went he "understood everything" (277). His power also spreads out from his body, as when the time of the bomb test nears and the "whole mesa seemed on edge, like some extension of Oppenheimer's nervous system" (446). As the detective, Connolly eventually subdues his own rationalist epistemology and replaces it with Oppenheimer's intuitive one in order to solve the crime. "The Oppenheimer Principle" (281), as Connolly puts it, is the physicist's problem-solving ability, so uncanny it becomes an immutable law within the novel and so powerful it becomes an all-purpose tool as useful in building atomic bombs and saving the world as in solving crime.[13] Dr. Friedrich Eisler, a fictional scientist at work in Kanon's Los Alamos, elaborates on "The "Oppenheimer Principle" when he calls it a "leap in the dark" (327), suggesting that it is more about intuition than it is about rational deduction. In any case, Connolly's solution to the crime comes at the same moment as the successful atomic test in the desert on July 16, 1945, a moment that aligns the knowledge Connolly acquires with the vital unlocking of the physical world's most fundamental principles.

"The Oppenheimer Principle" thus represents the paradoxical result of the assumption seemingly at play in Kanon's novel that history can be grasped *through* discourse as opposed to *as* discourse. Kanon himself, in an essay on the process of writing *Los Alamos*, stresses the importance of this kind of authoritative, transparent access to history: "It may be that because we now so readily accept spin in our public lives, we've come to demand more accuracy in our fiction" ("A Novel Idea" 24). Although Kanon acknowledges that he is creating "a *version* of" Oppenheimer (25), he nevertheless reveals his investment in historical accuracy and in the ontological certainty that supposedly comes with it: "I do like to get things right" (24). Kanon also laments the way that much revisionist history of the past fifty years has demonized the Manhattan Project scientists, and although he stresses moral ambiguity and the importance of historical context, he nevertheless admits to a recuperative approach in his depiction of Oppenheimer: "I thought enough mud had been thrown at Oppenheimer during his life—I didn't want, even inadvertently, to add to the damage" (27). Depicting him in what is, for Kanon, a positive light as a superhuman scientist, therefore, is intimately connected to understanding history as an objectively knowable entity. But as the previous chapter suggests, one of the consequences of this assumption—and of the mythical, superhuman scientist who emerges—is potentially the freeing of the scientist from his moral responsibility or even his absolution of sin. All-knowing, detached from his physical surroundings, dwelling on another plane altogether, this "version" of Oppenheimer is caught up in "the fascination of theorems and the ecstasy of sudden inspiration" (Dorsey 277) that characterize many representations of scientists. He thus need not concern himself with the physical effects of the technology he is about to unleash, and his omniscience and status as a mythological figure assure him (and readers) that the development of the bomb was the right and inevitable thing to do and that moral equivocation is not necessary.

History in *Los Alamos* is likewise not only accessible but usually under the control of its participants. Many of the novel's characters claim to be "making history on the Hill" (109–110), and Eisler endorses a particularly American version of this practice when he says, "I put the past behind me. The old world. Isn't that the American idea? Start fresh, leave everything behind?" (180). Eisler quickly answers his own question, though, and reveals that history is in fact powerfully determinative when he adds: "You don't believe in history here. Yet. Sometimes I think we don't believe in anything else" (180). His speech, consisting of the short sentences and juxtapositions literary scholars call parataxis, reveals his hesitation over the idealized American notion that history can be negated in favor of reinvention. In fact, his speech helps strengthen history by instantiating it in the novel as an elemental force or particle—as fundamental as gravity or protons. History becomes such a key constituent of the world of Kanon's novel that many of its characters—and its narrative voice—speak of history as backdrop. When an automobile becomes a clue in the mystery, for example, Kanon begins one chapter as follows: "They found the car on May 8th, the day the war ended in Europe" (257). A few pages later, another security officer says to Connolly: "The Germans surrendered, by the way, in case you haven't heard" (259). In both statements, history comes second—either as a point of reference for another, more prominently placed fact in the detective narrative, or as an aside. History, in this ostensibly historical novel, in fact recedes into the background and becomes axiomatic through its familiarity. The contradictory depiction Kanon provides of history as authoritative yet effaceable, as accessible yet elusive, is an aestheticized view of history—one that makes it both momentously groundbreaking (especially when aligned with the atomic test) and an inexorable given.

"History Is Over": *Oh Pure and Radiant Heart* (2005)

Strikingly different from Kanon's novel, Lydia Millet's *Oh Pure and Radiant Heart* directly confronts the contingency and mediated nature of history. Generic classification of Millet's work is challenging. With her dark sense of humor and magical realist tendencies, she works in the vein of Kurt Vonnegut, Joseph Heller, and Haruki Murakami. The scholar Samuel Cohen calls *Oh Pure and Radiant Heart* "the novel Raymond Carver would have written if he had written a novel—and abandoned realism" (211). The novel fits Linda Hutcheon's by now familiar definition of historiographic metafiction in that it examines its own status as a textual construct while also claiming real history as its subject matter (5). In its self-reflexivity, however, it constitutes an example of "recombinant fiction,"[14] which reveals how the capriciousness of imagination and memory influence historical narratives. In a book about how postmodern fiction in general is a response to the temporal crisis provoked by the bomb and its capacity to eliminate the future, Daniel Grausam states that such fiction "rethinks the ontological altogether (61)" and, in the process, provides the absurdity and fabulation necessary to engage with "the paradoxes of a national imaginary that is

continually located in a tense no longer available to it" (73). Millet, likewise, seeks meaning in the counterfactual and the anachronistic as both
a reflection of and a means of addressing postmodern skepticism over
the objectivity and accessibility of history. *Oh Pure and Radiant Heart*
depicts the picaresque adventures of Oppenheimer and fellow Manhattan
Project scientists Enrico Fermi and Leo Szilard when they find themselves
in twenty-first-century Santa Fe—alive and well, with no memories of
their lives beyond the moment the first atomic bomb was detonated in the
desert in 1945.[15] Shepherded through the early twenty-first-century by Ann
and Ben, a contemporary (and rather befuddled) American couple, the
physicists function as a historical rupture into 2003 (the year in which the
novel is set) and a literalization of the threat atomic weapons posed to the
domestic sphere during the Cold War.[16] *Oh Pure and Radiant Heart* offers
a decentered reading experience that echoes a decentered twentieth century following the development of atomic weapons. The novel oscillates
between the historical and the fantastical. It assails the notion of a single,
monolithic, authoritative history, presenting history instead as a reconfigu-
rable discourse or text. Such a view of history is one that dwells (especially
in a post-9/11 context, in which grim, neoconservative responses to the
terrorist attacks of that day were just getting started) in what Amy J. Elias
calls the "terrifying, chaotic, and humbling incomprehensibility" of the late
twentieth century (56). Millet accomplishes this partly by setting Oppenheimer against what are for him radically new forms of knowledge and
ways of knowing. By using him as a fictional trope, she brings together two
supposedly dichotomous ways of accessing the past: through mediation
(especially technological and visual) and through supposedly privileged
firsthand knowledge. Within the logic of the novel, Oppenheimer has just
witnessed the Trinity test personally, only moments before awakening in
2003, and is thus "best" positioned to negotiate the two different ways
of knowing. His submergence within postmodern forms of mediation,
however, leaves him with a desire to evade history and to absolve himself
of responsibility for the bomb and its twenty-first-century consequences.
Millet's novel does not allow this and depicts instead the impossibility of
circumventing history and the need to confront the legacy of the bomb in
meaningful ways.

Oppenheimer's appearance in the modern-day United States is Millet's way of exploring the multiplicity of that moment when the country ushered in the atomic age. The twenty-first-century presence of the physicists is deliberately disruptive and dramatizes the impossibility of satisfying a nostalgic desire to encounter history in a direct, unmediated fashion ("as it really happened"), even while it refuses to shirk the reality of history altogether. At once an emblem of postwar American heroism and a sharp critique of the militarization of science (and the militarization of American society at large) that fed such notions of heroism, Millet's Oppenheimer remains deeply equivocal. The history he evokes is a sublime force that both offers a playful engagement with received notions of the atomic bomb and that highlights the tragic, often terrifying sense of loss in the face of the reconfiguration of the world wrought by nuclear weaponry. Oppenheimer's defamiliarizing presence and actions in the novel, the "historical inaccuracies" that are frequently cause for complaints about historical fiction but that in this case deliberately establish an ironic distance from history, "create," as one critic notes, "what might be called a suspension of *belief*" (Jacobs 69). Suspending belief in history by focusing instead on its texts and contexts provides a means of questioning received historical narratives.

The novel's nostalgic gestures are well in evidence and reveal ways that nostalgia structures the knowledge of history.[17] Millet's opening sentence, for instance, reads as follows: "In the middle of the twentieth century three men were charged with the task of removing the tension between minute and vast things" (3). Like the opening line of Nathaniel Hawthorne's short story "The Birthmark" ("In the latter part of the last century there lived a man of science, an eminent proficient in every branch of natural philosophy" [Hawthorne 36]), Millet's first sentence uses a fairy-tale gambit to begin her tale about nuclear scientists. The apparent mismatch (in both Millet and Hawthorne) between form and content, between a fantasy genre and the supposedly objective scientist at its center, points to (and criticizes) a nostalgia for a prescientific age. Casting the scientist in fantastic terms, in fairy-tale language, in the allegorical framework suggested by Millet's invocation of the minute and the vast, harkens back to supposedly simpler, more mysterious times—times understood not through the lens of empiricism but conjecture or fantasy. Such a move points to the deep dismay at the core of many responses to the bomb. It points to a barely concealed desire to slot the bomb into a framework that will explain it in more familiar terms, that will simplify its exceptionally complex language, or that will simply to make the bomb go away.

Similarly, much of the humor in the novel comes from the befuddled physicists' encounter with a radically altered America utterly unlike the "kindler, simpler" times they remember. Szilard, for instance, comically discovers power brakes on modern cars and puzzles over the purpose of *Cat Fancy* magazine, while Oppenheimer responds to a profanity-spewing teenager with a quaintly archaic phrase: "What a surprising expostulation!" (119). *Oh Pure and Radiant Heart* provides, on the surface, nostalgic reminiscences of bygone days, of American innocence and porkpie hats, of nonchalant chain-smoking in restaurants and casual sexism, all underscored by their comparative rarity in the contemporary United States. The physicists' pensive, wistful meditations on "how times have changed," although in sharp contrast to the virtual omniscience of Kanon's Oppenheimer, are as much about the complexities of historical change as they are opportunities in this novel for fish-out-of-water gags.

In this way, nostalgia can have a critical edge. Used self-consciously, it does not evade the reality of the present or romanticize the past, and it thus constitutes an important critical device for Millet. As an example of the genre Cohen calls "the transhistorical fantastic" (207), Millet's novel uses nostalgia not because that is the only mode now available to postmodern writers who have rejected traditional understandings of history but because she wishes to question how traditional narratives have arisen and what limits they impose on understanding the past.[18] Millet is, first, carefully self-reflexive in deploying nostalgia. In one scene, Ann goes to a restaurant for an after-work drink: "A mariachi band was playing in the depths of the restaurant. It was the music of nostalgia, she thought, pure sentiment with words only for placeholders—as though that was the only function of music, to convey either nostalgia or longing, the same emotion in different tenses" (136). Ann's direct confrontation with nostalgia, her identification of it as such, allows Millet to signal that she is being critical about it. Her critique of nostalgia is especially biting when, for instance, she aligns it with a kind of psychosis: Ann's husband Ben, who remains skeptical that the scientists are who they say they are, worries about the mental health of his wife when she claims she sees "resurrected A-bomb scientists from World War Two...lurking in the bushes" (71).

Millet's skepticism about nostalgia also emerges from the ways she positions Oppenheimer against twenty-first-century forms of mediating the past, a process that underscores the variegated role of 1945 in constructing contemporary American ideology. Accompanying that moment's triumphal iterations is a warning against the danger and moral dubiousness of nuclear weaponry. And accompanying post-1945 constructions of Oppenheimer and company as heroes or celebrities is an implicit concern with the normalization and prevalence of American scientific militarism. All of this can be seen when Oppenheimer, on a visit early in the novel to the 2003 Los Alamos, is struck by the changes it has undergone since 1945: "He had wanted it," Millet writes, "to be a place that history had moved through once fleetingly, with no trace of the past blowing through the high silver braches of its solitary trees" (24). But, of course, this desire for nugatory history—and this Oppenheimer's self-effacing desire for his own historical obscurity—is thwarted by the technological and visual mediation of the past. His wistfulness turns quickly to despair when, at the Bradbury Science Museum in Los Alamos, he watches a video of the 1945 atomic test that, for him, occurred only days before:

> Watching the video he registered not the strange, anomalous cloud but the rest of what he had lost, the vacuum that was left....It was a sucking vacuum on the ground, blistering a hole in the sky. It was vengeance on them all: it was the unspeakable and the divine.
> It had taken everything. (26)

The nature of the blast—its unspeakability and its divinity—produces a rupture that transcends mere historical obscurity and that Oppenheimer cannot reconcile because it threatens the very existence of history itself. Even when foregrounding the mediated nature of the image, when running "the footage from the Trinity shot repeatedly, pressing the button that started the video again and again" (27), Oppenheimer cannot make familiar the results of his work. In fact, his repeated playing of the video might be another attempt to displace responsibility onto technology. Technologized, mediatized repetition, as opposed to the more familiar logic of historical linearity and its purported "accessibility," interferes with his memory. It obliterates more and more. In a series of increasingly abstract sentences, Millet writes:

> As he watched the shot, the cloud that transformed itself as it rose, he finally forgot about individuals, forgot about the others who had been there with him. At first he had remembered their gestures and habits, the texture of them had come home with startling force as he watched the cloud rise and burgeon, its pregnant violence spread rolling and tumbling over the sky, spectacular and obscene birth.
>
> But now he was losing them. (27)

History becomes an annihilative force, and for the time-traveling scientists, conventionally nostalgic invocations of the middle of the twentieth century become impossible once the scientists are aware of the concrete consequences of their work. Szilard, lecturing Ben on the recent history he has gleaned from the "fabulous invention" known as the Internet, talks about the uranium-tipped shells used in the first Persian Gulf War, wonders about the tons of depleted uranium left behind after the second Gulf War, and berates Ben: "You people don't bother to know the basic facts about what your government does to other countries" (128). He points to the Orwellian renaming—often lost to twenty-first-century familiarity—of the position of Secretary of War to Secretary of Defense. "Apparently these days the government likes to pretend that all war is defense" (150), he says, reminding readers of the prevalence of scientific militarism in so much U.S. history in the second half of the twentieth century: from the Cold War of the 1950s to the napalm and Agent Orange in Vietnam to Ronald Reagan's Strategic Defense Initiative to the so-called smart bombs in Iraq and drones in Afghanistan. Significantly, Oppenheimer also chastises the U.S. government for downplaying Japanese deaths at Hiroshima and Nagasaki and exaggerating the number of American lives saved by the sudden end to the war. Reading accounts of Hiroshima and Nagasaki, he is especially struck by the catalogue of horror they contain: radiation burns, charred and dismembered body parts, vaporized humans. Such observations, made by figures at once familiar to readers from the history books yet quite out of place in the contemporary United States, potently invoke the trauma of that historical moment. Such invocations occur through the ways Millet foregrounds mediation: reading history books, surfing the net, or watching museum video installations. Despite (or perhaps because of) its postmodern aesthetic, the novel nevertheless holds on to the notion of historical truth and is able to refer to it meaningfully despite the "competing subjectivities" (Berlatsky 1–2) so often in evidence in these types of novel. At the same time, it defamiliarizes historical truth through the very channels often thought to provide transparent access to that truth. Reading about the history he made is, for Millet's Oppenheimer, "a fierce and ugly act. He was afraid of it, but he had to persist" (143). Such persistence is evidence of the progressive power Lukács locates in historical fiction when he claims that its driving power lies in "the living contradiction between conflicting historical forces, the antagonism of classes and nations" (Lukács 53). The "living contradiction" of Manhattan Project scientists in the contemporary world prompts the reevaluation of history and, with it, human progress. Oppenheimer's resolve is an assertion of presence that ultimately defeats the desire for historical obscurity and allows him to take responsibility for the bomb. In this sense, Millet's novel contradicts literary scholar Daniel McKay's claim that "the signature objective of [Manhattan] Project novels has never been to enlarge upon—or even to engage in the slightest—with the decision that led to the bombings" (170).

The persistence of history, and Millet's diligent attempt to "read" its presence into the contemporary (signaled partly by her protagonist Ann's job as a librarian), is made possible by her whimsical but not merely nostalgic resurrection of the scientists. Their presence provides a narrative opportunity to acquire knowledge about the past. As living anachronisms, they illustrate the effect the present has on the past, the way today's mass mediation and its attendant visual repetition blunts the trauma of history at the price of ignorance. The full sublimity of history, the creative possibilities it contains but also its shock, finds echo in the subatomic science Oppenheimer and company were doing: unleashing the tension between the miniscule and the immense, "the pinprick and the vast desecration" (Millet 124). Effecting the shift from one state to the other is, moreover, figured as a loss of history. Oppenheimer forgets those with whom he worked—they are obliterated by the metaphorical vacuum of the atomic bomb in an echo of the actual obliteration of the Hiroshima and Naga-saki bombs—but as Millet writes, the Japanese survivors of Hiroshima and Nagasaki "spoke of the quality of their lives after the bomb as *muga-muchu*: without self" (181). The text too, as historiographic metafiction, obliterates the conventional subject by reinforcing its constitution through inescapable history and social context.[19] Altering that context alters our sense of historical self. Oppenheimer's presence teaches Ann in *Oh Pure and Radiant Heart* "that it was at the moment of the first atom splitting that material things gained final ascendancy and took the place of God" (61). Usurping God confronts the notion that history can be seen from an omniscient perspective or that history strives to place itself in an omni-scient position and thus questions the knowledge provided by received historical narratives. The changeability and circuitousness of historical narrative helps reimagine the future, not just the past, and attempts to create a future free of depleted uranium and vaporized bodies. Oppen-heimer thinks at one point in the novel: "As soon as we saw history as a line we also saw its end…because then it was not merely our deaths that we had to contend with but our extinction" (176). Despite his anxiety over the human desire to destroy history, his own imagined presence speaks to the persistence of history even in the face of catastrophe.

The second half of Millet's novel, however, interrogates the belief that history can persist embodied in the figure of one man. It takes Oppen-heimer's postwar celebrity and transplants it into early twenty-first-century culture in the form of a carnivalesque messianism. A crowd of wild-eyed followers glom on to Oppenheimer in the months after his appearance in 2003. Between propositioning him sexually and treating his cigarette butts and porkpie hat as holy relics, their vision of Oppenheimer as the second coming and the accompanying crypto-apocalypticism (replete with alien-worshipping subcults and other fatuous manifestations) serve to critique the hero discourse within which he was understood in the years immediately following the war. The mindlessness and fanaticism of his admirers, along with their willingness to commit violence for the cause they believe themselves to be following, speaks (hyperbolically, of course) to the failure of postwar hero discourse to account for the various meanings of what Oppenheimer and his fellow scientists had accomplished. His mad acolytes are Millet's fictive judgment on the discourse of mysticism— on Oppenheimer's frequently invoked identity as a visionary—that sits disconcertingly at odds with the objectivity and rationality supposedly at the center of the enlightened American scientist. Their rapturous fascination with the end of the world that Oppenheimer was, in their estimation, both bringing about and saving them from, clinches Millet's skepticism regarding blind faith in "the wonders of the atomic age" and the disturbingly self-satisfied certainty of the Cold War's doctrine of Mutually Assured Destruction. After the scientists disappear as mysteriously as they arrived (carried off, apparently, by a flock of whooping cranes), Ben concludes, Francis Fukuyama–like: "History is over" (479). His statement asserts the ability of one or two mortal men to embody the notion of history, an assertion that contradicts the novel's view of their undying legacy: "The bombs they had conceived remained, of course; the bombs in their various silos, trucks and trains, their submarines and aircraft, had been dispersed over the globe like seeds, and lay quietly waiting to bloom" (489). Such a contradiction helps reposition historical knowledge on the border between the fantastic and the objective. The excesses of Millet's conceit (not just the whooping cranes but the very premise of time travel) produce a narrative pleasure at the same time that the novel engages with a deep sense of loss.[20] It also embodies a profoundly dark vision—one that, as Cohen points out, makes even attempting to challenge the military-industrial complex in the twenty-first century an act of sheer fantasy (212, 215).

History in Millet's novel is thus indebted to the quantum-physical elimination of the boundary between "minute and vast things" (3). Nonlinear and unstable in its relationship to space, time in *Oh Pure and Radiant Heart* challenges binary oppositions such as past/present and forward/ backward and enacts instead simultaneously existing states in which Oppenheimer is (like Schrödinger's cat) both dead and not-dead, part of "then" and a messiah in the "now." Such simultaneity is a crucial component in representing Oppenheimer—crucial because his prominent role as cultural representative reinforces the difficulties of acquiring knowledge in the nuclear age, the counterintuitive knowledge that often results, and the role of mediation in the construction of the "reality" of that knowledge. Like Thomas Edison, who was nicknamed "the Wizard of Menlo Park," Oppenheimer worked in a realm perceived as magical.[21] The existential threat posed by the bomb, couched as it often is in both the language of the Enlightenment and the language of magic, challenges the very enterprise of knowledge acquisition and embodies that challenge in the figure of Robert Oppenheimer. *Oh Pure and Radiant Heart* reinforces the continuity between these languages and, in doing so, defies most conventional ways of understanding the individual and his or her place in history. By contrast, Joseph Kanon's fictional world in *Los Alamos* strives for a more conventionally historical register. In offering "The Oppenheimer Principle" as the fount of ultimate truth and knowledge, however, it seems to suggest that such knowledge depends as much on divination, intuition, and mysticism as it does on objective observation. The atomic explosion that sends the physicists to the future in Millet's novel, crucial as it is to the novel's premise, is absent from her narrative (not including Oppenheimer's repeated but highly mediated replaying of the test on a video screen), which reminds readers that her novel's metahistory locates the test outside the realm of realist narrative.[22] Kanon, by contrast, not only dramatizes the atomic test but aligns it with the climax of its detective protagonist's investigative procedure. Despite the paradoxes that seem inevitably to accompany representations of Oppenheimer, Kanon attenuates the physical and epistemological ruptures of the world's first nuclear detonation by aligning it at the end of the novel with the successfully resolved logical puzzle. Millet rejects such logic by disavowing, at least to an extent, the fantasy of unmediated access to "real" (i.e., nontextual) history. Both novels engage with the aesthetics (and the ethics) of renewal. In Millet's case, simultaneity and fabulation counteract the troubling nature of nostalgia and enact instead a chimerical history. In Kanon's case, linearity and knowability offset the troubling nature of history. Neither novel, however, puts Oppenheimer forward as its main protagonist which ensures that their aesthetics—regardless of their ideological underpinnings—constitutes an engagement with history as a text rather than an acceptance of history's "great men" as its primary movers. The relationship between history and fiction in these works, thanks to their related aesthetics, is nearly as multivalent as the bonds among atoms, nearly as varied as the stuff of the universe.

The history evoked in these novels is likewise contingent. Like a subatomic particle, which in its quantum-physical existence cannot have its position and momentum known simultaneously, history and fiction both offer in the scientists they depict speculation and approximation—likelihoods, odds, averages, potentialities, and uncertainties. Like a subatomic particle, which is real but which must be accessed through approximation, history is real but must be represented textually. In its textuality, it has challenged the godlike omniscience of "objective history" and the godlike omniscience often attached to science. Such a challenge can have, of course, unmooring effects, even in a time marked by an unprecedented accumulation of knowledge and, especially, in a time of renewed urgency for assurance. In taking a counterfactual form, such a challenge to science is also a symptom of postmodern ennui, in which individuals are seen as too weak to be real historical actors and to which fabulation is one of few possible responses.[23]

These imaginative representations inform the narratives of twentieth-century America's cultural, economic, and military ascendancy to the global stage. But they also illuminate the ways those narratives have come to serve as a contemporary means of renewal, of reinforcing national glory in the face of a variety of challenges, whether the shifting geopolitical relations of the Cold War, the upended social conventions and priorities of the culture wars, or the profound sense of loss that accompanied the terrorist attacks of 9/11. If nothing else, the atomic bomb and its human agents are, for many, a gruesome crescendo of the relentless modernist drive toward technological efficiency and mechanization—a device to halt the Nazi regime's assembly-line murder with an even more spectacular form of technologized mass murder—and the horrific centerpiece of humankind's most violent century. In that light, counterfactual history—fiction that, for example, forces Oppenheimer to confront the contemporary consequences of his creation—provides what Niall Ferguson calls an "antidote to determinism" (89), a discourse counter to science's perceived stoic march toward "progress." Even when it deemphasizes "great" figures such as Oppenheimer in favor of unknown and average figures and thus appears to embody Lukács's conception of the historical novel as one that affirms Marxist values of revolution and dialectical progress, historical fiction about the development of the bomb is often grim and nihilistic. That these novels foreground reconfigurability or flexibility as essential qualities nonetheless reveals their creative, renewing potency. They can, after all, ensure that nostalgia exceeds its idealizing or eliding tendencies, and they can act to address the malaise over how knowledge is configured, authorized, and understood in the postmodern age. Ultimately, that is one of the more powerful implications of novels such as Millet's: they disrupt that insistence on a single, inexorable, teleological historical narrative. When such texts deal with science, they also question the nature of progress. The imaginative power of their nostalgia-as-renewal invites readers to imagine nothing less than other futures.

PART II

VISUALIZING
OPPENHEIMER

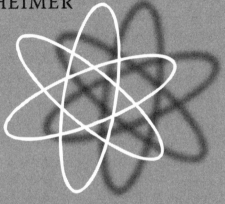

From the startling images of the unseen that marked Wilhelm Rönt-
gen's discovery of X-rays in 1895 to the "pinprick of a brilliant light"
(Lamont 235) and the solar metaphors that came to characterize
the Trinity explosion, many of the tropes in early nuclear science involve
sight, light, and other dimensions of visuality characteristic of Enlightenment thought (including the word "enlightenment" itself): revealing the
unknown, seeing is believing, the dawning of a new age, and so on.[1] At
the same time, the subatomic activity at the core of nuclear weapons is
invisible to the naked eye and must be depicted in terms of probability.[2]
Furthermore, and as Paul Virilio and Akira Mizuta Lippit have perhaps
most creatively explained, these new forms of light unleashed at the turn
of the century and over the next forty-five years are inextricable from the
knowledge of death and destruction—not only of physical structures and
human bodies but "the destruction of the visual order" (Lippit 4) itself
by this new regime of radiant energy. X-rays, an early inspiration within
atomic science, complicated the subject position of the Enlightenment-era
spectator by producing, in Lippit's words, "a phantom chiasmus, 'x'" (55)
that disturbingly reversed categories such as visibility and invisibility or
interiority and exteriority. At the same time, the atomic light unleashed by
the bomb reversed, for Lippit, the categories of living and dead: "At Hiroshima, and then Nagasaki, a blinding flash vaporized entire bodies, leaving
behind only *shadow* traces. The initial destruction was followed by waves
of invisible radiation, which infiltrated the survivors' bodies imperceptibly.
What began as a spectacular attack ended as a form of violent invisibility"
(86). And, ultimately, "the bombings were themselves a form of total photography that exceeded the economies of representation" (95) and thus
complicated the role of the visual in the construction of knowledge. The
visual rhetoric of an atomic explosion is simultaneously one that insists

on knowledge of itself through extreme visibility (a visibility so bright it leads to blindness) and one that is perpetually threatened with erasure. Thanks to the banality imparted to the iconic mushroom cloud by its repetition and cooptation, and thanks to its virtual imperceptibility granted by a five-decade long atmospheric test ban, the bomb's invisibility is one of its most conspicuous features. Those who produce these explosions are similarly balanced between conceptual realms; they require dead bodies—real or imagined—to secure the power of the bomb (see Gusterson 109), yet they themselves must be invisible to maintain that power. As the body behind the bomb, both obscured in his role as "executioner" and brought to the forefront of nuclear weapons by that paradoxically obscuring phrase "behind the bomb," Oppenheimer stands on this razor's edge of visuality. In his simultaneously self-aggrandizing and self-negating claim to have "become Death, the destroyer of worlds," and in his public visibility as a celebrity and his later self-exile, he and his relationship to knowledge are both clearly visible and opaquely invisible.

The first part of this book examined a variety of textual versions of Oppenheimer and explored how those biographical, historical, and fictional texts have constructed him and positioned him in relation to nuclear knowledge. Some of that exploration rests on the importance of visuality—of seeing deserts, seeing the life-destroying bomb in the light of the life-giving sun, seeing history in/as fiction—but because such iterations are all textual, they oppose, in a sense, the tropes of visuality they often evoke. Suggested but never fully enacted by the textual Oppenheimers discussed in part 1 is the relationship between word and image, between that which can be said and that which can be seen.[3] That relationship is made more explicit in part 2.

The importance of the visual to Enlightenment knowledge, the conflicts and problems that subatomic physics poses to visuality, the unstable relationship between the infinitesimal world of subatomic particles and their world- and star-sized consequences, and the destructiveness of a weapon conveyed through incomprehensible images of Hiroshima and Nagasaki or through the visual strategies of cinematic attempts to imagine nuclear holocaust all compel a closer examination of the visual. If sight is privileged—as a site of truth and comprehension—then seeing Oppenheimer and seeing how he has been seen next to that eye-searing pinprick of light that marked the first atomic test becomes crucial to understanding the knowledge he and his science have produced. Because the visual and the textual are intimately connected, part 2 begins with a brief discussion of comics—a genre operating simultaneously in the realms of text and image. It then moves into a brief discussion of photography, of "purely" visual representations of Oppenheimer (that as analysis shows is anything but pure). The rest of part 2 provides more sustained examinations of visual representations of Oppenheimer in cinema and television (chapter 4) and of material representations, within which the visual and the textual come together, in museum displays (chapter 5).

The Visual and the Textual: Oppenheimer in Comics

In bringing the textual and the visual together as a means of anticipating the next two chapters, I turn now to a form perhaps surprisingly conversant with the topics of Oppenheimer and the atomic bomb: comics.[4] This turn anticipates a discussion of the purportedly greater objectivity of visual forms such as photography and cinema by emphasizing the subjectivity of the hand-drawn image.[5] The self-consciously subjective nature of hand-drawn images grants comics a power to challenge received historical narrative, transcendent truth, and other products of the potentially problematic cultural investment in objectivity. Furthermore, it challenges the privileged position enjoyed by prose text by putting hand-drawn images forward as equally capable of "re-presenting" reality.[6] Comics make the constructedness of representation obvious. It is an ideal form through which to explore the relationship in Oppenheimer representation between the ephemeral and the material (a prominent relationship in many of the texts examined in part 1) because "the material" in Oppenheimer representation is often focused on the bodily, and the material aesthetics of comics depends partly on the body of the artist: "Comics works are literally manuscripts: they are written by hand" (Chute, "Comics Form" 112). At the same time, comics derive power from the disjunction between, as opposed to the synthesis of, text and image. In a seminal analysis of comics,

Scott McCloud declares that the form is neither writing nor pictorial art; rather, it is both and neither, "a language all its own" (McCloud 19). Likewise, Hillary Chute and Marianne DeKoven write: "In comics, the images are not illustrative of the text, but comprise a separate narrative thread that moves forward in time in a different way than the prose text.... The medium of comics is cross-discursive because it is composed of verbal and visual narratives that do not simply blend together, creating a unified whole, but rather remain distinct" ("Introduction" 769).

This distinction, a characteristic inherent in the medium's form, gains unexpected political power from the challenges it can mount to established social systems.[7] The participatory power of comics lies, according to these scholars, largely in the blank spaces between the images. McCloud, borrowing the term from the typesetting and printing industries, calls this blank space "the gutter" and argues that it is an empowering space, for it is there where the reader must imagine what occurs between one still pictorial image and the next (66). The "silence" between the panels is just as important, if not more so, as the panels themselves for constructing narrative and reconstructing the meaning and value of the social systems supporting those narratives.[8] Constructing meaning from absence, generating something from nothing, has been a vital process at work in many of the representations examined in part 1. That process helps characterize Oppenheimer as a mystical visionary (alongside his identity as a logical-minded scientist) and thus has characterized midcentury American science's quest for knowledge as a penetrating but ultimately inscrutable process. The complex relationships between image and text and between visibility and invisibility are key in representations of Oppenheimer as well as in the connections between part 1 and part 2 of this study. The uneasy relationship between words and images in comics often questions Oppenheimer's relationship to the privileged, (in)visible knowledge of nuclear physics. Such questioning will inform part 2.

One Oppenheimer comic pertinent to this line of questioning is *Fallout: J. Robert Oppenheimer, Leo Szilard, and the Political Science of the Atomic Bomb* (2001) by Jim Ottaviani and a number of graphic artists. *Fallout's* most striking feature—the pictorial diversity imparted by its use of multiple artists—has an important and influential effect: that of casting Oppenheimer (and Szilard and nearly every other recurring character in the narrative) into visual uncertainty. The abrupt variations in visual style marking the shifts from one segment to another, and one artist to another, lend him a variety of visual appearances and help create, in the gaps between sections, a "new" Oppenheimer each time. The ambiguities of the historical Oppenheimer are compounded visually in these shifts in style. *Fallout* thus underscores its own status as an object of mediation by reminding readers of the distance between reality and the "transparent" access to reality that the visual image appears to promise. The kaleidoscopic nature of *Fallout*, its tendency to depict Oppenheimer as changeable simply by virtue of its multiple graphic authorship, is an example of the ability comics have to challenge realism and to destabilize the privileged narrative position enjoyed by realism and verisimilitude.[9] Such instability reflects the cultural, geopolitical, and historical instability wrought by the creation of the atomic bomb, but it also challenges the instrumentalized, militarized science that emerged from the Manhattan Project. Furthermore, it complicates, by unstably joining textual and visual forms, the visuality at the core of Enlightenment science.

The challenging, motley style of *Fallout* and its frequent multivalent representations of Oppenheimer, however, tend to be smoothed over by other techniques the artists adopt. The text is bookended, for instance, by some editorial apparatus that work to restabilize its potentially transgressive aesthetic. A note at the beginning reads: "Though not a work of history, this book isn't entirely fiction either. We've fabricated some details in service of the story, but the characters said and did (most of) the things you'll read. And as the notes and references will indicate, many of the quotes and incidents that you'll think most likely to be made up are the best documented facts" (5). *Fallout*'s notes and references are surprisingly extensive; twenty-six two-column pages at the end of the work—pages with dark borders to signal their status as reference material distinct from the main text—detail all the ways in which the artists have deviated from "real history." Such a meticulous accounting of the distinctions between "fact" and "fiction" reveals a significant investment in the stability of such categories. Reasserting such categories means that *Fallout* constitutes an example of an attempt, by a form noted for its potent interventionary possibilities into received historical narratives, to resolve the ambiguously positioned Oppenheimer it creates.[10]

These ambiguities appear also in more recent examples of comics depicting Oppenheimer. Jonathan Fetter-Vorm's *Trinity: A Graphic History of the First Atomic Bomb* (2012), for example, does not even hint at the possibility that parts of the narrative may have been (or could be) fictionalized. Despite its identity as a supposedly straightforward historical account in graphic form, *Trinity* nevertheless offers the themes of vision and sight, specifically through a focus on Oppenheimer's eyes, as a means of reinforcing his role as a twentieth-century "visionary." The cover of *Trinity* features a detailed, close-up view of his eyes below the title and a mushroom cloud above it. His penetrating gaze, coupled with the mushroom cloud emerging overhead, exemplifies his role as scientific seer capable of imagining the bomb into existence almost by thought alone. This cover suggests that the visionary scientist makes concrete (and concretely destructive) the evanescence of his own thoughts while leaving behind (or, rather, below) the mere materiality of his body. Part of the *Oxford English Dictionary*'s first definition of the noun "visionary" illustrates that such a person is "capable of receiving impressions, or obtaining knowledge, by means of visions," which is consistent with the idealized portrait of Oppenheimer as a keen, powerful scientist that appears on the cover of Fetter-Vorm's comic. In contradistinction to this portrait, however, the *OED*'s second definition, stemming from the nonscientific and decidedly mystical connotations of the word "vision," helps characterize Oppenheimer as one prone to "fanciful and unpractical views; having little regard to what is actual or possible; speculative, dreamy." Within the pages of Fetter-Vorm's work, Oppenheimer is frequently depicted in this second fashion: wreathed in cigarette smoke that becomes clouds upon which mythological scenes play, or draped in shadows—especially cast by his own porkpie hat—and stylized as noir with all the obscuring murkiness suggested by that aesthetic's name. A particularly striking example of this simultaneous ambition to reveal and conceal occurs early in the text, when Fetter-Vorm provides on a single page a jumbled series of partial images of the physicist lighting a cigarette, which coalesce in a chiaroscuro head-and-shoulders image with a caption reading: "What this bomb needed was a visionary" (21). Oppenheimer is depicted as a figure who brings these disorderly and abstract images together much in the way the visionary "obtains knowledge"—and much in the way he brought the disparate parts of the Manhattan Project together—at the same time that he preserves the mystical and enigmatic connotations of the visionary.

The moment of the bomb's detonation in *Trinity* reiterates this dance between the visionary's power to reveal and to conceal. Captions providing a countdown appear superimposed over images of various attendees of the test, and as the countdown approaches zero, a trio of panels at the bottom of one page, each progressively smaller, zoom in on Oppenheimer's eye. The countdown reaches zero as his round pupil, evoking the numerical figure zero, fills the small sliver of frame remaining (69). At just the moment when his visionary powers reach their maximum—represented by another extreme close-up of his eye—the reader turns the page to encounter a very large, fully schematic, and ultimately imaginary look at the inside of the bomb at the moment its detonators fire and its radioactive core—rendered as a textbook cutaway—goes supercritical (70). This supremely penetrating image exemplifies, through the portal of Oppenheimer's visionary eye and the gaps between the panels that create a narrative of penetration, the esoteric knowledge to which such a visionary has access. Almost immediately, however, Fetter-Vorm's work acknowledges the imaginary nature of this image of the bomb, and the next six pages depict the detonation as inscrutable and ultimately unknowable. Almost wholly black pages, adorned with small, surreal drawings of the bomb going off in its first few milliseconds, obliterate the detailed knowledge produced by the schematic drawing and replace it with the unknown of the now postatomic world (71–76). An image of Oppenheimer shielding his eyes against the blast completes this section's oscillation between the desire to see and the necessarily obscuring practices of the mystical visionary (77).

Photographing Oppenheimer

Despite the insistent subjectivism of comics and the frequent contradictions that arise from their use of text and image, their complexities are in fact not that different from those of the supposedly pure visuality of the photograph. As light inscribed in emulsion, the photograph appears to register "the real world," but as many photography scholars have noted, the variety of ways in which it signals meaning also ensures its instability. Likewise, the material similarities between photography and nuclear bombs allow the ambiguity of the bomb to be traceable within the photograph. The visible light necessary for photography and the energies produced in a nuclear explosion are both forms of electromagnetic radiation (see Taylor, "Our Bruised Arms" 6). This commonality is the foundation for one of the most striking examples of the "chiasmus"—the conceptual categories reversed by the atomic bomb's new realm of visuality—of which Akira Mizuta Lippit speaks: the particularly horrific "photographic" effects of the weapons dropped on Hiroshima and Nagasaki. In the seconds after the bombs detonated, their intense heat and light left permanent shadows, imprinted on walls and roads, of the objects that were casting them at that moment: fences, ladders, bicycles, and, of course, people incinerated at the moment of detonation. As noted by Oppenheimer's colleague Robert Serber, who visited Hiroshima not long after the bombing, the shadows "gave a striking picture of how people were frozen in a set position when the bomb exploded. These shadows photographed the individual's actual position in relationship to the bomb" (qtd. in Laurence 251).[11] For Serber, this form of photography constitutes documentary evidence, "objective" knowledge of the location of individuals in space and time—a spatial and temporal "relationship to the bomb." For others, however, this form of photography, which in its inscription on the city's surfaces, marks an absence more permanent than that of conventional photographic images. It enacts an important conceptual and epistemological reversal: the body is simultaneously there and not there (see Lippit 93–94). These "images" represent both a new order of knowledge and the destruction of knowledge. As "human negatives," their presence signals their negation. As "shadow people," they are at once insubstantial (tenuous and tenebrous) and significant (human beings inscribed in concrete). They are forever visible in their invisibility and alive in their deaths. As Roland Barthes famously notes, "the Photograph is violent: not because it shows violent things, but because on each occasion *it fills the sight by force*" (*Camera Lucida* 91)—fills the sight, in this case, with the residue of violence but also with the permanent absence of those individuals. Such individuals exemplify "that rather terrible thing which is there in every photograph: the return of the dead" (9). The constructedness of photography, the aesthetic and ideological qualities that often deny a photo its idealized identity as a "recording" of reality, in fact aligns it closely with the subjectivity of a form such as comics.

These "atomic photographs" include the physical spaces of Hiroshima and Nagasaki, and many of the shadows imprinted on its surfaces are of its urban paraphernalia. One such shadow, of a valve wheel inscribed on a gas storage tank, redoubles the dialectic Lippit identifies in these images between visibility and invisibility: because the wheel is still there, its presence reinvokes the absence invoked by its own shadow (fig. 2). This image renders concrete the simultaneity of presence and absence, of visibility and invisibility. It inscribes it (in concrete) on the surfaces of Hiroshima and Nagasaki and within the visual economy of nuclear culture. Oppenheimer is, of course, absent from these images, but in his role as "creator" of the atomic bomb—its progenitor, its producer, its prime mover—and as

FIG. 2. *Hiroshima valve wheel. The United States Strategic Bombing Survey, May 1947.*

one responsible for its positing, he is present in his position "behind" the bomb, visible through his own invisibility.

While novelist Joseph Kanon's observation that, "like many charismatic people, Oppenheimer photographed well" ("A Novel Idea" 28) is assuredly true, one of the most famous photographs of Oppenheimer does not actually have him in the frame. In 1948, the American Institute of Physics began publishing a new journal called *Physics Today*, and its inaugural issue featured a similar dialectic of the visible and the invisible in its cover photograph "of" Oppenheimer: that is, of his trademark porkpie hat sitting on a piece of cyclotron equipment (fig. 3). The equipment, which echoes visually the valve wheel in Hiroshima, nearly overwhelms the hat, yet the image unmistakably evokes him even though he is not pictured. In a book released in conjunction with the 1980 BBC television miniseries *Oppenheimer* (discussed in chapter 4), Peter Goodchild writes about the cover of this journal, stating that "in the mind of the editor, Sam Goudsmit, it could symbolise to his readers only one man" and the "fact that the photograph was uncaptioned was a tribute to Oppenheimer's international reputation" (174).

More recently, Ray Monk's biography of Oppenheimer notes that he was "so famous that he did not actually need to be pictured in order to be represented" (536) The hat's inevitable depiction of "only one man," whose fame was so great it need not have been remarked on, indicates the power of synecdoche in discerning the meaning of Oppenheimer. The hat and the machinery "become" Oppenheimer, a visual act of personification that echoes and anticipates the personification of nuclear weapons. Likewise, the "uncaptioned" photo attests to the centrality of silence (of textual absence) in bringing him into existence rhetorically. Charles Thorpe elaborates on the image in his biography of Oppenheimer: "Awkward against the symmetric architecture of the machinery, the hat sits as it would be worn—pulled down to one side. It was a touch of personal style; yet underneath the hat, instead of a face, is still more piping, merging into shadow. Oppenheimer himself is physically absent from the photograph, lurking as an invisible presence. The very iconography through which Oppenheimer is remembered and celebrated has often seemed to hide the man rather than illuminate him" (*Oppenheimer* 15). Thorpe highlights not only the

TRENDS IN AMERICAN SCIENCE by Vannevar Bush . . . . *See Page 5*

VOL 1 NO 1 ● MAY 1948

FIG. 3. *Cover of* Physics Today, *May 1948. Lawrence Berkeley National Laboratory. Courtesy AIP Emilio Segrè Visual Archives,* Physics Today *Collection.*

prominence of silence and empty space in representing Oppenheimer but also one of the key ways in which his invisibility is in fact the visibility of something else: his juxtaposition with technology. Replacing his body with machinery signals his absence, but in its focus specifically on the hat and the head that it would otherwise contain, the photo simultaneously reasserts his presence as a cerebral form. Like the juxtaposition of absence and presence, this simultaneous mechanization and etherealization—a process that in fact disembodies him in what is arguably his most famous photograph—will figure into other ways of representing him visually. It will have important implications for how cinematic and other visual and material representations of Oppenheimer depict his relationship with the strange, often counterintuitive knowledge at the heart of atomic physics. Such knowledge becomes, through a variety of visual tropes, concrete and material at the same time that it suggests the terrifying dematerialization, the profound negation, of nuclear holocaust.

CHAPTER 4

THE GHOST AND THE MACHINE: OPPENHEIMER IN FILM AND TELEVISION

Photographs "of" Oppenheimer—images in which he is both present and absent—emerge from a twentieth-century convergence of technologies. The beginning of the century saw what Akira Mizuta Lippit calls the "extreme, even excessive modes of visuality" (30) offered by inventions such as X-rays and cinema, inventions that changed the very possibilities of sight, while the middle of the twentieth century saw the blinding light of the atomic bomb change the nature of war. The relationships between brightness and shadow, depth and surface, exteriority and interiority are at issue in both X-ray images and cinematic images, and as the Hiroshima and Nagasaki shadows discussed earlier indicate, such relationships characterize the bomb as well. Similarly, Paul Virilio argues in *War and Cinema* that a series of sight-related developments in twentieth-century warfare—from the use of searchlights in 1904, to the "cine-machineguns of fighter aircraft" and "the blinding Hiroshima flash which literally photographed the shadow cast by beings and things" (85)—made war indelibly cinematic. Virilio cements the parallel development of these images of war and the cinema in a chilling comparison: "the funerary handprints of stars left in the concrete sidewalk of Grauman's Chinese Theatre in Hollywood already prefigured the 'human negatives' of the atomic age" (61). The unearthly, deathly light unleashed at Trinity, Hiroshima, and Nagasaki is in fact kin to the light that inscribed iconic photographs of Oppenheimer in silver and emulsion, the same light that allows filmic and other visual depictions of Oppenheimer to be seen, the same light that "brings history to life" in these mediated forms.[1]

Technologically, cinema and television function through the interplay of light and shadow, by visually positing and withholding. Owing to the central role of visuality in Enlightenment science, as well as to the conflicted dynamics of seeing the unseeable that lie at the center of subatomic physics specifically, a discussion of the visuality of film and television will reveal some of the consequences that *seeing* Oppenheimer cinematically and televisually has on nuclear culture. This approach will focus mostly on the visual "languages" of film (cinematography, lighting, movement, and so on).[2] It is, first, too simple to assert that seeing Oppenheimer is equivalent to knowing him, that visibility produces unmediated knowledge. For one, cinema *produces* (rather than only reflects) the cultural values in which it was made, and a multiplicity of often contradictory cultural voices are articulated within individual cinematic texts.[3] Because of the complex relationship between materiality and visibility, the visibility of film does not mean it automatically conveys knowledge transparently. Cinema's stock in trade is dematerialization—light rather than matter (see Virilio 41). Film enacts a form of living death, in which absent actors are seemingly brought to life (see Barthes, *Camera Lucida* 92). Yet light nevertheless has substance, and absence has an often palpable presence. In their flat simulation of depth and their lively animation of death, "the invisible men and women of the cinema" (Lippit 93) at once confirm and confound the knowledge of their own present absence and absent presence. They make familiar and they estrange.

Film and television seem particularly suited to science's Enlightenment goal of making visible, in this case, nuclear physics and the process of engineering the world's first nuclear weapons. At the same time, these productions remain fascinated with Oppenheimer's mystical and poetic dimensions: his interest in Eastern religions, for instance, or his reading of Donne. In various ways, these productions attempt to negotiate, through their representations of Oppenheimer, the unstable terrain between scientific and technological knowledge on the one hand and mystical knowledge on the other. The inscrutable nature of the atomic bomb, the unfathomable destruction of Hiroshima and Nagasaki, and the unimaginability of nuclear holocaust means the "visual materiality of the tropology [used to depict these things] is marked by erasure and effacement" (Lippit 102). This paradoxical form of (a)visuality, furthermore, often sits alongside the materiality and corporeality of cinematic representations of Oppenheimer. These films confront (a)visuality directly by being self-reflexive about cinema, by interrogating their own means of seeing and knowing. These films imagine complex relationships between scientific knowledge and mystical or poetic revelation, between the embodiment of knowledge in a figure such as Oppenheimer and its diffusion throughout technology, and even between the human beings watching the film and the mechanical technologies through which they do so. The insistence with which such representation examines technology is a visual echo of the postwar observation in Don DeLillo's *Underworld* that "all technology refers to the bomb" (467). Such representation in turn resonates with popular understandings of nuclear weapons as simultaneously complex and impressive technological achievements and sublime and inscrutable forces, the products of supremely rational minds and a mad rush to destruction. Such representation also underscores the similarities between the rarified, privileged knowledge enjoyed by scientists and mystics alike.

Many of the motion picture and television productions that depict Oppenheimer date from the 1980s.[4] A decade marked by an invigorated political right in which conservative and neoimperial politics reigned, the 1980s saw a resurgence of aggressive nuclear policy, the sanity of which has been repeatedly questioned.[5] The period also saw a rise in the opposition to nuclear proliferation in the form of multiplying peace groups and mass protests, particularly in the early 1980s (see Gusterson 178). Within this volatile political and public arena, a spate of films and television productions appeared. Many of them—such as the TV miniseries *World War III* (1982) and the made-for-TV movies *The Day After* (1983), *Countdown to Looking Glass* (1984), and *Threads* (1984), as well as theatrical films such as *Testament* (1983) and *Red Dawn* (1984)—all imagine nuclear war and its cataclysmic consequences. Other productions, such as most of those I examine in this chapter, cast themselves as historical texts interested in recreating, at this tense and unstable period in the 1980s, the Manhattan Project and Oppenheimer himself. This decade thus seems to have contained an impetus to explore the meaning and the possible consequences of contemporary nuclear technologies through an exploration of their genesis. The connection between "the sight machine" of cinema and the increasing derealization of war in the postmodern era, which in part locates its origins in the invention of the bomb, helps account for this resurgence of interest in the Manhattan Project and in Oppenheimer.[6] The notion of derealization makes specifically fictional cinematic and television depictions fertile ground for exploring representations of Oppenheimer. This chapter therefore traces the ways in which a number of film and television productions—most from the 1980s—attempt a "making visible" of the bomb through dramatized representations of Oppenheimer. I will focus primarily on the seven-part 1980 television miniseries *Oppenheimer* (which did not air in the United States until 1982) and will conclude with a brief discussion of how these tropes also appear in documentaries.[7]

As depictions of a man intimately involved in the development of the twentieth century's most notorious technology, the films and the TV series discussed in this chapter use assorted visual rhetorics to link their representations of Oppenheimer self-reflexively to the technologies of mediation used to acquire nuclear knowledge. Many of these productions are fascinated, for example, with recording devices: tape and phonograph records, telephone wiretaps and photographic equipment, stenotype machines and typewriters, and the technologies of cinematic and televisual projection themselves. The appearance of such devices reflects, of course, the "reality" of the historical Oppenheimer; as a man pursued during and after the Manhattan Project by authorities for his alleged Communist ties, he had his phones bugged, his words recorded, and his movements documented. More than simply for "historical accuracy," though, the inclusion of such technologies in these productions reinforces the importance of technological mediation in general in knowing Oppenheimer. Such knowledge is frequently encoded as technological embodiment, a juxtaposition of Oppenheimer's physicality with the materiality of technology, which has variable effects on how such productions envision nuclear knowledge and the responsibility for such knowledge. Similarly, the technologies of

visual representation (film projectors and, later in the Oppenheimer narrative, TV screens) indicate the provocative connections between nuclear
technology and modern mass media. They also demonstrate a certain
degree of self-reflexivity, an awareness of how their own presences and
representational strategies lie between their viewers and the knowledge
they mediate. Like biographical texts, the often biographical films discussed in this chapter cannot be assessed simply on the basis of "historical
accuracy." Their often allegorical approach to their subject, as well as the
generally equivocal nature of film and television, mean that these media
productions continue to trouble the role of narrative in understanding
history.[8] The kind of "derealizing" historiography alluded to in chapter 3,
in which the focus shifts from the supposedly transparent truth of historical events to the narrative and other representational tools used to
depict those events, is equally possible in historical film—perhaps more so
because the visuality of motion pictures seems to promise but ultimately
withholds transparent access to the "truth" of history. Consequently, these
productions are often self-reflexive about the technologies of representation themselves. Self-consciously cinematic images in film and television
productions—including images of cameras and other technologies of
media reproduction—acquire the ability to create, as well as to modify or
eliminate, individual and national memories.[9] Self-reflexivity can thus be a
nuclear option in engaging cinematically with history's certitudes.

THERE AND NOT: *THE BEGINNING OR THE END* (1947),
FAT MAN AND LITTLE BOY (1989), AND *DAY ONE* (1989)

MGM's *The Beginning or the End* is notable less for its serviceable if bland
performance by Hume Cronyn as Oppenheimer than for its status as the
first major motion picture about the Manhattan Project to appear after
the war and, less obviously but just as influentially, for its self-reflexive
gestures. The film opens with a faux newsreel purporting to show a
time capsule's being sealed. Included in the capsule, to be opened in five
hundred years, is a copy of *The Beginning or the End*, along with a film
projector, presumably for screening the film in the future. The film that has

just been sealed in the capsule then appears to begin, with a shot of Cronyn's Oppenheimer behind a desk. This is quickly revealed to be another narrative frame, as Oppenheimer addresses the future audience directly to explain the film's raison d'être. Even once the film's main narrative finally begins, the self-reflexive gestures continue. At one point, the film makes obvious use of actual test footage to depict the Trinity explosion (an early example of what would become a standard trope: archival military footage within fictional cinematic narratives about the bomb), and later, when the military authorities brief the airmen about what they can expect after they drop the bomb on Hiroshima, *The Beginning or the End* shows them sitting in a darkened room in which a movie projector plays the same bomb test footage that was part of the film itself minutes earlier during the Trinity sequence. Such gestures highlight the importance of visual mediation in understanding the atomic bomb and its legacies, and they underscore the material technology, such as film projectors, through which that visual mediation occurs. The film's elaborate narrative framing makes cinematic mediation itself a prominent subject in the film, and its other self-reflexive gestures suggest that all its subjects, including Oppenheimer, gain access to knowledge about the bomb through recursive, circuitous, and highly mediated ways. Consequently, direct objective knowledge of the bomb is undone by the bomb itself and by the kinds of cinematic and narrative strategies, themselves compelled by the bomb, that would soon become characteristic of postmodernism.

After a notable lack of English-language film depictions of Oppenheimer during the 1950s, 1960s, and 1970s, renewed Cold War tensions in the 1980s spawned a significant resurgence of interest.[10] One of the best known and most critically acclaimed productions is the BBC seven-part television miniseries *Oppenheimer* (1980). With a running time of seven hours, *Oppenheimer* is one of the most sustained cinematic explorations of the development of the atomic bomb and by far the longest so-called biopic of the Manhattan Project's chief representative. Near the end of the decade, however, Roland Joffé released *Fat Man and Little Boy*, probably the twentieth century's splashiest Manhattan Project film, a film perhaps most (in)famous for its casting of Paul Newman as General Groves. The Paramount Studios film was, in Bryan C. Taylor's words, "commercially and critically unsuccessful," partly because of the "androcentric frame" it reinforces as part of a general tendency in nuclear cultural production to repress the contributions of women and minorities ("Register" 269).[11] Similarly, scholar Christoph Laucht notes the film's "Americanization," the way it minimizes the contributions of foreign-born Manhattan Project scientists in favor of a more homogenously American narrative of technological success. Although I do not dispute Taylor's or Laucht's identification of repressed and repressive narratives in nuclear culture, I believe *Fat Man and Little Boy*, consistent with the other films I examine in this chapter, also represses Oppenheimer in important ways. In positioning Dwight Schultz, who plays Oppenheimer, against atomic and other kinds of technologies in ways that obscure him or that cast the bomb in biological or embodied terms, *Fat Man and Little Boy* participates in an aesthetic of concealment. This aesthetic, in which *not* seeing Oppenheimer or the bomb become the film's primary visual tropes, implicitly raises the question of how knowledge production and acquisition in nuclear realms is related to understanding Oppenheimer.

Schultz's first appearance as Oppenheimer takes place in a car, as he drives down a California highway with his wife, Kitty, and brother, Frank, as passengers. Shortly thereafter, the film depicts his first meeting with Groves as taking place inside a bomber with engines running. These two early scenes assert a man-machine connection that the film sustains throughout. When Oppenheimer is shown calling former lover and Communist Jean Tatlock, for instance, the camera cuts to the Los Alamos switchboard, operated by a military official, and then pans slowly over to some reel-to-reel tape devices recording the private conversation. The technologies of surveillance mediating his voice electronically become, in that moment, akin to the technologies used to represent him cinematically. Los Alamos technology, broadly conceived, frames and in fact *confines* him in a number of ways. The film's focus, in the first fifteen minutes or so, on the construction of Los Alamos means that the town's physical infrastructure frequently restrains and even fragments Oppenheimer. Indoors, a number of scenes trap Schultz in a maze of glass and mirrored surfaces. Perhaps the most striking of such scenes follows a moment in which he airs some misgivings to Groves (and Groves reaffirms Oppenheimer's importance to the project), and then Schultz is shot reflected in a mirror after which a dizzying 360-degree panning shot provides a multitude of reflected and re-reflected Oppenheimers. Even outdoors, he is restrained by Los Alamos rather than inspired by it. Despite the known import of the landscape to his thought, work, and personal life, he is rarely shown outdoors, and when he is, he is in a military vehicle or otherwise contained. One scene, about halfway through the film, has him out on a deck telling Groves that he wants to leave the project. Spectacular scenery forms the backdrop of this scene, but the prominent railing, roof, floor, and support beams of the structure in which Schultz is standing hem him in and isolate him from the landscape. Schultz's Oppenheimer is diminished not so much by the sublime landscape but by the technology imported into the wilderness to shape and control nature.

The bomb, of course, functions as a powerful framing and defining technology. The film contains several verbal equations of man and bomb, such as when an on-site military official says, "if Oppie doesn't let up, *he's* going to explode" or when Groves asks, "are we working on [the bombs] or are they working on us?"[12] The film also contains shots of Oppenheimer from the bomb's point of view as it sits at the top of the test tower in the Alamogordo desert, shots that lend the bomb its own perspective and agency to delineate its human subjects. The very title of the film, together with a persistent visual trope, helps to align man and bomb. Although the bombs dropped on Japan, Fat Man and Little Boy, were originally code-named by Robert Serber after Dashiell Hammett characters (see Serber and Crease 104), the rounded Fat Man and the long, thin Little Boy visually echo the physiques of Groves and Oppenheimer, respectively, and Joffé's film repeatedly aligns them with the Manhattan Project leaders. The opening credits of *Fat Man and Little Boy* play against strange dark shapes that, as the camera pulls out, are revealed to be stylized silhouettes of the eponymous bombs. With Paul Newman's and Dwight Schultz's names playing over these images, and with other instances, such as when the two men stand side-by-side doubled by the bomb casings hanging side-by-side above them, the film conjoins the historical figures they play with the weapons those figures eventually developed (fig. 4). The prominence of the bombs provides a sense of technomilitary inevitability (we *know* how this story

FIG. 4. Fat Man and Little Boy *(1989). Courtesy of Paramount Pictures.*

will end), but their conjunction with Groves and Oppenheimer constitutes a reminder that individual human beings were likewise essential to the inevitability of the bomb.

Curiously, however, *Fat Man and Little Boy* seems relatively uninterested in Oppenheimer's relation to knowledge, scientific or mystical. He is not much of an academic in this film, and the producers take few opportunities to showcase his knowledge of physics. There is, for instance, only one brief moment in the film that takes place in his classroom. Schultz, projecting an image of Michelangelo's *The Creation of Adam* on the classroom wall for no discernable reason, plays the professor-as-flamboyant-ham, and the scene is so brief and nonspecific that it is not even clear what subject he is teaching. One of the only times Oppenheimer is seen reading poetry, he almost immediately gets up, walks over to where blueprints of the bomb are pinned to the wall across the room (emphasizing the strict separation between these realms of knowledge) and ponders the science of his gadget instead. The nondescript depiction of his relationship to knowledge seemingly results from two related ideologies at work in Joffé's film. First, as Taylor notes in his article on the film, Oppenheimer's apparent disavowal of knowledge could arise because Joffé depicts him as a betrayer of the other scientists and their ethical qualms. He is uninterested in further knowledge because his mind is made up, he is in the clutches of the army, and he will brook no dissent. Second, the film suggests a wide gulf between types of knowledge because of the technological determinism with which it understands the bomb and its accompanying mechanical contexts. There is a clear hierarchy among types of knowledge, and the film is clear about which type "gets results." Oppenheimer is thus wholly determined, and practically erased, by the technological. The machinery eclipses the embodied human "behind the bomb" (to use that phrase with both its obscuring and determining connotations). To efface him visually and conceptually is to lodge knowledge and power in the technology itself and thus to reinforce the narrative of inevitable technological "progress" as the determining force in the development and proliferation of nuclear weapons.

Director Joseph Sargent's television movie *Day One*, which aired the same year as *Fat Man and Little Boy* was in theaters, depicts an even more rudimentary relationship between Oppenheimer and strange or mystical knowledge. Unlike *Fat Man and Little Boy*, *Day One* practically refuses to align Oppenheimer with technology of any kind. In fact, it repeatedly dis-associates him from technology and diminishes his knowledge about and familiarity with machinery. One of the few times Oppenheimer, played by David Strathairn, is shown anywhere near a scientific experiment occurs nearly halfway through the film. Physicist Seth Neddermeyer, played by John Pielmeier, is doing outdoor implosion tests on lengths of pipe, while Oppenheimer assumes a position up on a hill some distance from the experiment to oversee it from a privileged position. Oppenheimer ducks down behind the hill at the moment of the test and, after Neddermeyer holds up the mangled pipe, pronounces: "Back to the drawing board." Oppenheimer's dismissive comment and his physical remoteness from the experiment reinforce his position as a manager of technology, not someone with deep or personal knowledge of it. Subsequent scenes in a lab and in the field with Neddermeyer have Oppenheimer ordering the other scien-tist to do more work and then demoting him in favor of chemist George Kistiakowsky, scenes that consolidate Oppenheimer as more a bureaucrat than a scientist. Later, when the scientists are assembling the device for the Trinity test, the visibly nervous Oppenheimer is asked twice in about three minutes of screen time to leave the assembly room. When he leaves, he begins coughing and anxiously pacing about, his body becoming ungov-ernable and betraying his capitulation to forces beyond his control. When

Day One depicts the raising of the bomb to the top of the Trinity tower, most of the shots come (shakily) from Oppenheimer's perspective, looking up warily at the bomb that hangs over his head. When the bomb is finally in place on the tower, he stands next to it, gazes up guardedly at the thunderstorm raging above his head, touches the bomb briefly, then steps back to separate himself from the device. He quite deliberately turns his back on it before starting to climb down. The decision in this film to dissociate him from technological apparatus, scientific experimentation, and ultimately the bomb itself perhaps indicates a desire to separate the man from the destructive technology, to absolve him of responsibility for this weapon of mass destruction. But such a reading would likely also rely on depicting his humanistic qualities, those poetic, mystical, religious, or ethical turns of mind he frequently used, as counterbalances to his work on the bomb. For whatever reason, though, *Day One* also ignores those tendencies.

Depicting Oppenheimer more as an administrator than a scientist, although historically accurate in the context of the Manhattan Project, is one of several ways the film divorces him from knowledge production, whether scientific or mystical. When we first see him, Oppenheimer is in a Berkeley classroom, supposedly a site of knowledge production and transmission, but he is not shown teaching. Rather, he is in conversation with Groves (played by Brian Dennehy) about the military potential of nuclear physics. The sequence uses a series of close-ups of the men in profile as they talk to reinforce the first scene's placement of Oppenheimer in military and political relationships rather than in the context of scientific knowledge. Further, Oppenheimer denies his own scientific expertise in this conversation with Groves, claiming that the field is "too new" to know of any applications and explaining to Groves how little he in fact knows about this new science. This lack of knowledge, often coded in the film as "modesty," pervades its representations of Oppenheimer. Without any scenes of moral or philosophical contemplation (he is never shown reading the *Bhagavad Gita* or John Donne's poetry, for instance), he comes across as a pawn for the military, a ruthless enabler of violence. He is shown having a cool, calculating conversation with Enrico Fermi about poisoning the German food supply, and his suggestion to Secretary of War Henry Stimson that the U.S. should bomb multiple Japanese cities again depicts him one-dimensionally as a cold-blooded rationalist capitulating to the military. The film seems to take pains to avoid his humanistic side and its accompanying equivocations. He never seems to entertain doubt as he contemplates vicious ways of attacking the enemy. Near the end of the film, as he views slides of Japanese destruction with the other Los Alamos scientists, several people leave the room in disgust. Oppenheimer whispers to his wife: "The reaction has begun"; Kitty replies: "What did they expect?" The cold scientific rhetoric with which he assesses how other Los Alamos scientists are behaving (and not, notably, how Japanese civilians have been affected), coupled with his wife's callousness, are strongly at odds with historical accounts of his briefly celebratory but then profoundly horrified reaction. But more than simply a historical inaccuracy, this depiction divests Oppenheimer of any ambiguity and any possibility of thoughtful contemplation—of his humanness, in short.

The film ends at Los Alamos in October 1945, when Oppenheimer is presented with a certificate of appreciation by the military. He delivers a jeremiad-like speech stressing the danger of atomic weapons and the potentially infamous legacy of his own work: "If atomic bombs are to be added as new weapons to the arsenals of a warring world, or to the arsenals of nations preparing for war, then the time will come when mankind will curse the names of Los Alamos and Hiroshima. The people must unite, or they will perish." As the speech ends with Oppenheimer's declaration of commitment "to a world united, before this common peril, in law, and in humanity," the film freezes his face and the credits immediately roll. *Day One* thus ends in a strangely abrupt fashion, without depicting any of the resonances of this complex speech. The film simply stops at the only significant instance in the film when Oppenheimer registers wariness over what he has done. His only real moment of equivocation comes in the very last frame before the credits. The nature of the cinematic freeze-frame, in which stillness is imposed on something whose filmic purpose is to move (see Chaloupka 73), brackets this moment safely off from the rest of the film's depiction of Oppenheimer as an instrument of the U.S. military. Perhaps the film's having been sponsored by AT&T, as announced in its first title card, helps explain this portrait. More than just a telecommunications company, AT&T was also a parent company of Sandia National Laboratories when this film was made. As a "sponsor" of nuclear weapons, they had a vested interest in portraying Oppenheimer as the administrator of a successful governmental initiative, as a man with "helpful" contributions to imaginative ways of destroying the enemy with little moral compunction. The resounding success of the Manhattan Project, sustained by that final scene, which abruptly cuts him off as he registers any doubt over the legacy of his atomic bomb, underscores the need for and value of such weapons in the U.S. arsenal. AT&T's financial investment in the film thus cannot help but influence, at least to some degree, the meaning of Oppenheimer that *Day One* conveys.[13] In separating him from the technology he helped engender and in obfuscating the moral ambiguities that suffused his work, *Day One* depicts an Oppenheimer who dutifully helped his country but who kept his poetic inclinations and his mystical tendencies out of the rationalist epistemologies of American science and technology.

HISTORY, TECHNOLOGY, AND KNOWLEDGE: *OPPENHEIMER* (1980)

The final section of this chapter consists of a discussion of the BBC television miniseries *Oppenheimer*. As its title suggests, this production is a biopic, a genre of cinematic biography with an ample genealogy.[14] Perhaps of central concern to *Oppenheimer*, the most biographical of the productions discussed in this chapter, is the sharp contrast between the "life narrative" provided by film and the death-dealing provided by the Manhattan Project at the center of that narrative. As Lippit notes, "to cinefy" means both "to make cinema and to incinerate" (Lippit 33), to animate through moving images and to destroy through the heat and the light of, in this case, an atomic bomb. To "cinefy" Oppenheimer is thus to unify these two concepts. That this production was, like *Day One*, a television production is also significant because, as the historian of television Joyce Nelson proclaims, "the two mass media that dominate our age—television and the bomb—cannot help but be intertwined in an ideological embrace" (12). Nelson identifies this ideology as patriarchal rationalism—a fixation, which achieved a cultural climax of sorts in the middle of the twentieth century, on technology and the scientific method as the solution to all possible problems and the source of a more "rational" (that is, patriarchal) society. This ideology is sometimes identified in Oppenheimer's apparent obsession with the "technically sweet" over the ethical. According to Nelson, thanks to the "extraordinary ritual and institutional power" (25) of television in the postwar age, its images, which are frequently of technology itself, contribute to elevating technocratic determinism—again, the power of technology and the scientific method, perhaps best embodied in nuclear weapons—to the highest cultural level. The intimacy of television, its presence largely in private, domestic spaces, resembles the intimacy of the biopic's focus on the individual. Thus, *Oppenheimer* cannot help but participate in the process of domesticating and normalizing patriarchal rationalism, of bringing the bomb into the living rooms of the world. At the same time, however, and as this section of this chapter will show, the production is also more self-critical than that.[15]

To discuss some of the visual strategies it uses to align the scientist with technology, it is first necessary to explore how this production (unlike *Day One*) sets up the complex relationship between scientific and mystical knowledge. Oppenheimer himself is the primary source of this contested epistemological landscape. As in *Day One*, the first time we see him is in the classroom, but unlike in Sargent's film, he is actually teaching, and *Oppenheimer* makes this scene its very first one. The scientist presents his Berkeley students with a physics problem. After some futile attempts to answer it, one of his students asks him for the answer. Oppenheimer grins and responds, "I don't know." After some grumbling from his students, he adds, more seriously, "nobody knows. Now it's exciting." As a curiosity-driven intellectual, he is excited by the unknown and by its equivocal possibilities, in contrast to his depiction in *Day One* as being modestly ignorant. His relationship with knowledge in *Oppenheimer* is one of exploration and exhilaration. Throughout the production, he manifests this relationship to knowledge as a verbal habit. In the fourth episode, he visits the Trinity site in anticipation of the test, and when asked if he thinks the device will work, responds: "I don't know. I think so. I don't know." In the next episode, Enrico Fermi asks him how he feels, and he responds, "I don't know. Excited." In the sixth episode, when he gets word that the

Atomic Energy Commission is beginning its investigation, Kitty Oppenheimer asks what will happen to them, and he responds: "I don't know.
Nothing. I don't know." This persistent verbal pattern in which he claims
a lack of knowledge, then provides an answer, then (more often than not)
reaffirms his lack of knowledge, reflects an equivocal relation to knowledge. In that such a pattern also identifies the fundamental uncertainties of
the project he is working on, it also presents him as a source of mysterious
knowledge and power by embedding answers, however qualified, within
expressions of uncertainty. His answers, informed by the "exciting" possibilities of the unknown, constitute a source of mysterious knowledge in
a morass of doubt over the technological and scientific feasibility of the
Manhattan Project.

The production also employs a series of tropes to depict the technology
that generates both the ambiguity and the mysterious knowledge embodied
in Oppenheimer. Again, one of the main visual tropes in the production is
to align the scientist with mechanical technologies. As one might expect,
the machines of physics and the apparatus involved in the construction
of the bomb are part of this strategy, but so are the technologies of mass
transportation (trains and automobiles) and mass communication and
mediation (tape recorders, typewriters, radios, and so on). These machines
serve to locate him visually in the technological realm in which he works,
but as in *Fat Man and Little Boy*, they also tend to efface him. They do
not render him immaterial (the insistent materiality of the machinery
precludes this), but they mechanize him. This man-machine tropology, a
cyborg aesthetic, has important resonances, as I discuss in the next section, for the conceptual and etiological legacies of the atomic bomb.

The film's title sequence, for instance, played at the beginning of each
of the episodes, starts with an extreme close-up of a tape player's control knob and a hand turning the knob from "stop" to "play." Two cassette
reels begin turning, and we hear what we find out in the third episode is
a secretly recorded conversation between Oppenheimer and intelligence
officer Colonel Boris Pash, which is later used to help revoke Oppenheimer's security clearance. The closing credits of each episode are also
run alongside two turning reels of tape. As a recurring motif that opens
and closes each episode, the tape player invokes those official institutional

attempts, forged by Communist paranoia, to bring Oppenheimer down and thus serves to highlight his downfall as a central component of the narrative. This downward narrative arc is reinforced visually by the anonymous hand turning the knob to "play" and thus divesting Oppenheimer of agency, again and again, at the beginning of each episode. Because he is first presented to viewers through a recording of his voice, this production's reiteration of the tragic component of his narrative also has the effect of mechanizing him.

Traditionally coded as "dehumanizing," such mechanization reinforces the film's tragic narrative structure, but it also serves several important conceptual functions. First, mechanical reproduction and representation are foregrounded as crucial components in the construction of selves. More than simply the mercurial, contradictory qualities of Oppenheimer himself, reproduction (particularly the mass electronic reproduction that has come to characterize the postwar era) lends Oppenheimer multiple and variable meanings. The opening sequence suggests a layer of self-reflexivity through the tape recorder reels' resemblance to those of movie projectors and by the way in which the hand turning the knob to "play" activates the film by replacing a static shot of the machine with a visually dynamic montage. As a reminder to viewers that they are in fact watching a cinematic construction (although through the rather different medium of television), these tropes emphasize the importance of media in "knowing" Oppenheimer.

Second, mechanizing Oppenheimer serves the crucial function of aligning him with technology, particularly with the bomb itself. For instance, after the hand turns the knob to "play," the opening sequence joins together snippets from various parts of the production, intercut with images of technology and machinery (scientific objects one might expect from a film about the Manhattan Project such as slide rules and detonators, but also the aforementioned typewriters and film projectors). As the opening sequence unfolds, the shots get shorter and shorter as the music approaches its crescendo. At the music's climax, there is a burst of light and the screen goes white, suggesting the successful detonation of the atomic bomb. Viewers then see the first title card. It consists of two lines of text. The first line reads "Sam Waterston as" and the second line, rendered in a much larger typeface, reads "Oppenheimer." In other words, this title card simultaneously provides the name of the lead actor, the name of the character he plays, *and* the title of the film. Oppenheimer, as played by Sam Waterston, is therefore also *Oppenheimer*, the film. In becoming the film itself, the historical figure of Oppenheimer undergoes a cinematically mediated resurrection, one that depends on the film's self-reflexivity and that points to the slippery relationship between embodiment and technology. Because the "explosion" at the end of the sequence fades into "Sam Waterston as / Oppenheimer," the climax of the Manhattan Project in the form of an atomic bomb becomes aligned with Oppenheimer, the man. This culmination of the race for the bomb also becomes, in this opening sequence, *Oppenheimer*, the film we are about to watch. This complex entanglement of historical figure, actor, bomb, cinematic production, and even representation itself reveals a film deeply invested in mechanizing Oppenheimer and in encoding his embodied relationship with knowledge as technologically mediated.

Consistent with the Frankensteinian dimensions of the Oppenheimer narrative, and anticipating many of the strategies a film such as *Day One* uses to remove his agency, significant portions of this production depict the bomb and its attendant technologies eclipsing or otherwise getting away from their perceived controller. In the first episode, for example, Oppenheimer meets with Ernest Lawrence, inventor of the cyclotron, in Lawrence's Berkeley lab. In this production, Lawrence's industrial-looking lab dwarfs and partially obscures Oppenheimer and Lawrence with complex machinery. As the two physicists discuss the mysterious wartime project into which they have both been recently recruited, a series of shots then not only overshadows the scientists with equipment but visually *replaces* them with machinery. Near the end of their conversation, the film uses a series of alternating shots: Oppenheimer to the right of the frame with a piece of mechanical equipment on the wall behind him and to the left, and Lawrence on the left-hand side of his frame with a similar piece of machinery on the wall behind him and to his right (fig. 5 and fig. 6). These mirrored shots allow for a visual replacement of the scientists (Oppenheimer in Lawrence's frame and Lawrence in Oppenheimer's) with pieces of technology. During their discussion of the secret project that would fill the next several years of their lives, the machinery in the set, as it obscures or supplants them, evokes the overwhelming nature of the endeavor and its tendency to impose the technological upon the human. A similar trope appears in, for instance, scenes in the fifth episode when Oppenheimer is rendered miniscule by the test tower in the Alamogordo desert, when shots from the top of the tower—a bomb's-eye point-of-view instead of a scientist's-eye point-of-view—diminish the men working below, or when he climbs the tower to inspect the bomb and is nearly completely hidden by the ominous device occupying most of the frame.

It would, however, be too simple to suggest that these tropes affirm the complete obliteration of human knowledge by technomilitary power. Despite his role as eminent man of science, Oppenheimer's mystical and humanistic qualities are frequently on display in this production, and there are instances in which the production offers some intricate links between knowledge mediated through technology and knowledge mediated by less scientific means. In the fourth episode, for example, Oppenheimer and

FIG. 5. Oppenheimer *(1980). Courtesy of the British Broadcasting Corporation.*

Groves are making their way to the Alamogordo test site in an automobile. As in *Day One*, Oppenheimer spends a lot of time in cars, suggesting again his interpenetration with mechanical technology. But in this instance an additional trope complicates what might otherwise be simply another "dehumanizing" gesture. Groves, irritable and anxious, finds the desert landscape through which they are driving tedious, and he expresses his impatience: "What am I going to do for five hours?" Oppenheimer, however, is laconic and enigmatic yet utterly confident that things are moving along properly. He spends much of the scene with a rolled-up coat under his head, either gazing at the landscape that Groves finds boring or with his eyes closed, speaking in mysterious aphorisms. When Groves is about to suggest a name for the test, Oppenheimer interrupts him with, "Trinity," and in a slow, hypnotic voice, he recites John Donne's "Batter My Heart, Three-Person'd God." In contrast to the distracted and nervous Groves, Oppenheimer is a Conradian Marlow, an inscrutable yet seemingly all-knowing figure who enters a Zen-like state through the landscape that

FIG. 6. Oppenheimer *(1980). Courtesy of the British Broadcasting Corporation.*

the philistine Groves finds dull. His quasi-altered state, gazing dreamily at the blankness of the desert while reciting poetry, sits uneasily yet suggestively alongside the technological mediation proffered by the automobile in which they move through this evocative landscape, and the result is a self-assured knowledge derived from seemingly mystical means. His technomysticism, a mechanical and poetic amalgam, correctly forecasts the successful test of the bomb and, in the process, constitutes a powerful potential link between the "two cultures."

The fifth episode of *Oppenheimer* climaxes with the successful first test. At the moment of detonation, director Barry Davis employs footage of the actual Trinity test. Evoking the stock footage of *The Beginning or the End*, and no doubt cheaper than creating original footage as Roland Joffé did for *Fat Man and Little Boy*, this decision nevertheless introduces an oddly jarring note of verisimilitude. I say "oddly" jarring not to point out redundantly the oddness of any jarring moment but to suggest that the moment is jarring when perhaps it should not be. *Oppenheimer* is, after all, striving for historical accuracy and realism, so why shouldn't Davis employ actual footage of the moment he has been anticipating fictionally for nearly five hours? What makes the climax of this episode oddly jarring is that plenty of actual footage exists of many stages and moments of the Manhattan Project and, later, of Oppenheimer's public life; the aesthetic consistency that this production is aiming for, the convincing and unbroken performance of Sam Waterston that compels the willing suspension of disbelief necessary to produce a certain kind of knowledge of Oppenheimer, would be shattered by the repeated inclusion of actual footage. Frequent juxtapositions of actual and dramatized people and events, as in the *American Experience* episode about Oppenheimer discussed in the next section, for instance, produces a significantly different aesthetic and thus a significantly different impression of Oppenheimer. This single instance of actual footage embedded in an otherwise seamless dramatization, however, singles out the bomb itself for an excess of verisimilitude in its depiction. Similarly, because the bomb test footage was well known in 1980, as it is today, the familiarity of the imagery jars with the unfamiliar reality of an exploding nuclear bomb. The supposed mundanity of stock footage is thus eclipsed by the self-reflexive use of such footage to depict an unfamiliar event and the self-conscious eruption of "real" reality into what has thus far been a "realistic" (that is, homogenous) production. Such self-awareness, a reflexive kind of knowledge in a production clearly concerned with how knowledge is acquired and managed, undoes the purported knowledge that comes with familiarity. If viewers are familiar with the imagery, then they believe themselves to be familiar with the bomb, but this excess of verisimilitude throws into question the very representational possibilities of depicting the bomb and thus the means by which it can be "comprehended."[16]

Some of Oppenheimer's supposed mystical knowledge or poetic intuition is reasserted immediately following the detonation. Intercutting original footage with archival footage of the mushroom cloud, the production depicts him emerging from the bunker, removing his dark glasses, and gazing up at the off-screen fireball. Shot from below, he appears larger than life, and with his mouth agape in silent reverence, his image is accompanied by Waterston providing a voice-over of the famous lines from the *Bhagavad Gita*: "I am become Death, the destroyer of worlds." Because Oppenheimer apparently did not speak the lines at the Trinity test but later recalled having thought of them at the time (most biographies make this clear), Waterston is not seen speaking the lines in the desert. The voice-over in situ, a classic cinematic device to indicate the thoughts of a character, is employed clairvoyantly in this scene to designate a thought he would only later claim to have had at the time. Like the rhetorical disruptions in Kai Bird and Martin J. Sherwin's biography, which I discussed in the first chapter and which signal an authorial omniscience that echoes the omniscient posture Oppenheimer sometimes assumes in that biography, the voice-over in this scene anticipates Oppenheimer's future. Thus, it takes the omniscience of retrospective narrative and places it within Oppenheimer as well. It also constitutes a reminder of the role played by cinematic mediation—signaled by the highly artificial device of having the actor provide a voice-over of his character's thoughts—in representing individuals and historical events.

His reaction to the use of atomic weapons on Hiroshima and Nagasaki later in the summer of 1945, as depicted in the fifth episode of *Oppenheimer*, is likewise part of the production's complex assemblage of the tropes of knowledge, cinematic mediation, and Oppenheimer's poetic and scientific sensibilities. Sitting in a seminar room with other Los Alamos scientists, Oppenheimer watches filmed military coverage of the attack on Japan. Over the mechanical hum of the film projector and the droning voice of one scientist reciting statistics of death and destruction, Groves lets out the occasional whoop of delight that contrasts with Oppenheimer's silence. Several shots feature the film projector itself in the foreground, its turning reels mounted one above the other and connoting the inexorable track of technological "progress." Full of cutaways of the horrified Oppenheimer, this lengthy segment of the episode features the actors watching a display of destruction and mangled bodies. *Oppenheimer* lingers on this footage, just as Oppenheimer does, and the film-within-the-film constitutes a twinned "making visible"—cinematic light and shadow, projected in a room full of actors in a production of light and shadow—that discloses the destruction wrought by the awful light of the atom bomb. As the episode ends, Oppenheimer gets into a car and drives away. The final shot of the episode sees him leaning, in profile, into the frame, nearly silhouetted by the bright window behind him, and for the first and only time in the miniseries, the turning tape reels that appear each time the credits roll fade in slowly over the scene. At the end of every other episode, the frame fades to black before the turning reels fade in; but here, superimposed over his stricken face and enclosed by the vehicle in which he sits, the reels are both a visual echo of the film projector reels that so horrified the scientist moments ago and another evocation of technological mediation as a central trope in the film. They help visually obscure him (as does his position in the car), but they also make visible the role of cinematic technology in the construction of the appalling knowledge he has just acquired (fig. 7).

It is important to remember that *Oppenheimer* was not a theatrical release but rather a television miniseries. As if to remind viewers that the knowledge they are acquiring about the Manhattan Project comes through television, a piece of technology whose development is intermingled with the end of World War II, the sixth episode includes a peculiar moment involving a television set. Beginning in 1949 and tracing Oppenheimer's appearance before the House Un-American Activities Committee and his tangles with Lewis Strauss of the Atomic Energy Commission, the

FIG. 7. Oppenheimer *(1980). Courtesy of the British Broadcasting Corporation.*

episode features a conversation between Edward Teller and Oppenheimer in Oppenheimer's home in 1950. As they discuss the hydrogen bomb, the television in the living room is on, and Senator Joseph McCarthy is interrogating suspected Communists. After Teller complains that too much public debate is delaying the production of the bomb and that the Soviets pose a pressing danger, Oppenheimer says, gesturing toward the television: "You'd rather the public stuck to that?" The production cuts to the television set, and at that moment the broadcast goes to commercial and a human-sized cigarette package tap-dances on a stage. Oppenheimer's remark disparages the investigation as lurid sensationalism, but his dismissive remark, coupled with a strangely extended shot of the TV set and its puerile commercial, has the effect of bringing television itself into question. The investigation becomes ridiculous not merely for its paranoia but also for its status as television entertainment. The inescapably commercial nature of television, reinforced by the disquietingly lengthy shot of the tap-dancing cigarette package, casts doubt on the very role television plays in making truth visible. The historical question of whether McCarthy's inquest had much value in exposing Communists is very nearly beside the point in this scene because television itself as a medium is ultimately what Oppenheimer's piquant question indicts. The glowing box depicted on the glowing boxes of those watching *Oppenheimer* constitutes a recursivity that questions the potential of a televised representation of Oppenheimer to depict reality.

The last shot of the seventh and final episode affirms the importance of the relationship between technology and knowledge. After depicting the denial of his security clearance, the last few minutes of the production feature the aging scientist after he has been "exiled to Princeton" (as visiting friend and colleague I. I. Rabi puts it). The final shot, taken from overhead and looking down at the grass as Robert and Kitty slowly move out of frame, echoes some of the shots employed in the depiction of the Trinity test in which the device itself assumes cinematic authority and "looks down" on Oppenheimer. This final shot is accompanied by voice-over narration. The narrator's voice, as it often does in film, connotes authority and omniscience (especially from its position high above and looking down) as it tells of Oppenheimer receiving the Fermi Award in 1963 and dying in 1967. Because much of this final shot is of an empty field, the Oppenheimers having moved off-screen after a morose conversation about Robert's "martyrdom," the production reiterates the flexibility of the scientist's meaning. The narrator has the final say, however, summing up his life from an authoritative position outside of history. The artificiality of the camera position—looking straight down at an empty field of grass in a production that has employed mostly conventional camerawork in claustrophobic interior sets—again reinforces the importance of cinematic construction. Such a commanding perspective, one so self-conscious about its power and positioning, allows *Oppenheimer* to end on an assertion of its own centrality in the meaning of Robert Oppenheimer. Such meaning—bound up productively and problematically in the knowledge of atomic science, the knowledge of a life lived for atomic science, and the knowledge produced by cinema itself as it depicts atomic science—is both brilliantly illuminating and destructively contradictory.

DOCUMENTING KNOWLEDGE: *THE DAY AFTER TRINITY*
(1981), "THE TRIALS OF J. ROBERT OPPENHEIMER" (2009),
AND *COUNTDOWN TO ZERO* (2010)

In many ways, the epic qualities of *Oppenheimer* make it the magnum opus of cinematic Oppenheimer representation. Subsequent productions, however, employ many of these same techniques to similar effect, and they do so in more "factual" formats, such as the documentary. I conclude this chapter with a brief discussion of three documentaries. The first, Jon Else's *The Day after Trinity*, primarily depicts Oppenheimer as an omnipotent master of knowledge. About a quarter of the way through, the film portrays how the various scientific fields—physics, chemistry, metallurgy, ordnance, and others—came together in early stages of the Manhattan Project. Viewers see a series of still images of scientific equipment ostensibly representing these fields. The images appear in quick succession and largely out of context, and the result is a profusion of visual iconography representing the baffling multiplicity of "science and technology." Over these images, audio from an interview with Hans Bethe plays. Bethe explains how Oppenheimer integrated this perplexing array of equipment and ideas: "He knew and understood everything that went on in the laboratory.... He could keep it all in his head and coordinate it." As Bethe speaks of Oppenheimer's powers of synthesis, the conjunction of the visual and auditory dimensions of the film serve to equate machine and man. This conceptual ideogram, a composite of machinery and Oppenheimer, is sustained throughout the production and helps produce an Enlightenment vision of the perfect man of science—another version of the cyborg aesthetic seen in other Oppenheimer representations.

A second documentary to employ these sorts of representational strategies, a 2009 episode of the PBS series *American Experience* titled "The Trials of J. Robert Oppenheimer," demonstrates considerable self-reflexivity about technologies of representation and thus brings Oppenheimer's omnipotence into question. Like *The Day after Trinity*, "Trials" provides, despite a focused title, a fairly broad biographical portrait. It, too, intersperses historical photographs, newspaper clippings, and other documents with interviews with historians (including Martin J. Sherwin and Richard Rhodes) and with physicists who worked with or otherwise knew Oppenheimer personally (Freeman Dyson, Marvin Goldberger, and others). A narrator weaves these disparate voices and media together into an authoritative narrative arc. However, featured prominently in the production and, as I assert, working against this authoritative narrative are dramatizations of the security hearing. David Strathairn, once again, plays Oppenheimer.[17] He is shown almost exclusively seated in the hearing room, nearly motionless, frequently obscured or distorted by extreme close-ups and acutely raked shots, and reciting the words Oppenheimer spoke during the hearing. The production provides a badge of historical accuracy at the beginning in the form of a title card: "The words spoken in the courtroom are taken directly from the transcript of the hearing in the matter of J. Robert Oppenheimer." As if to reinforce the production's investment in historical accuracy, shots of Strathairn are intercut with shots of a stenotype machine. Some of these are extreme close-ups of the machine, often shot in long takes, relentlessly recording his words. The stenotype's suggestion of historicity, of a keen desire to provide "the whole truth," contrasts with the various visual strategies that provide a minimalist portrait of Oppenheimer, one not infrequently obscured by the very recording technology that affirms the accuracy of the depiction. Other shots of Oppenheimer and the stenotype machine are wide-angle ones that place them on opposite sides of the room and of the cinematic frame, suggesting a gulf between actuality and representation. Depictions of communication and representation devices—lingering shots of telephones and recording equipment, mostly—are far more prominent in this production than depictions of scientific technology, and they obscure Oppenheimer both visually and conceptually in his identity as a scientist. The production's self-reflexivity, its own status as a "recording device," underscores its existence as a *construction* of knowledge rather than a transparent window into history. Oppenheimer thus appears as a *construct of* history rather than as an autonomous actor in the production of knowledge.

Documentary films concerned with nuclear weapons more broadly are interested in depicting Oppenheimer as well, and Lucy Walker's *Countdown to Zero* also explores his relationship with knowledge as part of an antinuclear weapons stance. Early in the film, narrator Gary Oldman describes Oppenheimer's reaction to the discovery of nuclear fission: "Robert Oppenheimer said, 'Impossible.' But within fifteen minutes he decided it was real. He realized it would release a great amount of energy, but you could generate power and make bombs." Central to Oppenheimer's reaction, as in Barry Davis's *Oppenheimer*, is equivocation—an almost simultaneous denial of possibility and affirmation of multiple possibilities. Such equivocation blurs the distinction between knowledge as a product of empirical accumulation of truth on the one hand and knowledge as mystical revelation on the other. Early in the film, Walker uses a well-known clip of Oppenheimer's appearance on NBC's 1965 documentary *The Decision to Drop the Bomb* in which he recites, haunted and forlorn, the passage from the *Bhagavad Gita*: "I am become Death, the destroyer of worlds." By positioning his desolate aphorism early in the film and by following it with impassioned pleas from scientists, politicians, and lay-people to abolish nuclear weapons, Walker portrays the quotation as a warning against the spiritual death of the human race brought on by its obsession with the physical death nuclear weapons promise. Walker's film is self-reflexive about this depiction of Oppenheimer in possession of prescient knowledge. It is cognizant of how this depiction violates the precepts of scientific thinking, yet it is simultaneously aware of its own cognizance. Similarly, the film represents his relationship to technology in primarily self-reflexive ways—that is, the technology that constructs Walker's vision of Oppenheimer is self-reflexively cinematic technology. The opening segment of the film, for instance, takes well-known moving images of nuclear bomb tests and destruction and runs them in reverse. An obvious visual evocation of the fantasy of "uninventing" the bomb, this opening sequence also takes the familiar imagery of nuclear destruction—terrifying images rendered banal through popular repetition—and defamiliarizes it. Running it backward renews the footage and makes it potentially disruptive to the political stasis or cultural inertia that has tempered the horror of this footage over the years. Such a political move, however, is accompanied by a self-reflexive comment on the nature of film itself: these images of destruction, by virtue of their easy visual consumption and compulsive repetition, have settled almost into invisibility in the public consciousness. By drawing attention to their status as film

images, however, *Countdown to Zero* also questions the culpability of its
own medium in the proliferation of nuclear weapons. A curious image
of Oppenheimer, appearing about halfway through Walker's film, features him slightly off-center against a white background, slowed down
slightly, and flicking his eyes slowly down and back up again. Reminiscent of how Errol Morris manipulates footage of his subjects' faces in
his documentaries, this image also foregrounds the role of cinematic
images—insubstantial in their flickering etiolation yet substantial when
suggesting three-dimensional reality and movement—in the construction
of multiple Oppenheimers in the realm of public knowledge.[18]

These media representations of Oppenheimer are all consistently interested in exploring his relationship with knowledge, and their status as
visual media ensure that this relationship is characterized by the interplay of visibility and invisibility. Fictional or nonfictional, cinematic or
televisual, they also explore their own operation as tools of mediation for
nuclear culture particularly suited to the postmodern age. The obscurity
into which Oppenheimer is frequently cast in these productions is perhaps, in some instances, simply denial—repressing the individual seen as
responsible for the existence of a dreadful technology and pushing back
against the perceived inevitability of the scientific method—but in other
cases, these instances of opacity ask pointed questions about the role television and film play in constructing knowledge. Can we say we "know"
how nuclear weapons came to be and what nuclear weapons mean if the
instruments for accessing them consist largely of media productions? In
what ways do visual mediations convey knowledge, in what ways do they
construct it, and how significant are the differences between these two
things? The next chapter will engage with these questions by extending the
notion of visual mediation into another form: nuclear science museums.

CHAPTER 5

"THE BONY TRUTH":
OPPENHEIMER IN MUSEUMS

Before discussing the representation of Robert Oppenheimer in museums, places in which the materiality of history assumes prominence in depicting the past, I wish briefly to discuss another "transitional" genre, one that (like novels and films) fictionalizes its subject but (like museums) makes use of material representation: drama. Theatrical productions about Oppenheimer frequently appeal to the material reality of the bomb. But like museums, which trade on "the bony truth" (Fortey 295) of physical artifacts and concrete, often three-dimensional representation, theater also confronts the transience of history with a tangible, in situ reality. The "liveness" of plays, the "presence" they depend on, and the sense of (potential) interactivity and (apparently) unmediated access they offer, make them an appropriate entry point into a discussion of museums, which offer many of the same effects. At the same time, an onstage Oppenheimer can only be experienced through the fictive and figurative strategies theater nevertheless employs.[1] Furthermore, one of the features of postwar atomic theater, in both the United States and Britain, is its repeated failure to depict the bomb.[2] Even when some of the most prominent dramatists in the United States during the 1950s and 1960s tried their hand at writing drama about the atomic bomb, they too failed.[3] The bomb, and with it Oppenheimer's (in)tangibility, thus does not appear very often on the stage during the Cold War despite the tantalizing and suggestive nature of the material.

When he does appear in drama, the plays in question demonstrate a variety of strategies for managing the relationship between Oppenheimer's embodiment and the immateriality of history and inscrutability of nuclear science. Some plays, such as German dramatist Heinar Kipphardt's *In the Matter of J. Robert Oppenheimer* (1964), are examples of "documentary theater."[4] They foreground historical verisimilitude and claim authentic access to the past.[5] In other plays, the Oppenheimer narrative has received more expressionistic treatments that, collectively, constitute an engagement with the poetics of history. But rather than asserting the discovery of Oppenheimer as a historical referent, they question the possibility of doing so. For instance, although Peter Sellars's libretto for John Adams's opera *Doctor Atomic* (2005) is drawn from original source material, the staging is highly stylized: productions in Amsterdam in 2007 and New York in 2008 featured video projections, animated physics equations, and a chorus ensconced in a giant periodic table. Along with the grandiose and nonrealist nature of opera itself, such techniques ensure that the production unsettles the notion of objective, transparent access to history. Carson Kreitzer's play *The Love Song of J. Robert Oppenheimer* (2003), a precursor to *Doctor Atomic*, also takes a poetic approach to Oppenheimer—evident through its title's evocation of T. S. Eliot, through its inclusion of mythical and Biblical characters, and through its surreal staging.[6] More recently, the Royal Shakespeare Company's production of Tom Morton-Smith's play *Oppenheimer* has drawn rave popular reviews for its extension of this tradition of stylizing Oppenheimer, with one reviewer calling the play a "dramatised graphic novel."[7] With the stage surface functioning as a giant chalkboard throughout the production, Morton-Smith's play affirms the conjunction of text and material image and, with it, the "writability" of the history being enacted. Collectively, these plays explore Oppenheimer's positioning among presence and absence, creation and destruction, and other fraught binaries and ultimately (un)substantiate on stage the elusive qualities of the bomb and the man. The existential threat posed by the bomb, its ability to destroy everything, seems to constitute an obstacle for some dramatists (as it does for many other artists) and, for others, generates a powerful desire to question the narratives of history and the possibility of objective, material knowledge of that history. Theatrical productions about the bomb do not occupy a prominent place in this book, despite the resurgence of science on stage in recent years,[8] but they do serve to introduce many of the negotiations between materiality and immateriality that can be found in atomic museums.

ATOMIC TOURISM: THE PLACE OF THE MUSEUM

When I visited the Bradbury Science Museum in Los Alamos in 2013, a banner outside the building featured an image of Robert Oppenheimer and Leslie Groves at the Trinity site with the following text: "Learn how Los Alamos National Laboratory scientists are using the latest technologies to solve today's complex challenges related to defense, energy, and the environment." This banner juxtaposes the past (signaled by the black-and-white image of Oppenheimer and Groves) and the present (signaled by the contemporary "challenges" identified in the text). But it also juxtaposes the role of the museum, one of interpreting and preserving the past, with the role of a public relations agency, one of promoting corporate science. What sorts of knowledge, then, does a museum like this one create, and with what kinds of authority? How does that knowledge support or challenge the narratives underlying the museum's content and those of modern museums in general as mechanisms for the production of truth?[9] This chapter addresses such questions in its exploration of how Oppenheimer is represented in museums devoted to the science and history of nuclear weapons. Thus, *The Meanings of J. Robert Oppenheimer* now moves from analyzing visual iterations of Oppenheimer toward iterations that combine textual and visual dimensions with spatial, material, and sometimes monumental ones. This move shifts the emphasis toward forms of representation that emerge from a science museum's exhibitionary practices. These practices of showing, which resonate with the larger scientific aim of making the world visible, are supplemented by the additional complications of moving spatially *through* a representation. The strange relationship between the concrete and the ephemeral at the center of the Oppenheimer persona becomes, in this chapter, an index to the aesthetics and ideologies of constructing knowledge in atomic museums.

Museums are educational institutions, but they are also implicated in tourist practices and local economies. They are invested in the production of truth and knowledge but do so within local power structures and particular sites (see Luke xiii–xviii). Thinking about museums in the context of tourism might mean that what is on display at, say, the National Atomic Testing Museum in Las Vegas sits uneasily next to institutions such as the Pinball Hall of Fame or Madame Tussauds. The situatedness of nuclear museums, as opposed to the global diffusion of television and other electronic media, also makes them particularly fertile grounds for exploring historical events such as the Manhattan Project and historical figures such as Oppenheimer that are strongly characterized by specific localities. Museums also make complex interventions into cultural, political, and historical debates. Their "politics" are complex and manifest not only in the overt statements they make but in their aesthetics: their architecture, their layout, their lighting, and the appearance of their text panels. They can be sites where certain historical, political, or technological ideas are normalized (see Luke xxiv), but they can also (or at the same time) criticize overt political ideologies (see MacDonald, "Afterword" 230). They can thus be ambiguous or even oppositional in their relationship with dominant culture and with their own authority as cultural institutions.

As a multibillion-dollar enterprise sponsored by national governments and functioning as a central pillar in the military-industrial complex, the nuclear weapons industry certainly relies on support from, and even tries to positions itself *as*, "dominant culture." Part of such positioning, consistent with the ideological function of a military or corporate museum, is to celebrate the bomb's development, to generate support for it, and even to domesticate it. The well-funded and governmentally authorized pronuclear field has many methods at its disposal for framing nuclear weapons. In his anthropological study of atomic sites and scientists, Joseph Masco traces the Cold War banalization of the bomb (a "making normal" always paradoxically inflected, however, by a sense of apocalyptic horror) and the movement from atmospheric testing to underground testing to no testing at all (at least in the form of detonation). In doing so, Masco argues that for nuclear weapons to remain on the national agenda, they must rely on what he calls "technoaesthetics" (22)—particular ways of visualizing, imagining, and cultivating the bomb. In response to the increasing abstraction of the bomb thanks to our inability to see mushroom clouds blooming on desert horizons or against palm trees in the Pacific islands, nuclear weapons, Masco argues, must be domesticated, rendered familiar, or otherwise made appealing by casting them in a particular visual regime. Museums are, in part, responsible for producing the bomb's "beauty." At the same time, museums offer the potential to resist dominant culture. Like resistance to the bomb in the form of protests, peace activism, test ban treaties, and other practices, museums can talk back. A science museum can engender subversive debates about technology, for instance, just as readily as it can provide a narrative of technological progress (see MacDonald, "Exhibitions" 9).

Such rhetorical conflict emerges at least partly from how nuclear museums represent Oppenheimer. I do not wish to suggest that his appearance in these museums determines, strictly speaking, the stance the museums take toward nuclear weapons or of the nature of the historiography they perform. Instead, I hope to discern ways in which the tropes and expectations of the Oppenheimer narrative echo or complicate some of the work these museums are trying to accomplish. The multimedia and multimodal nature of museums resonates with both the proliferation of Oppenheimer representation in numerous genres and with his own wide-ranging interests in science, art, religion, and philosophy. The touristic component of a museum—that is, the relationship between the museum and its location—echoes Oppenheimer's complex and generative relationships with American places, particularly New Mexico. His own conflicted relationships with science and politics find echo in the ways "politics has erupted publicly into the imagined sanctity of science and of museums"(MacDonald, "Exhibitions" 1). But perhaps most important, the physical experience of moving through the museum and the concrete or even tactile nature of many museum exhibits echo the concerns with embodiment apparent in the Oppenheimer narrative. The long-running interest in his bodily materiality reveals a complex awareness of the materiality and ephemerality of knowledge. More specifically, it reveals an interest in the material and bodily effects of a technology otherwise enmeshed in abstract, theoretical, and ephemeral science.

For fairly obvious reasons, none of the four museums I wish to focus on—the Los Alamos Historical Museum and the Bradbury Science Museum in Los Alamos, the National Museum of Nuclear Science and History in Albuquerque, and the National Atomic Testing Museum in Las Vegas—take an explicitly critical stance on the bomb. But none of these museums take a univocally or unassailably probomb stance either. Consistent with their political and financial material conditions, however, they often do take positions on the bomb that align with scientism (with the belief in the teleological movement of science and its attendant discourses of progress and improvement), and they often follow the process Masco outlines of aestheticizing the bomb. Oppenheimer's role within this process is an intriguing one. In some places in certain museums, he performs technoaestheticization; he becomes a familiar father figure, for instance, to "domesticate" the bomb, or a calculating machine to lend it a sense of inescapable logic. Thanks, however, to the complexity of Oppenheimer the historical figure and to the unpredictable nature of representation itself, these iterations of the scientist often move in unexpected directions. In some instances, he is represented as the elite technocrat he was, but in other instances, a counterdiscourse emerges that turns him into a mitigating force against aestheticizing, bureaucratizing, or otherwise domesticating the bomb.

Consistent with the approach I take elsewhere in this study, I make connotation and interpretation—the methodologies of literary, cultural, or film criticism—central to my analyses of museums. I enter museums with the understanding that they are *representations* of history and not passive vehicles for transparently conveying history—with the understanding that "science displays are never, and have never been, just representations of uncontestable facts" (MacDonald, "Exhibitions" 1). Furthermore, even if that were the case, these are technology museums rather than science museums. Aside from one or two places where, say, the difference between fusion and fission is explained in any detail,[10] this group of museums is more interested in the technology of nuclear weapons—and more invested in understanding technology as a force for securing and promoting "the

American way of life"—than in the supposedly disinterested, neutral science underlying it.

To carry out my analysis, I visit several nuclear museums in the U.S. Southwest and examine how they represent Oppenheimer. I begin in New Mexico, starting at the Los Alamos Historical Museum for an initial perspective on Oppenheimer (and for a broader perspective on Los Alamos in general) before moving a few blocks away to the flashier, generously funded Bradbury Science Museum, which functions as the public arm of Los Alamos National Laboratories (LANL). I then travel south to the National Museum of Nuclear Science and History in Albuquerque, where Kirtland Air Force Base (which houses a large arsenal of nuclear weapons) and Sandia National Laboratories (established in 1948 as both a rival and a partner to Los Alamos National Laboratory) make the city a central hub in nuclear weapons technology and nuclear culture. I then head east to Las Vegas, Nevada, where the bomb developed in New Mexico was tested, refined, and augmented within Cold War discourses of "national security." Although its fame as a tourist destination sometimes eclipses in the public imagination its role in nuclear technology and culture, Las Vegas is a crucial anchor for the Nellis Air Force Range and the Nevada Test Site (NTS), nuclear weapons development and testing areas to the northwest of the city. For years in the 1950s, part of the attraction of Las Vegas was being able to see bomb-test mushroom clouds from the city. Today, the National Atomic Testing Museum conveys the history of atomic weapons testing in the region and, like the Bradbury in Los Alamos, is a site of interrelation for the military and tourism industries. Each museum has a different story about Oppenheimer, about the technology he helped engender, and about the places in which this process occurred.

LOS ALAMOS, NEW MEXICO: LOS ALAMOS HISTORICAL MUSEUM

High in the mountain air of northern New Mexico and spread out over four mesas of the Pajarito Plateau, Los Alamos is a remote, spectacular place that became, in the 1940s, the centerpiece of the Manhattan Project.

Today, it is the site of LANL, a leading science and technology facility with a $2 billion annual budget, which continues classified nuclear weapons work. Los Alamos is an important—and contested—site, and its history can be found depicted in two museums. The first, the Los Alamos Historical Museum, is run by the Los Alamos Historical Society and is located next to Fuller Lodge, a massive log building that served as the main dining hall in the first half of the twentieth century when Los Alamos was a ranch school and that later became a social space for Manhattan Project scientists. The museum focuses on the Manhattan Project but is also committed to the larger history of the region. Beginning with ancient geological history and the arrival of Native American inhabitants in the twelfth century CE and, later, Hispanic and Anglo homesteaders, the museum also devotes a significant amount of its relatively small space to the Los Alamos Ranch School, founded in 1917.[11] The pre-Manhattan Project history on display is separated from the subsequent history of Los Alamos by the gate, brought up from 109 East Palace Avenue in Santa Fe, where arriving scientists would check in. Oddly, however, as visitors move through the gate into the Manhattan Project area of the museum, immediately to the right is a highly conspicuous panel, including two enormous panoramic photographs of Hiroshima and Nagasaki after the dropping of the bomb, titled "The Pacific War Ends." The layout of the museum is circular, so after passing through the gate, visitors have to go left to experience the history of World War II Los Alamos chronologically and to arrive, back at the gate, at the putative end of the story: the destruction of the Japanese cities. The direction to go left is clear, but nevertheless the first thing visitors encounter upon passing through the gate is the *end* result of the Manhattan Project. As a result of this layout, the bomb becomes a foregone conclusion, and the *process* of the undertaking at Los Alamos (recapitulated as one moves left, linearly through time, and witnesses the bomb as a work in progress) carries with it an inevitable result. Encountering this image frames the scientific work of Los Alamos as one that could only succeed in its efforts.

Within this narrative of inevitability, Oppenheimer is treated more or less as a hero. For instance, a famous photograph of him and Groves at the remains of the Trinity test tower appears centrally between two panels titled "Trinity Site: The Bomb Is Tested" and "Tinian: Departure for Japan," which again lends the narrative an air of surety thanks to Oppenheimer's reassuring presence at the center.[12] Similarly, images depicting his speech at Los Alamos on his last day as director in October 1945 appear next to ones depicting his burgeoning postwar celebrity and thus (like the freeze-frame at the end of Joseph Sargent's film *Day One*, discussed in the previous chapter) gloss over the concern he expresses in that speech over whether "mankind will curse the names of Los Alamos and Hiroshima" (qtd. in Smith and Weiner 311). However, the layout of the museum, which forces viewers (because of the museum's space constraints) to see those panoramic photos of destroyed Japanese cities first, produces a chronological disruption that brings its largely reverential treatment of Oppenheimer into question. Encountering the massive devastation wrought on Japan before encountering representations of the Manhattan Project prefaces everything exhibited between the 109 East Palace gate and the end of World War II with a violent act of destruction. Such a preface urges an interrogation of the scientific work that went on in Los Alamos. Such questioning is sometimes encouraged within the museum (as in the text panel reproducing Oppenheimer's concern over the legacy of Los Alamos and Hiroshima), but the appearance of a massive visual instantiation of nearly unspeakable destruction, at just the point where the narrative of scientific success is supposed to begin, is powerfully subversive. It forms a counterdiscourse to the official narrative of the bomb by revealing "progress" to be in fact destruction. The sobering effect such a preface has on visitors, even (or especially) when they leave the museum and continue their travels through Los Alamos and New Mexico, brings the very enterprise of Los Alamos into question.[13] It constitutes a reminder of the omnipresence of nuclear weapons, poised to rain down destruction yet hidden away in the landscape of official secrecy.

LOS ALAMOS, NEW MEXICO: BRADBURY SCIENCE MUSEUM

Several blocks away is another curious amalgamation of visibility and secrecy: the Bradbury Science Museum. What is now the Bradbury began in 1953 as a means of housing artifacts and documents related to weapons development at Los Alamos. Renamed in 1970 after Norris Bradbury, the second director of LANL, and moved in 1993 to its present location in downtown Los Alamos, this museum functions as the public arm of LANL. As such, overt criticism of nuclear weapons development and its consequences are relatively hard to come by. The physical layout of the museum, for example, supports the officially sanctioned identity of the institution. Its square footage is weighted toward showcasing the current research and defense work performed by LANL, and to reach a "Public Forum"—a small corner containing two text panels presenting arguments for and against the use of the atomic bomb on Japan and a comment book in which visitors can record responses—one must exit the relatively small section of the museum dealing with the Manhattan Project and pass through considerable space devoted to other kinds of science. The popular interest in such scientific work (my visit in 2013 coincided with displays on environmental research, nanotechnology, supercomputing, and LANL technology on Mars), not to mention the relative ease with which such work fits narratives of scientific progress and improvement, helps condition visitors to be more positively predisposed, by the time they reach the Public Forum, to the nuclear weapons technology that spawned these other types of research.[14] The alcove's physical location within the museum thus partially mitigates its ability to give voice to antinuclear activists in Los Alamos (see Masco 241).[15] Similarly, visitors must pass through displays devoted to "progressive" research (such as "Fuels from Algae") to reach the part of the museum dedicated to atomic bombs (including replicas of Fat Man and Little Boy), modern weaponry, and underground testing. Thus, in addition to representing the Manhattan Project as the fount of helpful and cutting-edge technological development, the museum seems to be suggesting that scientific research, with its Enlightenment connotations of teleology and forward progress, "naturally" (i.e., inevitably) leads to nuclear weapons proliferation. Although the Bradbury is less overt in its displays of patriotism than the National Atomic Testing Museum in Las Vegas, nuclear weapons are understood (thanks to a 9/11 memorial to Pentagon employees located outside the museum's entrance) to be tightly bound to the discourses and practices of national security. The Bradbury does not provide transparent, neutral access to technological history. Rather, it flexes its institutional authority to help construct the dominant meaning of nuclear weapons.[16] In an article on the contested meaning of the Bradbury, Bryan C. Taylor quotes 1992 museum director Jim Street's candid assessment of the museum's corporate purpose: "We're not a true museum. We're a company store" ("Revis(it)ing" 137). In associating America's nuclear "store" with the rationalized (and thus purportedly unassailable) processes of research, militarism, defense, and corporatism, the museum carefully limits opportunities to question and criticize the ethical value of such work.

At the same time, resistant readings at the Bradbury are possible, just as they are at the Los Alamos Historical Museum (and, indeed, at all museums). And the Bradbury, despite its close association with LANL, can be a vital critical space in Los Alamos.[17] As in my discussion of the Los Alamos Historical Museum, I wish to focus on the relatively small section of the Bradbury devoted to the history of the Manhattan Project, a section that likewise contains some intriguing representations of Oppenheimer and Groves. An analysis of how these representations manage the corporeal presence of the Manhattan Project directors—as well as the relationship between the body and the intellect—will reveal some more possible ways of counterreading the Bradbury's ideology. Such a counterreading might, more generally, help complicate the process of technoaestheticization that Masco stresses is crucial to the public acceptance of nuclear weapons at the same time that it works against the hagiographic approach to Oppenheimer and Groves on evidence elsewhere in Los Alamos.[18]

Like other representations of Oppenheimer in a variety of media, the Bradbury's depictions connect his bodily presence with his role as an intellectual. For instance, a screen in the section of the museum dealing with the history of the Manhattan Project runs a seven-minute biographical video that begins with a description of the boyhood illness that sent him to the healing climate of New Mexico in the first place. The narrator points out how "the once-frail Oppenheimer" went on to become a dynamic and effective leader whose job was to contribute the Manhattan Project's goal of "outthinking the enemy." Consistent with the mystical "healing" dimensions of the place in which Oppenheimer is situated, and consistent with popular understandings of the scientist as capable of transcending corporeality, this video foregrounds the ephemerality of the intellect by framing the Manhattan Project as a thinking competition. At the same time, however, the video's narration inevitably highlights Oppenheimer's physicality when it suggests that a bodily illness early in life is at least one of the reasons Los Alamos came into existence as a key space in nuclear culture. Attempting to imagine the scientist as more mind than body, more intellect than matter, just as often as not draws attention to the physical. The bodily individual who emerges to complicate this idealized portrait of science also complicates the notion that scientific knowledge is produced by disinterested "forces" rather than particular, embodied individuals.

One of the most striking exhibits in the "History" section of the Bradbury is a pair of life-size papier-mâché statues of Groves and Oppenheimer (fig. 8). Like the bronze statues of the two men created by artist Susanne Vertel that stand several blocks away outside the Los Alamos Historical Museum, these figures prompt an almost idolatrous reverence through their imposing presence.[19] The papier-mâché statues in the Bradbury stand astride a display headed "The Manhattan Project is born." To the right of the Oppenheimer statue, a text panel prominently quotes the scientific director on his 1943 vision of Los Alamos: "We shall be one large family doing work inside the wire." Sexual, birth, and family metaphors are, as a number of scholars have noted, everywhere in nuclear culture (see Cohn; Easlea; Gusterson). Such metaphors, along with the position of the statues on either side of a video installation on the Manhattan Project, frame the two men as parents and the bomb as their progeny. Constructing Groves and Oppenheimer as paternal figures, as "family men," is part of the Bradbury's generally positive portrait of the builders of Los Alamos and is congruent with its representation of the atomic bomb as necessary and beneficial. To "give birth" to the bomb—a metaphor premised on an image of the productive human body—assists in making familiar and domestic, and in technoaestheticizing, a supremely destructive technology.[20] The body becomes a means of familiarizing the often alienating twentieth-century relationship between scientific knowledge and society. Inevitably, though, the result of this conflation is the uncanny fusion of life and death.[21] Foregrounding his body is part of this process of domestication, and the process produces a portrait of Oppenheimer as a beneficent, familial presence, a figure familiar to us as our own bodies but one linked indelibly to the ability to destroy bodies. This fraught process of familiarization also serves to link the image of the nation as protector with the image of the nation as destroyer.[22]

Despite such technoaestheticization, it is possible to read against the grain at the Bradbury. One potential counterdiscourse arises out of the built-in limits of corporeal metaphors. If visitors are encouraged to envision Groves and Oppenheimer as parents and the bomb as their child, then the bomb becomes fragile when it comes to be seen as organic.[23] Such fragility works against the masculinist, militarist discourse on display in the museum and, consequently, against the "security" supposedly guaranteed by nuclear weapons. The statues of Groves and Oppenheimer, especially in contrast to the bronze versions outside the Los Alamos Historical Museum, are also conspicuously, almost acutely, fragile. Unlike other exalted representations of Groves and Oppenheimer, these statues stand on the museum

FIG. 8. *Groves and Oppenheimer statues at the Bradbury Science Museum (2013). Photograph by the author.*

floor, unprotected by any barriers, so their accessibility partially divests the men of their sacrosanct auras. The statues are unpainted, as well, and their ghostly white pallor produces a cold, distancing effect rather than one of comfortable, paternal warmth. Unlike, say, wax figures whose uncanniness would derive from the disjunction between their striving for verisimilitude and their obvious inanimateness, these statues foreground themselves first and foremost as representations, and their clear artificiality works against the discourses of nature and organicism that otherwise domesticate the bomb. In addition, papier-mâché does not wear well, which leaves the statues looking somewhat haggard. The "familiarity" of seeing Groves and Oppenheimer as parents and the supposed security engendered by their "procreative" act are thus undone somewhat by the material in which they are rendered and their strange, ghostly appearance that results. Perhaps the museum's most striking example of this "hauntology" is in an item they do not currently display.[24] The director of exhibits at the Bradbury informs me that the museum is in possession of the chair Oppenheimer used while director of the laboratory from 1943 to 1945.[25] The chair, like the statues, is a concrete object intended to "bring history alive" or to connect visitors to "the real Oppenheimer" by evoking with its presence Oppenheimer's materiality. But when on display, the chair is, of course, empty. Like the comforting invisibility of nuclear weapons evoked paradoxically by their being "on display," the empty chair reminds visitors that absence is often the most striking characteristic of history. The chair has not been on display since 2006, which compounds this evocative absence.[26]

The gender identities in this "family portrait" are complex, too. As "fathers" of the atomic bomb, Oppenheimer and Groves elide female procreative power in what scholars have noted is an example of co-opting that power and masculinizing it.[27] Two fathers can be, of course, manlier than one, so this scenario confirms the masculinism frequently identified in nuclear weapons culture and in science, more generally.[28] However, within the logic of family, Oppenheimer and Groves become a same-sex couple. Two fathers are, according to heteronormative thought, *less* manly than one. The dissonance of this scenario thus undercuts the virility associated with "fathering" the atomic bomb and the masculinism of militarized science in general. Furthermore, calling Oppenheimer the "father of the atomic bomb," as many do within the androcentric narrative of the Manhattan Project, leaves the bomb's "mother" unidentified. Perhaps the interest in the corporeality of this odd couple—particularly in their diametrically opposed physiques that seem to have considerable value in determining the meanings of the two men—reflects a desire to identify Groves as a mother figure. The accessibility of the statues means visitors frequently touch them, and the whiteness and fragility of the papier-mâché, in contrast to the apparent imperviousness of bronze or stone in most statues and monumental art, allows such touching to leave discernable marks. In the case of the Groves statue, the protruding stomach is noticeably darkened by the hands of visitors. Clearly, the most prominent part of Groves's body, his large stomach, invites contact reminiscent of the often irresistible impulse, familiar to many pregnant women, possessed by strangers to touch their bellies. This gesture of excessive familiarity, transferred to the Groves statue at the Bradbury, reflects the public interest in the corporeality of these two "parents," but it also has the effect of feminizing Groves. The family metaphor, which familiarizes the bomb within the orbit of technoaesthetics, gets complicated by the need to feminize one of these male figures. Such a need arises perhaps in response to the repressed narratives of femininity that scholars identify in nuclear culture. Interestingly, it is not the thin, effete, intellectual, poetry-reading Oppenheimer who is feminized here, but rather the bulky military man.[29] Such a process works against much of the patriotic and national security rhetoric, so dependent on masculinity, found in the museum and within nuclear-military culture in general. After all, domesticity is unstable and often uncanny in its disappearances and reappearances within such a repressively masculine narrative as the one governing the Manhattan Project.[30] Casting Groves as, on the one hand, a feminized figure consistent with gender stereotypes that envision the female body as "incubator" or as "matter" to be shaped by the creative spark of the masculine and, on the other hand, as a military man expected to display what Gusterson calls "a particularly disciplined form of embodiment" (102), reveals the instability of nuclear discourses and narratives. As one of the "fathers"/"mothers" of the atomic bomb, Groves's corporeality reminds visitors of the real, material bodies at stake in deploying nuclear weapons—the men, women, children (and the narratives of futurity they often construct) that sit as targets in geopolitical nuclear posturing.[31]

In a striking contrast to Groves's belly, the part of Oppenheimer most darkened by the visitor's touch is the statue's left hand. This public display of tactility acknowledges how implicated Oppenheimer is in the concept of manipulating, of *handling*, physical forces, primeval universal energies, or (as discussed in chapter 1) the desert landscape itself. His ability to manipulate the natural world, consistent with his role as an intellectual, is part of the Bradbury's depiction of him as an idealized scientific figure, as a theorist actively and deliberately seizing the world and shaping it. But like Groves's destabilizing belly, his hand connotes his physicality more than it does his intellect. Like the "hand" that emerged from the desert at Trinity, his hand represents, in addition to his ability to open up the natural world, his capacity to unleash bodily destruction on the world. Touching his hand represents an attempt to engage with the past through a material object that apparently represents that past and to come to terms with the threatening legacy the past has left for the present. The visible traces of such engagement work against the investment in closure and fixity usually ascribed to statues and monuments.[32] As the statues change over time through visitor interaction, the metaphoric function of the Bradbury as "corporate store"—its institutional identity—can potentially change as well.

As such metaphors become unstable, they can become highly dissonant.[33] Encountering Groves and Oppenheimer in discordant ways poses difficult questions. In what ways do Oppenheimer and Groves, as "parents," complicate the militarist, nationalist, and patriotic discourses attached to nuclear weapons? When hypermasculinity diverts attention from the fragile, organic life it threatens, how does this process reconcile itself with attempts to domesticate nuclear weapons? How familiar (and how uncanny) are nuclear weapons when the structure governing how we think about them in this instance is based on organic and corporeal metaphors? In what ways do unstable bodies complicate the figurative language nuclear scientists and military figures draw on to consolidate their regimes of power? The museum's own layout seems to offer evidence that it is wrestling with such questions. For instance, the second half of the museum, dealing with other forms of scientific work that LANL conducts, is explicitly a work in progress that reflects the processual nature of science itself. The museum takes a conflicted attitude toward simultaneously depicting nuclear science through familial and corporeal metaphors and promoting nuclear science as a military expediency. Perhaps this conflict reflects LANL's own conflicted identity as an institution. The struggle between scientists and the military, embedded in the narrative of Los Alamos from the first tales of animosity between authoritarian soldiers and scientific "longhairs," inevitably produces these sorts of divergent representational strategies and thus possibilities for counterdiscourses.

Like the chronological disruption effected by the layout of the Los Alamos Historical Museum, the Bradbury also engages directly with its own understanding of history. At the far end of the bomb display, past the section dealing with the Manhattan Project and past examples of the weaponry developed since the 1970s, are replicas of Fat Man and Little Boy. This chronological rupture, like the rupture of the boundary between living and inanimate that the personalizing names of the bombs accomplish, reminds visitors that history itself, the stuff of which museums are made, is constantly under reconsideration. In fact, on the walls leading up to and surrounding the replicas, the Bradbury has installed a new set of panels, denser with text than their counterparts in the earlier "History" section of the museum, recapitulating the history of World War II. Although the differences between these panels and the earlier ones are beyond the scope of this chapter, they likely would reveal some of the ways the museum has undertaken the intriguing project of recasting history—a recasting that nonetheless imagines as central those two bomb casings. Despite its professed job as mouthpiece for a nuclear weapons laboratory, the Bradbury exhibits a complex history of nuclear knowledge construction and its ideologies and reflects some of that history in the roles into which it casts Groves and Oppenheimer.

ALBUQUERQUE, NEW MEXICO: NATIONAL MUSEUM OF NUCLEAR SCIENCE AND HISTORY

As one comes down from the Hill (as wartime residents of Los Alamos called it), passes through Santa Fe, and takes the I-25 south, the Sandia

Mountains rise in the east and help define the sprawling city of Albuquerque. What is today the National Museum of Nuclear Science and
History (NMNSH) began in 1969 as the Sandia Atomic Museum located
on the grounds of Kirtland Air Force Base and run by Air Force staff. It
was renamed the National Atomic Museum in 1973 but did not receive a
national charter until 1991 when it also gained affiliation with the Smithsonian Institution. After changes in security protocol at Kirtland following
9/11, the museum was relocated to a former retail space in the Old Town
district of Albuquerque. In 2009, the institution assumed its present
name and moved to its current location on Eubank Boulevard adjacent to
Kirtland and a Sandia National Laboratories facility. Like the volatility of
shifting nomenclature, the situatedness of museums, their "spatial fixity,"[34]
comes into question when a museum moves around as this one has. Like
most museums, the NMNSH's "fixity"—spatial, representational, and
ideological—can never be taken for granted.

Oppenheimer's position within this museum is highly paradoxical.
He is, as one might expect, a central figure in its history of nuclear science—so central, in fact, that the museum is mostly offering the history
of a specific *kind* of nuclear science: weapons science. In that sense, this
museum does what science museums, according to some scholars, tend
to do in their more conservative iterations: promote consensus about
the value and function of their subject matter by stabilizing historical
narratives and making instrumental the science that underlies the technologies on display.[35] The narrative of the NMNSH, like that of many
science museums, is one of evolution, with each subsequent weapons
technology constituting "progress" over its predecessor.[36] Because Kirtland, in many ways the museum's continuing benefactor, remains so
important to the U.S. nuclear arsenal, this museum (like the Bradbury)
is clearly invested in bolstering the U.S. nuclear military-industrial
complex. In the words of Robin Gerster, it pays "proud tribute to
national nuclearism as an expression of American acumen and entrepreneurial spirit" ("The Bomb in the Museum" 213). Yet this museum
also exhibits a number of decentering strategies when it comes to representing Oppenheimer and, thus, nuclear weapons. Such strategies

result in another museum that offers complex, fluid meanings often at odds with its alleged ideology.

The NMNSH begins, in part, with Oppenheimer when it places a prominent photograph of him in "Pioneers of the Atom," a timeline display at the entrance to the museum exhibit. This prominence and primacy of Oppenheimer is consistent with how other museums showcase nuclear culture and serves as an important framing device. Across the top of the display, dates demarcate the decades of the twentieth century, and beneath them are clustered what the museum considers to be each era's most prominent "pioneers" of nuclear science. Marie and Pierre Curie, for instance, appear under the first decade of the twentieth century, coinciding with their Nobel Prizes. Oppenheimer's photograph is, along with Niels Bohr's and Ernest Rutherford's, one of the larger ones (while Einstein's is quite small). Unlike other museums, however, which largely associate him with the 1940s and the Manhattan Project, Albuquerque's National Museum locates Oppenheimer's photograph in the 1960s. Although the part of the Oppenheimer narrative that extends into the 1960s—which includes his advocacy against the thermonuclear bomb, his fall from grace at the hands of the AEC, his being awarded the Fermi medal, and his death—is, arguably, as important to the narratives, aesthetics, and meanings of atomic culture as the Manhattan Project, it is not as well known. Positioning Oppenheimer in this way decouples him somewhat from the Manhattan Project and thus decenters him, although his familiar visage and prominent appearance at the entrance to the museum exhibit simultaneously ensure his centrality. The NMNSH thus employs a paradoxically centralizing and decentralizing aesthetic that also characterizes many of its other instantiations of Oppenheimer and that indicates where the production and instrumentalization of nuclear knowledge sits within twentieth-century American scientific narratives.

In its focus on the Manhattan Project, the museum devotes considerable space to its scientific director and depicts him in sometimes surprising ways. For example, a series of image and text panels describes the difficult and privative conditions of early Los Alamos, with one panel, titled "Baby Boom," noting that "Oppenheimer did his best to keep the scientists and their families happy and productive." His role in this instance is not that

of theoretical physicist or even of administrator but rather that of care-
taker, a feminized role that places domestic peace ahead of technological
innovation or national security. The "productivity" alluded to refers to the
lab work of the scientists, of course, but conspicuous by its syntactical
placement in the sentence and by its contextual position in a text panel
about the "baby boom" in Los Alamos in 1944, the word also refers to
the exceptional fertility of this group of young men and women. Apparently overseeing this escalating birthrate like a hardworking midwife, he
seems a far cry from the coldly rational technocrat he was expected to be
as leader of the Manhattan Project.[37] This distancing strategy, along with
the domestication accompanying it, seems common in representations of
Oppenheimer, possibly as a way of disavowing the destructive power of
the bomb, the ultimate fruits of Oppenheimer's labor.[38] This instance of
domestication at the NMNSH, like those at the Bradbury, helps subdue
the deadly connotations of weapons work with connotations of nurturance and life. At the same time, its complex representational resonances
often serve to feminize him (as it sometimes does with Groves) and thus
to complicate further the displays of masculinity characteristic of nuclear
weapons culture.

In another domesticating strategy that helps contain Oppenheimer's
explosive multiplicity, a biographical panel at the NMNSH comments
on his birth in 1904 and calls him a "child of the scientific age." Although
the rest of the panel details in fairly heroic terms his academic career and
work on the Manhattan Project, that initial characterization invokes a
determinist narrative. It renders him as a product of his time, as well as a
perpetual "child," caught up in historical waves over which he has little control. The biographical panel also invokes the oft-seen "great love for New
Mexico's deserts and mountains," the uncontrollable emotional reaction to
the sublime landscape that, like the irresistible social forces that made him
a "child of the scientific age," controls his fate. The end of the panel reminds
visitors that "Oppenheimer was selected by General Leslie Groves to head
the Manhattan bomb project." Given Groves's role as the commanding
general in charge of the Manhattan Project, he was Oppenheimer's super-
visor in the military chain of command that governed the venture, and
thus the subordinate role into which Oppenheimer is cast in such a phrase

is historically accurate. But the effect is to render Oppenheimer subject to the whims of others. A later panel, "Oppie and Groves," elaborates on this role. It calls attention to the physical differences between the two men ("Groves was a heavy-set, conservative, practical-minded administrator and military man, while Oppenheimer was a slender, left-leaning intellectual and sophisticate"[39]), casting Groves clearly in the dominant role. Emphasizing that Oppenheimer was a distant third choice for Groves after Ernest Lawrence and Arthur Compton secures his subordinate role.

From the initial sentence of a panel titled "First Test of a Nuclear Weapon"—which reads, in part, "the first atomic device was tested at the Trinity site"—textual representations of Oppenheimer use passive language in their depictions of the Trinity test. That panel notes: "There's no consensus on the naming of 'Trinity,' but most sources attribute it to Oppenheimer." Even when he is granted agency, the museum text casts him in a passive role, as the figure *to whom* the naming has been attributed. Those "sources," which the text panel does not identify, become the grammatical actors of the sentence, and Oppenheimer is relegated to the status of indirect object. Similarly, the second half of that panel notes: "The sight of the explosion inspired Oppenheimer's famous quote from the *Bhagavad Gita*: 'I am become death, the destroyer of worlds.'" In this case, the subject of the sentence is the sight of the explosion, an abstracted and anonymous visual perspective, which inspires not Oppenheimer, but rather (somehow) the act of quotation itself divorced from its quoter. Again, the text removes Oppenheimer's agency and resituates it elsewhere. Doing so helps produce another narrative of inevitability, one in which institutional forces and the acquisition of scientific knowledge efface his materiality and lead unstoppably to their conclusion independent of the potentially messy ethical equivocations of the narrative's main figure.

In addition to divesting him of agency textually while apparently acknowledging his importance, the museum also (de)centers him through the historical chronology it establishes spatially. For instance, following a display case containing the U.S. flag that was flown over the Trinity site, a replica of the Fat Man bomb casing, and a plaque detailing the use of the bomb on Nagasaki, the museum's narrative strangely returns visitors to Trinity. It displays the vehicle used to transport the plutonium core from

Los Alamos to the test site and, further along, a mock-up of the Trinity bomb. A text panel provides more detail on the test and concludes by reintroducing the test's scientific director: "J. Robert Oppenheimer made one final inspection, as described in the book The Making of the Atomic Bomb by Richard Rhodes: 'Sometime early that evening Oppenheimer climbed to the tower platform to perform a final inspection. There before him crouched his handiwork....His duty was almost done.'" As discussed in chapter 2, Rhodes's description delineates Oppenheimer in passive terms. With the bomb crouching before Oppenheimer, Rhodes's characterization is consistent with how the National Museum has, to this point in its narrative, characterized Oppenheimer as well: as a passive object to larger forces. Quoting this passage from Rhodes is thus tempting—but singularly strange. In addition to displacing the moment out of historical sequence, quoting Rhodes displaces it from the museum's narrative voice. These words stand as more or less the only "quotation" in the museum and thus represent a rupture in the means through which the museum creates its narrative. As such, this part of the museum disruptively foregrounds the constructed and textual nature of history by revealing history's indebtedness to writers such as Rhodes.

Once the museum resumes the postwar narrative, Oppenheimer next makes an appearance on a text panel titled "Truman's Directive & Oppenheimer's Opposition." The panel begins with the Soviet nuclear test of 1949 and President Truman's directive to proceed with hydrogen bomb development. "Robert Oppenheimer and some of his colleagues," the panel continues, "recommended against launching any program to build the hydrogen bomb. They instead recommended expanding research into fission bombs. They were overruled and the 'superbomb' project was underway." The panel includes two photographs: one of a serious-looking Truman in profile, at his desk, and one of a rumpled-looking Oppenheimer in front of a chalkboard full of equations and staring at the camera. Countless photos exist of Oppenheimer in front of chalkboards. The trope reinforces his identity as an academic and theorist, but in this instance, it is associated with his being "overruled" by savvier political forces. His identity as an intellectual comes up short, and his pleas for restraint in weapons development, possibly rooted in his philosophical contemplation (as opposed to the political action signaled by Truman at work), go unheeded.[40] There is thus a sense in this panel that the intellectual labor of the academic and theoretician, the role to which he has returned following the war, is insufficient and misguided in the production of knowledge for the "new reality" of the Cold War.

Consistent with the museum's initial visual positioning of Oppenheimer in the 1960s, when he was speaking out against the hydrogen bomb and other forms of proliferation and when he was the target of the AEC investigation, subsequent displays produce a subtle critique of Oppenheimer by minimizing his agency or even neutralizing him. The period in which he supposedly "betrays" the nation becomes the moment that, in the museum's ethos, defines how he is to be represented throughout. Even in its depiction of the Manhattan Project (the period invoked most often when Oppenheimer is lionized as a genius for begetting the bomb), the NMNSH adopts a series of passive textual constructions and tropes (from Greek *trepein*, to turn or move away from) that decenter him. The museum does not appear to make any overt attempts to eliminate or otherwise censor Oppenheimer, but its representational decisions consistently cast him in passive terms and envision him as the object of the whims and actions of others. Such a strategy is perhaps consistent with historiographic trends in which the "lives of great men" narratives have fallen out of favor and been replaced by more contextual narratives. But for a museum so intimately connected to American nuclear weapons, the NMNSH nonetheless invites visitors to consider the Manhattan Project's prime mover as a displaced force and as essentially helpless in the postwar military-industrial complex.

Such a strategy relies on some problematic assumptions. First, the colonialist and peremptory connotations of the "pioneering" language into which Oppenheimer and other nuclear scientists are cast at the beginning of the museum's exhibit help clear the conceptual landscape for the technocratic and patriarchal ideologies that produced globe-threatening weapons under the auspices of "rationality." Calling him a "pioneer" invokes the language of Western frontiersmanship and reminds viewers that nuclear science is as much a forceful intervention as was the construction of a military laboratory on a New Mexican mesa. Second, the strategy of "feminizing" him by casting him into the role of midwife or nurturer relies on damaging or generalizing assumptions about femininity (as inherently weak, as enabling rather than creating, as more social than intellectual) to question or undermine his role as one of the leaders of the Manhattan Project. Such assumptions are, of course, also aligned with his supposedly effete or "sophisticated" inclinations. Third, calling him a "child of the scientific age" and delineating the bodily differences between Groves and Oppenheimer in a section of the museum devoted to biography is also problematic. These strategies are forms of historical and biological determinism. They make dubious assumptions about gender and bodily materiality, and they render history as an immutable force, processes that help "justify" the development of atomic weapons as an inevitable product of abstract forces. Atomic weapons become a historical inevitability or even a biological instinct rather than the result of conscious decisions. The process of representing Oppenheimer, especially when he is divested of intellectual rigor by a focus on his body or his "love" of New Mexico, is thus implicated in positioning atomic weapons in this way. Finally, the way the museum depicts his opposition to weapons proliferation and his being "overruled" by stronger political forces depends on many of the same anti-intellectual postures assumed against science and scientists within the public sphere. With all these complexities, the NMNSH remains a site of strange representation. The contested meaning of Oppenheimer therein is a testament to the contested meaning of nuclear weapons in general. Its historical, economic, and ideological ties to the U.S. military and to the largest city in New Mexico make it a formidable force in the state, yet as in Los Alamos such authority is often challenged.

LAS VEGAS, NEVADA: NATIONAL ATOMIC TESTING MUSEUM

As my late flight from Albuquerque arrived at McCarran International Airport, I was struck—as no doubt countless visitors have been—by the contrast between the explosion of colored light and incongruous buildings that are Las Vegas and the stark blackness of the Nevada desert beyond. Indeed, the aesthetic of Las Vegas is the juxtaposition of desert apocalypse and thriving American capitalism.[41] Likewise, what this region simultaneously reveals and conceals about atomic bombs is striking. The aesthetics of removing the bomb from sight, the implications of the representational strategies that produce its technoaesthetics, are perhaps nowhere else more evident than here. About sixty-five miles northwest of Las Vegas, the Nevada National Security Site (previously known as the Nevada Test Site, and earlier still, as the Nevada Proving Grounds) was the location for more than nine hundred atmospheric and underground nuclear weapons tests conducted between 1951 and 1992.[42] These tests were conducted in a region often seen as empty wasteland, as off the American cultural radar and thus out of sight in "a national sacrifice zone"—and of course many of these tests were conducted underground, literally out of sight. Hiding these tests effaced the bomb, but doing so also made nuclear fear more mobile in its invisibility and more capable of infiltrating the cultural imagination.[43]

To "make visible" these tests and to explore the national, military, and cultural contexts in which they occurred, the Atomic Testing Museum opened in Las Vegas in 2005. In another instance of how unstable nomenclature reflects the ambiguities of these places, it achieved affiliation with the Smithsonian Institution in 2011 and the following year was redesignated the National Atomic Testing Museum by the Obama administration.[44] With a long list of corporate, military, and governmental sponsors (including Bechtel, the Department of Energy, Lawrence Livermore National Laboratory, Lockheed Martin, Los Alamos National Laboratories, Nellis Air Force Base, Northrop Grumman, Sandia National Laboratories, and Wackenhut), the museum does not conceal its vested interest in the national nuclear weapons arsenal. As in the Bradbury Science Museum, overt critique of nuclear weapons is virtually nonexistent. A number of voices have castigated the Las Vegas museum's celebratory tendencies: from the so-called Downwinders who protest the site's effects on their health to Edward Rothstein, who comments in the *New York Times* that the museum is "almost promotional in outlining current site activities, which include research with hazardous waste and national defense systems."[45] Sociologist Matt Wray states, "it is fair to say that the museum's narrative has essentially been scripted by the DOE" and "paid for and designed by the scions of the military industrial complex" (469,

471). Verging on glorifying nuclear testing, the arms race, and nuclear war itself, the museum frequently reiterates the ideological and discursive structures, advanced primarily by Republican conservatives, that claimed the United States would prevail in the Cold War because of its techno-logical supremacy.[46] Text panels throughout the museum repeatedly remind visitors of the role of government agencies in providing "national security" and in doing so specifically through nuclear weapons.[47] The museum maintains militarist and paternalist tones connoting strength and protection throughout, supporting these notions with quotations such as Eisenhower's avowal: "History does not long entrust the care of freedom to the weak and timid." Furthermore, the last artifacts visitors see as they leave the museum—a ruined steel I-beam and a crumpled piece of sheet metal from the World Trade Center—suggest that the Nevada Test Site, like the Bradbury Science Museum, is in the process of evolving to serve the technological and ideological demands of the so-called war on terror.[48] One historical wrinkle in this kind of brazen display of military power, and a significant obstacle for a museum that could otherwise organize itself entirely around spectacular mushroom clouds in dramatic landscapes, is the Limited Test Ban Treaty of 1963. This agreement pushed all nuclear tests underground, dramatically altering (and, as this museum sometimes suggests, impoverishing) the aesthetics of the bomb. No longer visible to the naked eye, mediated instead by layers of mechanical devices and electronic representation, nuclear weapons verge on incomprehensibility (and thus risk funding cuts or diminished public support). In places, the museum laments this shift underground. It articulates the supposed dan-gers of concealing one's military light under a bushel and, more dubiously when one considers the omnipresent discourse of secrecy, suggests that hiding the tests from sight deprives citizens of information and is thus undemocratic. To make the bomb visible again, the museum replicates the historical narrative of bomb testing physically and spatially by having visitors walk through and down a tunnel into an underground area of the museum where more knowledge of the bomb is then acquired. In making visible that which is hidden, the museum fulfills the supposed purpose of the scientific epistemology underlying weapons development. To reveal the bomb is to magnify its role in national security discourse. And yet, as

Masco and others have argued, moving nuclear weapons underground and effectively out of mind has also had for hawkish politicians the fortuitous result of concealing the apocalyptic and destructive associations of this kind of "national security"—of removing, in effect, those ironic quotation marks and creating less complicated public feelings of safety. The museum's intriguing and contradictory engagement with this logic of concealment is, by now, unsurprising.

Perhaps a little more surprising, however, given Oppenheimer's relative detachment from the Nevada Test Site during this period of nuclear history, is how seminal he becomes in the museum's representational strategies. And, as I have been arguing throughout, representing Oppenheimer frequently has unexpected disruptive effects on the historical narratives, aesthetic manifestations, and ideological angles of nuclear culture. In that sense, even though most of the Las Vegas museum has nothing to do with him, Oppenheimer functions as a catalyst—an initiator—in how the museum depicts nuclear weapons. Despite his status as one of the "technocratic elites" (Wray 470) responsible for the bomb, he complicates the frequently celebratory and promotional tones taken in relation to those elites. Passing through an entry gallery, visitors first encounter four images of the Trinity test, laid out in a grid and, to the left of the quadriptych, a text panel titled "Establishment of the NTS." The panel begins, as most do in this museum, with a quotation from some nuclear "authority." In this case, it opens with the well-known Oppenheimer quotation from the *Bhagavad Gita*: "I am become Death, the Destroyer of Worlds." Placing the Trinity test at the beginning of the story of atomic bomb testing is logical enough. Placing Oppenheimer on the first text panel as the "authority" quoted before the exposition is likewise consistent with the museum's representational strategies. But doing so (and doing so with this particular quotation) also has an unexpectedly disruptive effect. For a museum that supposedly rehearses official history and that generally praises nuclear weapons for the "national security" they provide, foregrounding death and destruction by using Oppenheimer's quotation as an epigraph seems in fact to suggest a counternarrative— or at least a counterdiscursive current—that many critics of the museum claim is lacking. Such an ominous evocation of loss and ruin work against the museum's supposed interest in promoting or celebrating atomic bombs as devices that secured American freedom and democracy as a global standard. The Cold War logic of deterrence, which runs through significant portions of the museum and which operates in accordance with the idea that the bomb will *prevent* apocalypse, is brought into question from the outset by Oppenheimer's grim assessment of what science has wrought. That his words come from ancient scripture also supports this counterdiscursive current. In discussing the museum's celebration of the military-industrial complex, Wray writes: "there was, to my eye, no visible critique of the foundational tenets of scientism—the ideological belief that superior technology liberates us and serves as the guarantor of freedom and democracy" (473–474). Such a remark does not acknowledge that Oppenheimer, despite his ostensible role as a rational embodiment of science, had a strong mystical streak. In opening with the words of a sacred text, as spoken by a scientist, the museum does indeed complicate the discourse of scientism, the discursive dominance sought by weapons manufacturers, and the Enlightenment rationality and teleological thinking that has been used to justify these kinds of weapons. Unquestionably, the museum is designed to evoke awe in the face of nuclear technology, but Oppenheimer's complicating presence is not insignificant. Thanks to the pivotal role he played in the development of the bomb and thanks to his catalyzing position at the beginning of the spatialized narrative of the bomb offered by the National Atomic Testing Museum, Oppenheimer helps disrupt this museum's seemingly monolithic discourse.

The physical position of the images and texts in the entry gallery similarly complicates the museum's ideological stance. Like most of the displays, the four images of the surreal first milliseconds of the Trinity test are, as visitors face them, on the right, while the text panel is on the left. Consistent with the tendency to read from left to right, and congruent with the Enlightenment equation of visuality with truth, the display encourages visitors to read the text first, then have it "confirmed" by the images or objects accompanying the panel—a sense of progression toward ever-illuminated knowledge. However, because the entire first display appears on the right-hand side of the entry gallery, visitors tend to encounter these images first and their accompanying text second. This order positions the large photographs of the Trinity test as an irrefutable, visual scientific artifact first and the encounter with the text panel second. Reversing this progression from textual truth to visual truth means Oppenheimer's presence in the display disrupts the intellectual teleology apparent nearly everywhere else in the museum. The order of the objects in this first display, and the order in which visitors tend to experience them, turn the objective scientific revelation promised by an image into a strange mystery. The mystery is apparently "solved," when visitors then read the text, by mystical revelation—occasioned by a religious quotation. This configuration inverts the Enlightenment narrative at the moment that Oppenheimer is introduced as a defining figure and, in its position at the beginning of the exhibit, works against the logic of scientific progression that the museum tries to consolidate elsewhere. Such a reversal, in a museum otherwise devoted to narratives of technological progression, foregrounds the mysticism and the notions of gnostic revelation attached to Oppenheimer and (as the name Trinity itself suggests) to the rarified world of nuclear technology.

The notion of mystical revelation has the potential to disrupt received scientific narratives, but it also may be contributing to formulations of atomic weapons as different not just in scale but in kind—unprecedented devices somehow above and beyond traditional means of governing warfare. Oppenheimer's presence in the entry gallery, a reminder of how science and mysticism are intertwined, inflects the aesthetics of revealing and concealing that help tell the story of underground nuclear testing. As Wray notes, much of the rest of the museum's "eight thousand square feet of exhibition space is given over to displaying and explaining the massive technological achievement involved in building and testing nuclear weapons" (472). Yet the aesthetics of making visible and comprehensible, of "displaying and explaining," come parceled with the concealment and derationalization introduced by Oppenheimer in the entry gallery. Moving from the entry gallery into the "Atomic Age Gallery," for instance, visitors might notice, around the corner and slightly out of sight for anyone proceeding straight ahead, a small glass case devoted to the Trinity test. But visitors also might *not* notice the case. The marginal physical position occupied by the Trinity test in this gallery, further isolated from visitors by its glass case, is in noticeable contrast to the prominence of the same test in the entry gallery. Positioning the Trinity test in such ways reflects the uneasy relationship between revealing and obscuring that has been part of the development of nuclear weapons since their origins—origins themselves shrouded in secrecy yet presented as essential to the national good. Such mystification, couched as revelation, capitalizes on assumptions about Enlightenment science to more firmly ensconce the control of nuclear weapons in a contemporary technocratic elite. It at once acknowledges the roles Oppenheimer and Trinity played in the history of atomic weapons and obscures them. This dual function reveals how complicated the narrative of knowledge acquisition can be when such a narrative takes place within the context of nuclear culture.

Commemorating U.S. nuclear tests in general involves the museum's complex combination of lamenting and aestheticizing the movement of testing underground. Such a movement, with its elimination of the visually iconic mushroom cloud and its reliance on the mediation done by computers and other scientific prostheses, inevitably abstracts and mystifies the process and locates the truth it contains in the increasingly rarified hands of physicists and technicians. To "reveal the secret of the atom" in the case of underground testing means to conceal it with tons of earth and many inscrutable scientific devices and their equally inscrutable data. When Western notions of knowledge predicated on making visible become the standard by which such a process (and the commemoration of such a process) is evaluated, frustration with the increasing obscurity of this kind of scientific work might set in among the scientists conducting the research, the political forces arguing for its increasing necessity, and the public who often foots the bill.[49] Although Oppenheimer's mystical penchant, highlighted in the opening space of the National Atomic Testing Museum, likely contributes to this frustration, the kinds of mystification outlined in this discussion challenge, as Oppenheimer himself did, the often monolithic voice of scientism. Such a challenge is especially germane to a field such as subatomic physics in which probability and ambiguity—famously exemplified by Einsteinian relativity and Heisenbergian uncertainty—are the order of the day. Such a challenge must also overcome the ways the nuclear tourism industry often evokes nostalgic responses to the Manhattan Project and the Cold War. Such responses in turn help preserve nuclear weapons (and their ideologies) as usable technologies (and as operable ideologies) into the twenty-first century.[50] But the counterdiscourses this museum offers are also vital to constructing a vigorous defense against a technomilitary elite that uses nuclear armament to threaten the human race and the entire global ecosystem.

PART III

KNOWING
OPPENHEIMER

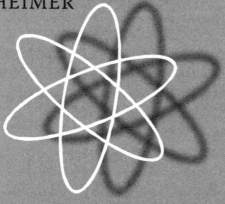

In 1982, about one million demonstrators gathered in New York to protest nuclear weapons. Earlier that same year, in Paris, philosopher and historian Michel Foucault delivered the lectures that would eventually be published as *The Hermeneutics of the Subject*. Although his focus was not nuclear arms, Foucault's development of the notion of ethopoiesis helps illuminate the objects of analysis in the final chapter of this book and their relation to the deep anxiety over nuclear weapons that would characterize the 1980s. Ethopoiesis derives from Foucault's study of classical thought: "*Ethōpoiein* means making *ethōs*, producing *ethōs*, changing, transforming *ethōs*, the individual's way of being, his mode of existence" (237). This production of the self, in Foucault's reading of the Greeks and Romans, was performed largely through writing. At once the private exploration of the self's interiority, writing about the self was also an act of objectification—the production of a self as an object in society. To produce text was to produce both a self as a subjective unit and a self in relation to social formations. The practice of ethopoiesis, according to Foucault, empowers the subject and "enables him to stand firm not only against the many beliefs that others wish to impose on him, but also against life's dangers and the authority of those who want to lay down the law" (240) When "authority" consists of the military and bureaucratic forces in charge of nuclear weapons, and when to "lay down the law" means launching nuclear war, ethopoiesis takes on especially important resonances.[1]

As discussed in earlier chapters, much Oppenheimer representation is characterized by invisibility, diffusion, obscurity, and other characteristics of a dispersed self. At the same time, these aesthetics frequently serve lionizing or idealizing purposes. Drawing on what literary and cultural theorist Roland Barthes calls "the prestige of the individual" ("Death of the Author" 143), texts possessing the aesthetics of erasure nevertheless frequently assert and consolidate Oppenheimer as a "great man of science" or an "important historical figure." In an attempt to make sense of these conflicting impulses, the final chapter of this study frames Oppenheimer as a celebrity in order to look at some specific instances of how he produced a self. It examines some of the things he wrote in his role as a public intellectual speaking to a dramatically changing political and cultural public.[2] This final chapter argues that the self he fashions in these texts, despite his use of absence and dispersal as tropes, paradoxically serves to reinstantiate the human form. His self-presentations serve as reminders that individual human beings—with all their corporeality, vulnerability, knowledge-seeking activities, and dignity—are at stake in a nuclear world.

In the months and years after the war, the secrets that enabled the construction of atomic weapons began to reveal themselves. The sudden disclosure of a massive, covert government project contributed, in the view of many scholars, to a significant midcentury change in American epistemologies. In the twentieth century, the atomic bomb lends texture to everything from individual psychosis to postmodernity to conspiracy theory culture. But the role of secrecy in particular deserves some unpacking.[3] First, secrecy is, like many of the concepts discussed in this study, marked by antitheses. It has a contradictory role in U.S. history: despite the prominence of visibility and clarity as key concepts—apparent, for instance, in the "self-evident" nature of the truths expressed in America's founding documents—secrecy lurks in countless arenas of American history and identity.[4] As one scholar of American secrecy notes: "From Puritan to postmodern paranoia, McCarthyite purges and Red Scares, Cold War containment and virtually enforced conformity, racial segregation and conflict, fears of ethnic and religious dilution of American identity, sometimes rabid distrust of government and its corporate ties, even epidemiological hysteria, America has maintained the open secret of its own self-defensive and self-constitutive employment of the ambivalent strategies of secrecy" (Liste-Noya 2). The bomb, too, is constituted by this schema. Discourses of secrecy are largely hostile to discourses of democracy, and they prevent citizens from knowing about the weapons they fund and that seemingly defend them. Similarly, the "right" to secrecy reveals an abiding faith in American exceptionalism that absolves the nation of its responsibility for more equitable global participation. Exceptionalism is, to many scholars, a form of self-delusion that prevents U.S. citizens from understanding or questioning American imperialism. At the same time, possessing the ultimate weapon yet disavowing it as a "secret weapon" gives rise to a sense of vulnerability, frequently repressed yet frequently evident in, for example, fantasies of self-destruction. Such fantasies—in millennialist religion, postapocalyptic novels, Hollywood disaster films, and attempts to comprehend terrorist attacks—represent the "secret" knowledge of the American imperial venture. The destruction wrought on Japan in 1945 returns in the form of the "Ground Zero" of 9/11.[5] This constitutive yet ultimately destructive fantasy of secrecy sits at the center of twentieth-century American identity and serves as a key to understanding Oppenheimer's self-fashioning.

Oppenheimer's exercise in constituting a self operates according to the relationship between secrecy and subjectivity. This relationship posits first a strict separation between secret and nonsecret (and between those who hold secrets and those who do not) and then presupposes the agency—the intention and the will—to discern between those categories. As the philosopher Sissela Bok notes, this capacity for "discernment, the ability to make distinctions, to sort out and draw lines...underlies not only secrecy but all thinking, all intention and choice" (6) and thus structures subjectivity itself. The agency necessary for keeping secrets helps establish the self, Bok asserts, yet the existence of the secret and its vulnerability to revelation threaten to undo the sanctity of the self and open it up to invasion (28). To disclose the knowledge concealed by secrecy is to empty out the self and remove its agency. Secrecy undoes itself even earlier, as soon as it becomes a secret because a secret must be known to at least one person: the secret holder. As the possessor of atomic secrets, Oppenheimer participates in this enigmatic process of constituting the secret and the self by denying them. The French term for "denial," as philosopher Jacques Derrida notes, is *dénégation* ("How to Avoid Speaking" 25), and the double negative of "de-negation" points to its role in constituting Oppenheimer: his secrets are a negation—a concealment or a denial of knowledge—while their revelation denies their own essence but establishes Oppenheimer as public, if often impersonal, persona.

In 1957, the same year Barthes published *Mythologies*, his study of the creation of modern myths, the French sociologist Edgar Morin published *Les Stars*, an analysis of film stars as modern myths. Although Oppenheimer was no cinematic star, his identity as public celebrity allows him to function as a focal point for the postwar renegotiation of national mythologies. One of the most significant ways in which he denegates himself—ethopoetically posits a self through negation—is through his status as a postwar celebrity. More specifically, he bears conceptual affinities with Morin's characterization of the film star as one who "straddles both sacred and profane, divine and real, aesthetic and magic" (84) and thus likewise embodies fundamental tensions. These tensions in turn allow Oppenheimer the celebrity to embody a multiplicity of meanings as he serves, in various public roles, to reconcile national mythologies.[6] This multiplicity arises in him because of another conceptual opposition within the figure of the celebrity: the tension between the private and the public.[7] The national mythologies his celebrity engages with, frequently connected to democratic ideals, are upheld or altered partly through the textual manifestations of celebrity that will be the subject of this final chapter.[8] The word "celebrity," as Boone and Vickers note derives "from the Latin nouns *celebritas* and *celebratio*, both of which signify the presence of a multitude, a large assembly or gathering, a crowd" (903). His self-fashioning thus transcends the self and reaches toward the multitude. Invoking the masses and drawing them together also brings with it religious connotations in which celebrities become imbued with mystical, unfathomable power (903–904). Terms such as "icons," "idols," and "heavenly bodies"[9] hint at these connotations, and the distancing effect they have is essential to the production of celebrity.[10] This sense of mystery persists in spite of celebrity's origins in the performance of intimacy and renown that comes, in Oppenheimer's case, with being on the lecture circuit. For him, this mystifying effect in turn helps confound nuclear weapons at the same time that it appears to concretize knowledge of them in the embodied form of the man who helped invent them.

His ambivalence about his postwar celebrity was, as nearly every biographical and historical source notes, an integral part of the real, material Oppenheimer. How much that ambivalence is a retrospective creation engendered by the conceptual ambiguities of quantum physics or the paradoxes of nuclear weapons or the contradictions of celebrity, and how much is a reflection of his "actual" ambivalence, is difficult if not impossible to resolve, however. This final chapter does not propose to resolve these questions about the "origins" of representing his ambivalence, but it will engage with the public persona evoked by his rhetorical self-fashioning and the contexts in which it appears.[11] Such a persona, I believe, emerges in the postwar period out of evolving concepts of celebrity and changing impressions of secrecy—flux generated by the revelation of the massive secret that was the Manhattan project.

CHAPTER 6

IN HIS OWN WORDS:
OPPENHEIMER'S WRITING

In 1916, when he was only twelve years old and after having been in correspondence with several New York area geologists, Robert Oppenheimer
was invited to give a talk to the New York Mineralogical Club. Unaware
that they had invited a young boy, the club was bemused when he showed
up, laughed when he could not see over the lectern, but gave him a "hearty
round of applause" (Bird and Sherwin 15) when the awkward child finished
his talk. For the precocious child this early foray into public speaking, complete with a belittling audience response followed by emphatic acceptance,
would be a sign of things to come. In the years following World War II,
when he attempted to return to his research and teaching, Oppenheimer
found himself instead drawn into an extraordinarily public life, in which
his job seemed to be to interpret modern science and its cultural consequences.[1] In addition to directing the Institute for Advanced Study in
Princeton, New Jersey, he served in advisory and leadership capacities for
a number of governmental committees and organizations until his fateful
security hearing. Almost to the end of his life, he traveled the world giving
lectures and speeches, and published many nonscientific essays in mainstream journals and magazines. He frequently drew large audiences and
was praised as an eloquent and inspiring speaker. He rose to prominence in
a conflicted time (a time of crisis that he, in many ways, helped precipitate)

and urged his audiences to appeal to science, history, and reason to make sense of that crisis.[2] He was, despite (or perhaps because of) his downfall and rehabilitation, a celebrity. His public appearances functioned in no small degree as an antidote to the secrecy surrounding the project that made him famous, but he frequently reiterated in those appearances the secrecy of the knowledge he possessed.[3] Like so many other concepts attached to Oppenheimer, his transparency is qualified by its opposite: an opacity that renders him distant and strange. In a review of several books about Oppenheimer published in the 1980s, for instance, Michael Sherman notes that Alice Kimball Smith and Charles Weiner's collection of his letters focuses on "Oppenheimer's youth and early professional years, before he disappeared behind the security screen of Los Alamos or the even more opaque wall of a public life in the years after Los Alamos" (100). Sherman's metaphors of opacity are intriguing, especially with regard to the striking suggestion that Oppenheimer's *public* life muddied the understanding of his selfhood even more than the supposed "privacy" granted by the secrecy of the Manhattan Project. That one's public persona conceals elements of one's private persona is both counterintuitive and entirely obvious. Oppenheimer becomes one of the paradoxical "intimate strangers" we call celebrities.[4] The "exposure" of public life is simultaneously a means of obscuring one's private self. This nexus of visibility and invisibility, which underlies the relationship between the "private" and the "public" self and which is central to the representational strategies in many of the works thus far explored, becomes crucial to analyzing Oppenheimer's own self-presentation. I argue that the opacity of his public self-presentation in fact clarifies, perhaps contrary to much of the indeterminacy in Oppenheimer representation, a sense of self.

It would be a mistake, however, to assume that his own writing constitutes the definitive Oppenheimer, the final word on who he "really" is. After all, even Foucault's most optimistic sense of ethopoetic self-fashioning is still bound by regimes of social power. The opacity that helps constitute anyone's public persona precludes any public text from providing transparent access to "the real person." Likewise, it would be problematic to assume that the historical moments in which Oppenheimer delivered these lectures constitute "the real" and that they take primacy over the mediations that are the subsequently published texts of the lectures. Collectively, the representations of Oppenheimer discussed so far are primarily reactions to a scientist with uncanny provocative abilities. The writings at issue in this chapter, however, establish in some ways Oppenheimer's public response to being appropriated. To finish fleshing out my analysis (while acknowledging that it will forever be incomplete), the final chapter examines the reciprocity of this portraiture: Oppenheimer's own self-presentation as it manifests in his published work.

Discussing this public presence means focusing on a few texts of a particular nature. Before the war, Oppenheimer's writing was quite resolutely scientific and not at all intended for general public consumption. This chapter will not examine these highly technical papers—on subjects such as quantum tunneling, mesons, and neutron stars—as instances of public self-fashioning, important as they may be in their fields.[5] Essential as they may have been to establishing his intellectual and academic identity, they lack the public displays of self-reflexivity that would come after the war to a man tapped as a sage and as an interpreter between the scientific community and the general public.

Similarly, and thanks to the presumed "truthfulness" of private texts— letters, diaries, and so on—over the presumed "artifice" of public ones, it might be tempting to imagine that analyzing, for example, Oppenheimer's private correspondence might yield better access to "the truth" about who he "really was" or what he "really meant." Many biographers work with this assumption, as do Smith and Weiner in their edition of Oppenheimer's letters.[6] Although private texts certainly produce specific kinds of knowledge about historical individuals, this book has been (and remains in this chapter) committed to exploring how representations of Oppenheimer work to produce meaning culturally rather than the purported accuracy of their truth claims. Thus, when I refer to Oppenheimer's writing, I am referring to the public texts, those essays and speeches that form his public persona, rather than the personal ones.[7] I hope to analyze less the knowledge that has been "concealed" by his public persona and more the knowledge that *is* his public persona. At the same time, and as already noted, his own self-fashioning is not the final and definitive articulation of Oppenheimer's meaning—"authorial intent" is, as always, but one point in a constellation of meanings. Rather, what he says about himself in his own published writing should be considered—as with all so-called life writing—one text among many that offer representations of this influential figure.

The focus in this chapter is on the three books of essays and lectures published in Oppenheimer's lifetime: *Science and the Common Understanding* (1954), *The Open Mind* (1955), and *The Flying Trapeze: Three Crises for Physicists* (1964). Although I will briefly discuss the two collections published posthumously, *Uncommon Sense* (1984) and *Atom and Void* (1989), most of his rhetoric pertinent to my argument will come from the first three books. Even though the primary objects of analysis in this chapter are texts, I want to avoid simply returning, in the final part of this book, to textual iterations of the scientist. After all, these books are made up mostly of transcriptions—textual copies of speeches he delivered orally—and thus exist somewhere between the textual and the oral.[8] Without privileging either the textual or the oral as more "authentic," I wish to draw attention to the unique status of these texts and to the relationship within them between the textual and the oral. As one might expect from books produced "on the lecture circuit," the three books, as well as the two posthumously published ones, are quite similar in style and content and are often quite repetitive. They can be considered, in that respect, one large text of self-fashioning. These books must also be contextualized within a larger, multimedia performance of his celebrity, a performance that included lectures, television appearances, and other mediatized and multitextual representations. All these representations—these *re-presentations* of self—serve to disclose the nuclear secret, to negate its status as secret and thus to denegate (that is, to produce) the self.

With their origins in speeches, these books are textual traces of in situ performances. They are, of course, words on the page, but they evoke—both implicitly in their repetition and explicitly from time to time in their situational addresses—what were once instances of the visual, material presence integral to the incarnation of celebrities.[9] As discussed in part 2, however, visibility does not always grant access to the reality of the thing made visible. The visibility of the individual confers the "illusion of intimacy" (Rojek 19) essential to the notion of celebrity, but in helping to create the celebrity, visibility also ultimately serves to distance the individual from his or her observers. The visibility of Oppenheimer at a lectern in a particular place and time, therefore, has more in common with the books published after the fact than it might first appear; his enshrinement on stage as a celebrity mediates him in ways related to the mediation conferred by reading a book of his essays. Despite his "liveness," experiencing Oppenheimer on stage involves a remoteness and a dissociation not dissimilar to reading his words years or decades later. His appearances and these books, as well as the experience of reading them, are the material traces of the revelation of a secret and thus straddle the boundaries between many of those categories essential to understanding the meanings of Oppenheimer: embodiment and disembodiment, text and speech, visibility and invisibility, originality and repetition, and presence and absence.

In addition to surveying knotty and elusive topics such as the atomic bomb, nuclear energy, and the social responsibilities of scientists, these books construct a self partly through their affinities with autobiographical writing.[10] Contrary to the expectation that a celebrity's books should reveal the self, there are few personal references in Oppenheimer's books. As I will show, however, they nonetheless produce a textual self in the way autobiographical writing, as a "technology" for sharing private subjectivity, produces a self.[11] More than just to thwart readers' expectations, the rhetorical strategies Oppenheimer uses to effect his self-fashioning depend on an aesthetic of absence and synecdoche similar to those in evidence in previously discussed representations. His self-fashioning, in other words, often takes the form of self-effacement or denegation. This self-effacement, although both essential to the objectivity attributed to scientists in general and related to the principles of uncertainty in twentieth-century quantum physics in particular, exceeds mere humility. Self-effacement in fact evokes permeability—to other scientists, to political maneuvering, to the general public—and although apparently operating in the service of fashioning Oppenheimer, it in fact reinstantiates all that is put at risk in a nuclear world: human culture, human institutions, and, indeed, corporeal human beings.

NULLIFYING THE SELF: *SCIENCE AND*
THE COMMON UNDERSTANDING (1954)

The BBC's Reith Lectures, begun in 1948 and named for Sir John Reith, the first director-general of the public broadcaster, offers annually a series of lectures by "some acknowledged authority in a particular field—it may be sociology, literature, history, public affairs, or economics" ("Reith at 60"). Oppenheimer delivered six addresses for the 1953 Reith Lectures, which were published the following year by Oxford University Press as *Science and the Common Understanding.* As its title suggests, his lectures and book discuss the nature of science and the identity of the scientist, together with their relationship to social knowledge. As in almost all his public writing, he constructs a portrait of the scientist in that book with little explicit reference to himself. The self at the center of the Oppenheimer phenomenon, the man who had become by 1953 an "acknowledged authority" sought out by the BBC and a celebrity in the public mind at large, appears only faintly in the text of these lectures. In what would become a characteristic mode of his writing, he fashions a sense of self through negation, abstraction, and other strategies of nullification. However, annulling the self means, within the realm of Oppenheimer representation, to posit something else, and *Science and the Common Understanding* in that sense underscores the importance of community. His first book, in negating him as part of its contribution to his celebrity, places community at the center of what is put at risk by nuclear weapons.

The style and subject matter of the essays in *Science and the Common Understanding* are prototypical. Although only a small amount of material in these essays is densely technical, they are nonetheless remote, abstruse, and often mystical. One of the more technical essays—the second one, "Science as Action: Rutherford's World"—stresses the importance of putting science into the services of "the inquiring human spirit" (36). The sense of liberal inquiry, as well as the ineffability of the "human spirit," ensures that the tenor of these essays remains metaphysical even as it delineates supposedly more concrete human concerns. The metaphysical language and the allusive and elusive cultural meditations that are hallmarks of

Oppenheimer's writing frequently help form that opaque wall that scholars and writers often claim constitutes his public persona.

Science and the Common Understanding contributes to this opacity with a number of examples of diminution or self-effacement, the kinds of phrases often taken as evidence of Oppenheimer's humility. Phrases such as "bearing in mind my limited area of experience" (95) and "we will have to accept the fact that no one of us really will ever know very much" (54) pepper his prose and serve to undercut both the celebrity that led to his giving the Reith lectures and, more generally, the process of positing a self. There are also some curiously double-edged locutions that on the one hand posit a self but on the other hand deny or nullify the self. In the first essay, he asserts the "deep, intimate, and subtle" connections between scientific knowledge and metaphysics before the following claim: "If I did not believe that, I should hardly be addressing these lectures to an attempt to elucidate what there is new in atomic physics that is relevant, helpful, and inspiriting for men to know" (3–4). He appears to be asserting something about himself: that he believes the arcane field of atomic physics does indeed hold relevance for the wider human community, that the work he does contributes to progress and betterment in a general sense. He is, however, making this assertion by denying its opposite. With typically convoluted syntax, he postulates that *if* he did not believe in this relationship between science and the common understanding, then he would not be "here," as it were, either orally in the Reith lectures or textually in the subsequent book. His assertion of a believing self occurs through an implied absence— a version of a process in much Oppenheimer representation—and that absence, thanks to this rhetorical device, exists alongside the presence the sentence ultimately asserts.

The science carried out by this both posited and negated scientist is likewise paradoxically both present and absent. On the wiliness of quantum physics, Oppenheimer writes:

> To what appeared to be the simplest questions, we will tend to give either no answer or an answer which will at first sight be reminiscent more of a strange catechism than of the straightforward affirmatives

of physical science. If we ask, for instance, whether the position of
the electron remains the same, we must say "no"; if we ask whether
the electron's position changes with time, we must say "no"; if we ask
whether the electron is at rest, we must say "no"; if we ask whether it
is in motion, we must say "no." The Buddha has given such answers
when interrogated as to the conditions of a man's self after his death;
but they are not familiar answers for the tradition of seventeenth-
and eighteenth-century science. (42–43)

He strikes a distinction between ancient mystical practices and more
recent scientific ones, alluding to the distinction as part of the reason for
the apparent incomprehensibility of the new physics, but at the same time,
he unifies these practices by suggesting that ancient wisdom "anticipated"
modern science. This paradoxical strategy is, of course, quintessential
Oppenheimer, but the structure of the comment is important, too, for
understanding the troubling nature of the public knowledge he and his
fellow physicists produce. His hypothetical questions all posit something
(that is, they are framed positively), yet the answer is always "no" (negation).
Simultaneously positing and negating, and the production of paradoxical
answers, becomes part of the epistemological framework of the new science but also part of how Oppenheimer himself is perceived. In a comment
such as this one, he is unwilling to exploit his identity as a scientist (or,
by extension, popular conceptions of science as a discipline that provides
"straightforward affirmatives") to announce pat answers in all-knowing or
sagelike manners. His status as celebrity scientist serves to mystify science itself, to affirm in the public imagination the troubling but inescapable
direction science has taken away from certainty and into uncertainty.

These patterns of negation—of the self and of science's ostensible task
of providing "affirmatives"—are prominent in the parts of the book that
reflect the word "Science" in the title. The scientific practices themselves,
abstractions such as "the scientist" or "physicists" that Oppenheimer
employs, and the infrequent but telling personal references to himself
as scientist are all characterized by their rhetoric of negation. Yet such
patterns inevitably help construct, in a positive and what Oppenheimer
might call "inspiriting" way, the second half of the book's title, "Common

Understanding." Articulated variously as a global network of scientists, as a kinship between scientist and nonscientist, and as that generic (but troublingly noninclusive) term "men," his sense of community arises out of the negation of the individual. In the final essay in the book, "The Sciences and Man's Community," he writes: "Each of us knows from his own life how much even a casual and limited association of men goes beyond him in knowledge, in understanding, in humanity, and in power" (101). The extension alluded to in such a phrase, the seeking of knowledge beyond one's personal limits, expands the concept of the self from its confines as a singular unity. Such expansion leads inevitably to an unstable self, referenced in the many instances of self-negation, but instead of simply provoking anxiety, in this essay the unstable self points toward a wider community. This final essay also contains an extended metaphor, in which science is a house and its subdisciplines are rooms in the house, that also sheds light on the relationship between the individual and the community. The occupants of this house are both scientists and "men," and their individual negation also helps articulate community. "Even in science," Oppenheimer writes, "and even without visiting the room in its house called atomic theory, we are again and again reminded of the complementary traits in our own life, even in our own professional life. We are nothing without the work of others our predecessors, others our teachers, others our contemporaries. Even when, in the measure of our adequacy and our fullness, new insight and new order are created, we are still nothing without others. Yet we are more" (107). As one of the expressions of humility common in his writing, his self-denial ("We are nothing") is tempered by a measure of not only adequacy but fullness, a "fleshing out" of the human individual put in such dire straits by the political instrumentalization of the room of the house Oppenheimer calls "atomic theory." The "fullness" of the individual, material self asserted in this passage against the growing political machinations of the 1950s, which would eventually come to reduce individuals to the status of "collateral damage" in a nuclear war, asserts a palpable human presence—a humanity—in the face of all such negation. Seeking nuclear knowledge is, as always, ambiguously about both learning and publicizing the "secret" knowledge of nature and somehow finding a way to live with its dangers.

In a group of essays characterized by negation, self-effacement, and other forms of erasure, his equal insistence on the importance of community—not only additive but exponential in its cumulative effects—ensures that his own writing "fleshes out," as it were, the meaning of Oppenheimer as discussed in this study. The "fullness" of which he speaks *posits* something—presence and humanity—in the face of the negation and absence that has gone before. "We" are indeed "nothing," as he says, without community, just as we would become nothing come the full flowering of atomic weapons. But the insight and order that emerge from community, that transcend both the individual and the transience of human culture, remind readers of what is at stake in a nuclear world: nothing less than the human race and the many individuals it contains.

ASSERTING THE SELF: *THE OPEN MIND* (1955)

The Open Mind, the title of Oppenheimer's second collection of lectures, refers to a broad philosophical attitude or even personality trait—the commonly understood "open-mindedness" required for inquiry, scientific and otherwise—but it also has a more specific application: the governance of atomic bombs. Oppenheimer speaks frequently in this collection of the importance of international cooperation to the regulation of atomic weapons and thus of the openness required to achieve cooperation. His sense of openness therefore encompasses a sincere effort to grapple with the kinds of potentially lethal tensions growing between the United States and the Soviet Union during the postwar period these lectures span (1946–1954). But that sense of openness also underscores the importance of sharing technical information and broadening public understanding of these new technologies. Oppenheimer advocates in that book for "examining with great care how great the area of openness can be, that it may not be merely a piece of technical information but an area of technical understanding" (35). The breadth of this openness encompasses political openness; it should be supported, he emphasizes, not only with the aim of preserving science's methods of inquiry but also to dispel the American political hegemony enabled by preserving "atomic secrets." These different kinds of openness—scientific and political—often come together, particularly when he discusses the frightful consequences of closing down discourse and keeping secrets: "With deep misgivings," he writes, "we are keeping secret not only those elements of our military plans, but those elements of our technical information and policy, a knowledge of which would render us more subject to enemy coercion and less effective in exercising our own" (52). Official secrecy made the nation weak—both vulnerable and incapable of wielding influence—while providing a confusing illusion of strength. He seems to hold out hope that this notion of open-mindedness exemplifies the scientific spirit and thus could clarify an increasingly incoherent postwar world.[12]

At the same time, Oppenheimer is cognizant of the dangers of total openness. His statements on openness are frequently tempered by concerns for national security and a patriotic sense of "competition" with other nations. He acknowledges the value of having diverse scientific communities working together to solve problems but recognizes that openness "would follow ideally if we had no worry that there were a competitor anywhere in the world" (39). Such qualified openness might stem from his perception of the Manhattan Project itself. The construction of the atomic bomb, as he says in the title lecture "The Open Mind," "owed its whole success and its very existence to the possibility of open discussion and free inquiry," yet it "appeared in a strange paradox, at once a secret, and an unparalleled instrument of coercion" (50). Although he acknowledges the power of secrecy as a political instrument, he laments its bureaucratic implementation in the Manhattan Project. As something of an atonement, he asserts the importance of openness "to the dignity of man, and in making possible the taking of decision on the basis of honest conviction" (51). He celebrates "the openness of men's minds and the openness of whatever media there are for communion between men, free of restraint, free of repression, and free even of that most pervasive of all restraints, that of status and hierarchy" (51).

Such a strongly worded endorsement of "freedom" emerges from the selves at the cores of liberal humanism, Enlightenment subjectivity, and American individualism. The connotations of the metaphor of openness, however, complicate such an assertion. An open self is a porous self, a

self with unstable boundaries, a self permeable to otherness, a self at odds
with the notion of the monad, and in the connections Oppenheimer draws
between the open self and international control of atomic weapons, a self
at odds with American individualism and exceptionalism. In the book's
penultimate lecture, he rejects much of the philosophical tradition that
has produced these Euro-American notions of the self: "We therefore have,
in so far as we have at all, a philosophy that is quite anachronistic and, I
am convinced, quite inadequate to our times. I think that whatever may
have been thought of Cartesian and Newtonian reforms in the intellectual
life of Europe, the time when those were what the doctor ordered—all
that the doctor ordered—is long past" (128–129). The "inadequacy," as he
says, of the Cartesian subject and the Newtonian physics that determine
his relationship to the world undermines conventional notions of the self.
The open self upon which so much depends is the effaced self in *Science
and the Common Understanding* and in many of the representations of
Oppenheimer discussed earlier. *The Open Mind*, despite its assertion of
freedom and its condemnation of coercion, often contains Oppenheimer's
self-nullifying discourse. And such discourse again helps reiterate what is
at risk in a world governed by nuclear weapons.

His self-effacement recurs in the apparent gestures of humility in his
prose. He calls his first lecture "a very incomplete and very one-sided talk"
(3), frequently interrupts his own pronouncement with comments such as
"and here I am speaking about matters of which I know even less" (39–40),
and he sometimes urges his listeners and readers to "deal with [ideas] more
fully and more wisely" (120) than he has. He frequently emphasizes the
limitations of science (100) and notes that using science to predict "the
course of civilization...is not my dish" (135). He uses passive constructions
in many of the lectures, pointing out the "things you will hear described
today" (7), for instance, and employs abstractions such as "I think one must
agree with this" (12) rather than direct statements. Such divesting of ego
appears writ large at the national level, as when Oppenheimer, in calling
for several things that must be in place when devising national policy for
the control of nuclear weapons, notes the importance of "a touch of weakness" (69) in the nation's character so better to facilitate unity with and
the commensurate strength of "our friends in the Free World" (69). This

national vulnerability is a typical Oppenheimer paradox: it is a *required* weakness, one that gives the nation strength in the world.

There are, of course, moments of overt self-assertion in *The Open Mind*. He uses the personal pronoun "I" as often, if not more so, as he uses the impersonal pronoun "one" or the collective pronoun "we," and unlike in *Science and the Common Understanding*, he frequently uses personal anecdotes. Such anecdotes are still short on intimate revelation of the self and are frequently cloaked in distancing strategies, but they also succeed in embodying Oppenheimer within the material world. They sometimes appear to be part of the numinous self he constructs, but they in fact reveal a powerful investment in the physical world, its inhabitants, and the palpable threats they face from atomic bombs. He makes one such assertion at the beginning of the title lecture when he claims: "A few weeks ago the president of a college in the prairie states came to see me. Clearly, when he tried to look into the future, he did not like what he saw" (45). Such an assertion of self through personal anecdote lacks detail (he never specifies who the president was, what state he came from, or the specifics of his consultation), and in establishing himself as one to be consulted on matters concerning "the future," Oppenheimer strikes an oracular pose. The anonymous prairie college president making a pilgrimage to see the Eastern sage contributes to an Oppenheimer characterized by distance and mystical inscrutability. Aware of the enigmatic quality of his own celebrity, however, he immediately dispels this mysticism by claiming that the theme of the lecture—"enlisting time and nature in the conduct of our international affairs"—is "not meant mystically, for the nature which we must enlist is that of man; and if there is hope in it, that lies not least in man's reason" (46). Time and nature are not inscrutable concepts but rather the very objects of a physicist's rational inquiry. Like those objects, atomic bombs need to be central in international politics. In other words, they need to be confronted rationally as part of the real world because that is ultimately what hangs in the balance of a nuclear confrontation.

A later lecture, "Physics in the Contemporary World," reiterates these secular concerns. It also contains a personal anecdote, recounted using a similar strategy: "When I was a student at Göttingen twenty years ago, there was a story current about the great mathematician [David] Hilbert, who perhaps would have liked, had the world let him, to have thought of his science as something independent of worldly vicissitudes" (88–89). The anecdote details Hilbert's claims that science and technology, science and society, science and the world of ordinary men, "have nothing whatever to do with one another" (89). Oppenheimer concludes the anecdote by dismissing Hilbert's antiquated view: "Today the wars and the troubled times deny us the luxury of such absent-mindedness" (89). Hilbert's otherworldly concerns, like the mystical gnosis ascribed to Oppenheimer and resting uneasily against his pragmatic empiricism, are irresponsible and perhaps even dangerous in the nuclear age. Dispelling the view that atomic scientists had become mystical prophets—a view engendered by the often paradoxical nature of the science itself, by the religious and otherworldly references Oppenheimer and others sometimes used, and by his celebrity status itself—was a leading cause for Oppenheimer by the time *The Open Mind* was published in 1955. "In the arts and in the sciences," he writes wistfully in the book's final lecture, "it would be good to be a prophet. It would be a delight to know the future" (134). But the long list of scientific questions that follows that impossible desire—questions such as, "What happens in the brain to make a record of the past?" and "What are the physical features which make consciousness possible?" (134)—reveals just how little scientists know. He further qualifies these questions by noting that "the pressing ones will be transmuted before they are answered, that they will be replaced by others, and that the very process of discovery will shatter the concepts that we today use to describe our puzzlement" (134). In doing so, he emphasizes the systematically self-interrogating nature of science and, ultimately, the confidence it instills in order to show how unlike prophecy the work of producing scientific knowledge is.

The openness of which he speaks, then, helps produce a self in *The Open Mind* riven by uncertainty but nevertheless committed to pragmatic truth. Extended to the national level, this open self reveals the importance of dispelling absolute secrecy from policymaking. At the center of *The Open Mind*, an essay titled "Atomic Weapons and American Policy" articulates Oppenheimer's belief that public opinion, a crucial component of "political vitality in our country" (71), suffers under the policy of official secrecy. "No responsible person," he says, "will hazard an opinion in a field where he believes that there is somebody else who knows the truth, and where he believes that he does not know it" (71). He acknowledges the limited usefulness of secrecy but claims that "knowledge of the characteristics and probable effects of our atomic weapons, of—in rough terms—the numbers available, and of the changes that are likely to occur within the next years, this is not among the things to be kept secret" (72). He disputes especially strongly the argument that secrecy is essential for keeping scientific information from enemy hands: "My own view is that the enemy has this information" (72). The collaborative nature of science is capable of being extended to national policy. Such policy, in turn, affects and is affected by all the other nations that together constitute his vision of global unity. Such unity is threatened by atomic weapons (and by the misguided secrecy that promises to "contain" them) and thus must be safeguarded through the knowledge enabled by openness and through the democratic work enabled by knowledge. The open self offering these visions in the lectures that make up *The Open Mind* becomes, in a process akin to turning ephemeral lectures into material text, the tangible yet fragile self imperiled by the world's new atomic order. The community of human beings fashioned in and by these lectures and then later in and by this text once again comes to represent the bodily materiality of those now threatened by that atomic order.

EMBODYING THE SELF: *THE FLYING TRAPEZE* (1964)

The third and final book of lectures published during Oppenheimer's lifetime bears the curious title *The Flying Trapeze: Three Crises for Physicists.* It consists of three essays derived from speeches he gave as part of the 1962 Whidden Lectures at McMaster University in Hamilton, Ontario. The lectures are, as expected, quite abstract despite their being addressed to a general public, but in contrast to the first two books, which come with little contextual material (brief biographical notes and perhaps a line or two at the beginning of each essay indicating when it was delivered and to whom), *The Flying Trapeze* includes some revealing editorial apparatus. In a foreword, E. T. Salmon, the principal of University College at McMaster in 1964, notes that the Whidden Lectures were established ten years earlier in memory of a former chancellor of McMaster and that their "purpose is to help students cross the barriers separating the academic departments of a modern university" (v). Before interdisciplinarity became an academic buzzword, the Whidden Lectures affirmed the value of seeking knowledge broadly and selected, as their 1962 speaker, a scholar and public figure who himself exemplified a breadth of interests in a variety of disciplines. Reinforced by this foreword, the setting of the lectures collected in *The Flying Trapeze* affirms Oppenheimer's identity as a celebrity academic whose interdisciplinarity allows him to circulate as a scholarly star among a wide range of listeners and readers.

In the short biographical sketch that Salmon provides in his foreword, Oppenheimer "is perhaps best known to the man in the street as the Director of the Los Alamos Scientific Laboratory during the Second World War" (vi). Rhetoric that evokes "the common man," those listeners and readers who contribute to "the common understanding" Oppenheimer writes about in his first book, enables Salmon to shape the audience for *The Flying Trapeze*. The Whidden Lectures, with the gravitas furnished by their annual recurrence and the mass appeal provided by their interdisciplinary speakers, help solidify a man who is, in the abstract and pontifical language he uses, remote in his celebrity sagacity. At the same time, in being oriented toward "the man in the street," *The Flying Trapeze* is also broadly appealing. The readership for *The Flying Trapeze*, as for the first two books, is general, so Oppenheimer circulates in these books as a remote figure who is nonetheless expected to meet the needs of a wide audience. Such a combination—of unapproachability on one hand and radiant communicativeness across a general audience on the other—is the essence of celebrity.

The preface that follows, written by M. A. Preston, McMaster professor of theoretical physics, provides some editorial detail that also helps determine the representation and circulation of the Oppenheimer produced by *The Flying Trapeze*. The lectures, Preston notes, "were given by Professor Oppenheimer from only sketchy outline notes, and were recorded" (vii). Thus, even before readers arrive at the first essay, Oppenheimer has been repeatedly mediated: through an oral performance, through a technological intermediary, into textual form, and yet again through these editorial apparatus. Preston underscores the frequent tension among these forms of mediation when he writes: "It was a revelation to me when I looked at the word-for-word transcript of the lectures to see that such sparkling addresses, so clear to the listener, contained so many sentences sufficiently involved to make reading difficult" (vii). The act of "translating" Oppenheimer from an oral performance to a textual one is not, therefore, straightforward. Yet Preston downplays the editorial work he has done as merely making "the verbal transcript more readable" (vii). This process, however, is never *only* an act of clarification of the "more authentic" verbal performance. Rather, it constitutes a separate instance of mediation that, in its textuality, is different from the self-fashioning Oppenheimer performed in 1962 at McMaster University. To privilege the verbal performance is to privilege one version of Oppenheimer (as the "authentic" Oppenheimer) over others and to overlook the fact that all versions are representations. Such privileging can be seen all over, for instance, in a 1965 review in *Science* of *The Flying Trapeze*, in which the book is judged "authentic, vintage Oppenheimer" (Henderson 811). But such privileging elides the ways in which the legacy of a historical figure or a celebrity is formed. Preston tries to reinforce the "authenticity" of the verbal performance when he notes that "the reader may be assured that, although they have been occasionally rearranged, all the significant words are Professor Oppenheimer's" (viii). The authority conferred by imagining Oppenheimer in possession of "his" words, together with the investment in the transcendental reality of the verbal performance, reveals Preston's commitment to the notion of the unmediated self, even as he highlights the various layers of mediation that went into producing *The Flying Trapeze*. Like the contrast between Oppenheimer's remoteness and the public appeal of these lectures, Preston's juxtaposition of "authentic" and "mediated" selves helps form the complex representational landscape in which one finds Oppenheimer, his ideas, and the legacy of those ideas.

The abstraction of the lectures is matched by the rhetorical strategies Oppenheimer uses to present an abstract self. The title of the book, for instance, hints at the precarious position of the physicist in the postwar world, a position of danger that, however thrilling, constitutes a series of crises on a global scale that must be negotiated. Another reviewer notes that "the first two are crises of understanding, that is, the theory of relativity and the quantum theory. The third is the crisis of war and peace" (Steenberg 285). Again, the challenging, paradoxical knowledge produced by theoretical physics becomes an obstacle to—a crisis in—the public's understanding of the new nuclear political order. In that sense, Oppenheimer's job ought to be to bring this information to "the common man" in accessible form. But as he notes in the first "crisis" in *The Flying Trapeze*, quantum theory "introduced an element of discontinuity into physics" (6) that makes physics extremely difficult to convey, in nonmystical fashion, to a lay public. Thus, he finds himself in the position of, and indeed constructs himself as, the sage on the stage, bringing difficult and counterintuitive knowledge to a broad audience. He constructs this sagelike identity through some now-familiar strategies of self-effacement. "I think some understanding of the concepts of physics can be conveyed with very limited use of mathematics," he notes in the first lecture, "and I propose so to restrict myself" (7). This intellectual restriction—or, rather, a restriction in his public presentation of himself as an intellectual—is both consistent with his ascetic persona and essential to the process of "translating" obscure knowledge into publicly consumable knowledge. His intellectual humility, apparent in the restricted conclusions he reaches about certain topics and expressed in phrases such as "that is about all that I am clear about in hindsight" (60), echoes the mass puzzlement and anxiety that greeted the atomic age. Such restrictions, limitations, and humilities are self-conscious attempts that Oppenheimer makes to "humanize" his public persona, but as negations, they form a void—an empty space on the lecture stage or a gap in the text—from which knowledge emanates incorporeally.

Even when Oppenheimer does locate himself materially and bodily in space and time, the text seems to undo those assertions. In an example that he says he likes of the relationship between physics and everyday life, he states: "When I write with the chalk it is part of me and I use it without any separation between it and my hand. When I look at it and get interested in what it is and put it under a microscope, it is an object of study" (54). The self he constructs relies again on his identity as an academic—his scenario has him at a chalkboard, working through equations—but it also posits a porous self. The initial sense of the chalk as a *part* of him, rather than simply a tool he uses, renders that self open to the outside world. The distinctness of the individual is rendered permeable by a mere piece of chalk. When he thinks about the chalk differently—"When I look at it and get interested in what it is"—the subject and the object separate, but the reassertion of this distinctness relies on a deliberate epistemological shift, a change in the way he thinks rather than a shift in ontological reality. One's observations, following Werner Heisenberg, do indeed affect the world.

Similarly, the first lecture in the book, significantly titled "Space and Time," contains Oppenheimer's expression of a scientist's desire to describe a problem objectively and universally. He tells his McMaster audience: "we would like to give a description which is just as valid in Chicago as it is in Hamilton" (18). This self-reflexive reference locates the talk (together with Oppenheimer's self-presentation in the form of a talk) in a particular place and time, echoing in real, material form the physicist's ideal description of the objective world. However, as soon as the lecture becomes part of *The Flying Trapeze* (after the layers of mediation Preston identifies in the preface), he becomes a dispersed, textual construction. His topical reference to the place he found himself in at that moment in 1962 serves to position the textual version of him in the past and in a location most readers of *The Flying Trapeze* will not be in as they read. The immediacy and materiality of his reference to Hamilton in 1962 transforms into the obscurity of history. These instances of invisibility, even when they occur while Oppenheimer appears to posit a material presence, produce the kind of disembodiment that makes talking about physics seem like divine inspiration.

The third lecture is titled "War and the Nation," and despite this grandiose and remote title, it contains by far the largest number of personal references among the three lectures. Oppenheimer talks about his own career (58), and phrases such as "I remember that [George] Uhlenbeck" (57) and "I was told by Dr. [Vannevar] Bush" (59) allow personal reminiscences and references to friends and colleagues to illuminate his points about the geopolitical implications of atomic physics. Such references help disperse his identity among the constellation of people—scientists and nonscientists—within which he circulated. Looking back on the discussions held at high government levels after the Trinity test over whether or not to bomb Japan, he contextualizes his thoughts "synoptically, briefly, on the basis of my memory of the time and of talk with many historians who have grappled with it" (59–60). The self-fashioning in such a phrase contributes to a portrait of a remote and superior Oppenheimer casting his eye comprehensively over the landscape, but it also reveals an individual self interpenetrated by other scientists, historians, politicians, and the public. As he brings the lecture to a close, he allows the scientific community about which he is nominally speaking to expand to include the global community.

> We are as a community really rather clear as to what our duty is. It is, in the first place, to give an honest account of what we all know together, know in the way in which I know about the Lorentz contraction and wave-particle duality, know from deep scientific conviction and experience. We think that we should give that information openly whenever that is possible.... We think that it is even more important, and even more essential, to distinguish what we know in the vast regions of science where a great deal is known and more is coming to be known all the time, from all those other things of which we would like to speak and should speak in another context and in another way, those things for which we hope, those things which we value. (63–64)

The collective pronoun "we" encompasses Oppenheimer (with his technical knowledge of "the Lorentz contraction and wave-particle duality") and the international scientific community (invoked in his calls for "openness"), but it also grows to include the world as a whole ("all those other things of which we would like to speak"). In calling, in the final line of this final lecture, for "above all, a world without war" (65), he reminds listeners and readers that nuclear war poses a monstrous threat to each and every one of those people within the global community, in their individuality and their collectivity.

The selves articulated in *The Flying Trapeze*—in Oppenheimer's chalk example or in his self-reflexive reference to his own material position in Hamilton in 1962 or in references to his personal contributions to history—are material selves. They are the individual selves functioning within collective formulations such as society, humankind, and community. They are intimate, personal selves, yet they are theatrical and highly qualified performances of a self. They are marked by permeability to other people and other ideas. They are open selves that help counteract the kind of closed-off, detached scientific practice he describes in the second half of his chalk example—the kind of practice that sees the bomb as "technically sweet" and that overlooks the individuals and communities it can destroy.[13] In the published version of these lectures, Oppenheimer thus circulates throughout the globe, drawing on the celebrity's ability paradoxically to construct a public self and a nonself, a material and embodied self that is also ephemeral in print and image, but that, in its openness, evokes the millions of individual selves targeted by nuclear weapons.

RESURRECTING THE SELF: *UNCOMMON SENSE* (1984) AND *ATOM AND VOID* (1989)

The other two collections of lectures and essays that form Oppenheimer's oeuvre—*Uncommon Sense* and *Atom and Void*—were published after his death and consist in varying degrees of republished material. Approximately half of *Uncommon Sense*, according to its editors, has appeared before, and all the essays in *Atom and Void* come from the three books published during his lifetime. These two books are, however, worth discussing briefly for how they reiterate the themes, rhetorical effects, and conceptual reversals discussed in this chapter. *Uncommon Sense*, for instance, oscillates between abstracting Oppenheimer through the aesthetic of negation and distance and substantiating him through community. Its title, a play on *Science and the Common Understanding*, first characterizes the knowledge he imparts as unusual, exceptional, or extraordinary and thus makes him remote and sagelike. It provides a sense of the uncommon in its "uncommon sense."

Uncommon Sense also reiterates this effect visually, through its inclusion of photographs. The photograph—with its genealogical roots in icons, idols, and relics—is crucial to modern celebrity.[14] It conjoins a "realistic" ontology—the potential to depict subjects "as they really are" at a particular moment of time—with the kind of representational capacity for mystifying subjects and rendering them numinous. For instance, the photograph accompanying the first essay is in fact *not* an image of Oppenheimer but rather the famous cover of *Physics Today*. Represented solely by his hat, Oppenheimer is presented visually in *Uncommon Sense* through the aesthetic of removal and abstraction. Retrenched into symbol, he becomes mysterious and unknowable. The rest of the images in the book, however, work against that aesthetic and serve to locate him within a broader sense of community. Only one or two of the images are of a solitary Oppenheimer. Other people, visible or implied, surround him in these images: at the 1947 Harvard University commencement, at various panel discussions, with Jawaharlal Nehru or Lyndon Baines Johnson or Albert Einstein, with other scientists and Manhattan Project colleagues, and with his family. These images of communities—scientific, political, and personal—ensure that *Uncommon Sense* depicts him as a material human being, intimately connected to and substantially defined by others around him.

The second posthumous collection of essays, *Atom and Void*, enacts a similar dialectic between presence and absence and between the unknowable and solitary sage and the interpenetrating knowledges of community. The title comes from Alfred, Lord Tennyson's poem "Lucretius," which references Epicurean theories of the atom to articulate the transitory nature of the universe:

> But he, his hopes and hates, his homes and fanes
> And even his bones long laid within the grave,
> The very sides of the grave itself shall pass,
> Vanishing, atom and void, atom and void,
> Into the unseen for ever—
>
> (ll. 244–258)

As a word denoting indivisibility, "atom" affirms presence and solidity. Its relationship with "void," however, reiterated in Tennyson's poem through the repetition of the phrase that would become the title of Oppenheimer's collection, ultimately undermines the surety of the atom and confirms the impermanence of the world, even beyond death. The perpetual dance of engaging and disengaging atoms confirms the transitory nature of the universe but, at the same time, is the universe's only constant. This dialectic—like the ones in his other books and, indeed, in much Oppenheimer representation generally—echoes the wavering between defense and attack, creation and destruction, light and shadow, subject and object, and life and death characteristic of nuclear weapons and nuclear culture. Such equivocation itself emerges from the ambiguities of seeking out this kind of knowledge: the public intellectual's claim that ascertaining knowledge of the world is everyone's responsibility, and the understandable but fundamentally irresponsible desire to discharge ourselves of the potentially apocalyptic knowledge unleashed by the atomic bomb.

Oppenheimer and His Readers

Finally, the publication and circulation of Oppenheimer's books as material objects further compounds the importance of individuals and communities in the nuclear age. As much as they contain technical treatises or political disquisitions, these books became objects of consumption for a sizable postwar public that had developed a fascination with Oppenheimer. Although these books likely manage to evade the agglomerative literary genre of autobiography, they nonetheless have the capacity to construct a self. They reiterate the singularity of Oppenheimer, but they also help generate the collective identity of their readers. As a number of scholars have noted, autobiographical books (like histories) gesture strongly toward the world outside of themselves—that is, they refer to specific individuals, living or dead, and their material and cultural contexts.[15] Their circulation as material objects within those same contexts, furthermore, provides a recursive field in which the reader actively reconstructs, rather than passively receives information about, an individual. Purchasing and reading Oppenheimer's books grants readers an agency to participate, in a dispersed and indirect but still meaningful way, in the postwar conversation about nuclear weapons. Even purchasing the books *because* of his renown rather than out of an interest in what he has to say, a response to fame often derided for its apparently superficial capitulation, is a connective act. Such an act is an affective response. It seeks to negotiate with nuclear culture through the material circulation of a piece, as it were, of that culture's prime representative in the immediate postwar period. Such an act reflects the desire to belong to a larger community that is also trying to sort out the meaning of nuclear culture. In a more restricted but comparable sense, attending an Oppenheimer lecture in the 1950s or 1960s provided a similar leveraging of agency. The physical presence of Oppenheimer at a specific time and place (along with the material ephemera of the encounter: programs, photographs, and the like) made concrete for attendees the materiality of the sage on the stage. This materiality, which Oppenheimer produced as an act of self-fashioning, makes his presence and the presence of his books in one's library a means of envisioning a future self unencumbered by the threat of nuclear weapons—a new self whose existence potentially revolves around resisting the bomb. Oppenheimer's embodiment in those moments helped transcend the dissociation that often accompanies both celebrity and science and thus, in a more general sense, helped transcend the abstraction of nuclear arsenals and geopolitics. And this embodiment of both Oppenheimer and the physical bodies destroyed or threatened by nuclear weapons encroaches on the mediascape that was developing concurrently with Oppenheimer's fame. The prevalence of television, in particular, and his appearances on programs such as Edward R. Murrow's *See It Now* (1955) on CBS and the British television documentary series *Panorama* (1960), brought him visibly into living rooms around the world. Grounded in the compulsive visibility inherent in celebrity and anticipating the interconnected and instantaneous media that help generate celebrity in the twenty-first century, Oppenheimer's textual presence in his books, his material presence on the lecture circuit, and his disembodied yet domesticated presence on television secure his role in the process of coming to terms socially and publicly with nuclear culture.

CONCLUSION

In a farewell speech delivered to the Association of Los Alamos Scientists in November 1945, Oppenheimer began with a disclaimer about his participation in postwar nuclear regulation: "I could not talk, and will not tonight talk, too much about the practical political problems which are involved. There is one good reason for that—I don't know very much about practical politics" (qtd. in Smith and Weiner 315). A characteristic moment of self-effacement, the comment reveals the fraught position of nuclear scientists in the years following World War II. Those responsible for the bomb had assumed remarkable public presences, in part because the figure of the scientist had long been associated with strange and mysterious forces, regarded with complex mixtures of awe and suspicion, fascination and disinterest, and had occupied rare and often exalted positions in Western society,[1] but also because they bore significant responsibility for creating the device that catapulted the United States into the category of global superpower after the war. In other ways, however, they assumed positions of prominence after expressing powerful misgivings about the weapons they had made and intense desires—a sense of obligation, in many cases— to intervene in the political and cultural forces shaping future nuclear weapons even as they proclaimed, as Oppenheimer did, their ignorance of such forces. Such conflicted positions, especially when their holders assume them suddenly, are precarious ones.

The postwar veneration of physicists and of scientists more generally, rooted in perceptions of their omniscience, lent them a powerful platform from which to shape public awareness of nuclear science, scientific militarism, and scientists as a group. Their forays out of the insular world of theoretical physics and the relatively stable world of the academy and into global politics gave them an unprecedented and influential national and global standing. At the same time, the perception that they had meddled in affairs too remote and dangerous for humankind or that they had initiated a destructive new relationship between scientific knowledge and military power made them pariahs in many quarters. The Manhattan Project had redefined, after all, how governments, corporations, and universities interact and what they do with the results of the pursuit of knowledge. Contemporary problems such as the corporatization of universities, the drive to commercialize knowledge, and the systematic starvation of ways of knowing not amenable to a narrow, neoliberal business agenda can be traced back, in not insignificant ways, to how the Manhattan Project altered knowledge production at midcentury. And, of course, the atomic scientists had created a palpable yet unpredictable tool for bringing about the end of the species. This conflicted view of atomic scientists and the Manhattan Project in particular and of the relationship between knowledge and society more generally has informed understandings of seventy years of literary, cinematic, popular, and other cultural instantiations of science and scientists. To focus on scientists exclusively as defining figures would be to miss crucial dimensions of this age—not to mention the contributions of politicians, journalists, members of the military, and countless other figures at various levels of visibility—but the towering presence of scientists and their highly disputed role must be accounted for. In that sense, *The Meanings of J. Robert Oppenheimer* is something of a demystification project. As Michael Day notes, Oppenheimer "was more a figure to be quoted than studied" ("Nature of Science" 88), and that propensity to quote—to evoke by allusion and to confine to textuality—obscures what can be revealed by a more transdisciplinary study such as this one.

In its analysis of a variety of different kinds of representations of

Oppenheimer—textual, visual, material, embodied—this book has been arguing that these productions frequently contribute, in the words of Paul Boyer, to the "image of the scientist as idealistic crusader for peace…balanced by the counterimage of the morally blind, technologically obsessed sociopath" (270). I have also been arguing that these representations are often constructed out of presence and absence, visibility and invisibility, and other oppositions of the manifest and the latent. Such oppositions come to characterize the twentieth century's most influential technology as one rooted in an ephemeral science yet generating inescapably material effects on landscapes, bodies, and geopolitics. At the same time, and in the ways they come to form a complex likeness of Oppenheimer, one of the twentieth century's central figures, such oppositions constitute no less than a portrait of the postwar era.

This relationship between absence and presence is everywhere in Oppenheimer representation. It is immanent in the desert tropology that animates the biographies. It operates alongside a dynamic of strangeness and familiarity within the solar metaphors so common in atomic bomb historiography. It both obscures and highlights the role of imagination and fiction in any narrative or textual representation of Oppenheimer. In visual or material representations, absence and presence juxtapose the technological and the corporeal in their depictions of Oppenheimer both to suggest affinities between the two realms and to demarcate the troubling differences between them. In these operations, the relationship between absence and presence reveals the troubling process of seeking out knowledge of the natural world and discovering hideously destructive potentials. This relationship is thus crucial for understanding the discourse through which nuclear weapons are articulated. The biography of their chief representative can be understood, through the absence connoted by the desert and his own seemingly inevitable presence, as a quintessential narrative of American triumph that justifies the production of nuclear weapons or that presents them as an existential risk. The familiarity and inevitability of the bomb can, through the very tropes that render it familiar and inevitable, become strange and terrifying in a process vital to resisting nuclear weapons. Although the Oppenheimer of fiction can secure the rational but potentially overwhelming knowledge of science, he can also help imagine alternative futures. And the juxtaposition of the technological and the corporeal can be both a dangerous elision of the human victims of nuclear weapons and a striking visual reminder of their fragility. The representational ambiguities identified in this study can thus help counteract the dangerous tendencies that technological instrumentalism can have, especially when manifested in nuclear weapons, of concealing other modes of knowledge and of dominating the conversation about knowledge.

These tropologies map with striking congruence onto the ways in which postwar and contemporary culture understand nuclear weapons. Nuclear weapons hide in silos, in submarines, and behind veils of official secrecy to sublimate their terrible violence. Likewise, the science that produced them, with its invisible rays, subatomic energies, and quantum entanglements, is jarringly opaque for a practice purported to be the "purest" of the fruits of the Enlightenment. The knowledge of technology becomes inscrutable in the light of an atomic blast. At the same time, these tropes are necessarily incomplete. As Oppenheimer writes in *The Open Mind*: "We learn that views may be useful and inspiriting although they are not complete. We come to have a great caution in all assertions of totality, of finality or absoluteness" (94). Such circumspection is valuable for thinking about a technology so wrapped in mystification—valuable because the lessons learned to date from atomic weapons could potentially do more than simply imperil the human species—and is thus an appropriate legacy for him to leave behind.

Twenty-first-century society's inheritance from Oppenheimer is a tormenting and provocative one. Whether or not it should be, it is also a defining one. Although responsibility for the construction and use of atomic bombs is dispersed among many individuals, bureaucratic structures, and even nations, Oppenheimer has become its public face. Neither fully a hero nor some techno-embodiment of evil, he has equivocal effects on the understanding of the bomb. As a conceptual mainspring, he sits—visibly and invisibly—at the center of the enormous shift in Western culture that occurred at the end of World War II, when late capitalism, mass mediation, the ever-increasing power of the military-industrial complex, and other forces surged into position to dissolve boundaries between public and private, real and simulated, subject and object, and the nation and the globe. As a central but sometimes overlooked figure in the history of the postmodern era, the representational strategies that construct him for public circulation are also vital to the cultural aesthetics of postmodernity and the official logistics of the post-9/11 security era. As an American scientist, he has come to represent the bureaucratization and rationalization of knowledge for the sake of the ultimate "defensive" technology, but he also functions—in having "become Death"—as the conscience of a nation that has produced a device that could end the human race.

Such rationality has been little more than a strange fantasy in the twentieth century. In the last seventy years, science has produced an astonishing array of new technologies (including nuclear weapons), but those same decades have also produced hundreds of millions of deaths through Stalinist purges, Nazi atrocities, "rationalized" war, and "democratizing" imperialism.[2] As its ever-increasing speed and electronic mediation moves war toward a state of invisibility, the irony of the twentieth-century liberal faith in rationality will only become more mystifying. The attacks of 9/11, with their rhetorical tropes such as "Ground Zero" replete with nuclear resonance not acknowledged as such, have profoundly challenged that Western philosophical reliance on rationality and history. The nuclear specter that continues to accompany terrorist threats, the nuclear aspirations of "rogue" nations, and ecological disasters such as Chernobyl or Fukushima only reinforce the instability of nuclear culture and compel its continued examination.

With the Cuban Missile Crisis receding from public memory, the urgency of nuclear weapons was once again abating by the late 1960s. This capitulation coincides, of course, with Oppenheimer's death in 1967. The meanings of nuclear culture are not, however, permanently or inseparably linked to him. Meanings change, and although such changes are themselves sometimes indebted to the tropes I have been arguing are attached to Oppenheimer, their trajectories cannot be reliably predicted. For instance, when nuclear infrastructure, from missile silos to testing grounds, is allowed to deteriorate and to succumb to nature, those natural forces undermine the Cold War notion of eternal political and ideological confrontation. Even when such infrastructure is preserved, monumentalized, or commercialized (as in the context of nuclear tourism), such a process helps mediate the relationships between remembering and for-getting, between celebrating and criticizing Enlightenment narratives of progress, and between mastering and being mastered by the nuclear past.[3] In the last case, the (in)visibility coursing through the nuclear narrative and associated so strongly with Oppenheimer becomes a site for negoti-ating rather than for fixing meaning. The nuclear future is potentially as volatile as the nuclear past.

NOTES

INTRODUCTION

1 This phrase comes from the well-known and frequently recounted moment when Oppenheimer, on first seeing the mushroom cloud in the New Mexico desert, supposedly thought of a line from the *Bhagavad Gita*: "I am become Death, the destroyer of worlds."

2 I draw the phrase from Porter xi.

3 Writer Eric Schlosser calls the bomb "the most dangerous technology ever invented" (480); historian H. Bruce Franklin believes that the "decision to use nuclear weapons on two Japanese cities was perhaps the most important conscious choice in human history" (149) and that such weapons "have transformed the fundamental conditions of human existence" (155); anthropologist Joseph Masco claims that the "Manhattan Project was not simply a technoscientific success; it was an act of world-making" (333); and historian Gerald DeGroot begins his study of the bomb with this claim: "Nothing that man has made is bigger than the bomb" (viii).

4 Philosophies of science broadly called "social constructivist"—in which social interaction, historical context, and other contingencies work to produce what we call "objective reality"—are multifaceted and have had considerable influence on the basic premises of this book. For influential studies of the social construction of scientific knowledge, see Latour; Latour and Woolgar.

5 For a discussion of secret U.S. geography, see Paglen. Hunner also discusses the role of secrecy at midcentury, identifying it as the generator of a

significant epistemological shift: "Since Trinity, Hiroshima, and Nagasaki...
atomic secrets had changed what the American people could know" (*J. Robert
Oppenheimer* 212).

6   Although the relationship between the Manhattan Project and contemporary conspiracy theory culture is beyond the scope of this book, an uptick
in the number of conspiracy theories and a change in their nature can be
observed following World War II. Before the war, conspiracy theories in
America were largely about the dangers posed by outsider groups (Jews or
Europeans, for instance). After the war, conspiratorial thinking amplified
long-standing distrust of the government (going back to the beginnings of
the American experiment) and made the supposed inner rot and corrup-
tion of the U.S. government itself the primary target of paranoid suspicion.
This transition is particularly interesting because many Manhattan Project
scientists were both Jewish and immigrants from Europe. In particular, the
technological dimensions of the Manhattan Project may also have primed
a shift toward more technologically oriented conspiracy theories, of which
UFOs are perhaps the most obvious manifestation. There is a growing body of
scholarship on contemporary American conspiracy theory. See, for example,
Dean; Fenster; Knight; Lee; Melley; O'Donnell. In keeping with conspiracy
and the "pathology" of the atomic bomb's legacy, Weart speculates that the
UFO phenomenon, which saw its genesis in the 1940s and 1950s, represents
"an 'atomic psychosis' brought on by fear of the bombs" (282).

7   For a discussion of Big Science, see Hughes 7.

8   For a discussion of this relationship in the context of the science of radiation,
see Malley 173–191.

9   For an extended discussion of the conjunction of the mythological and the
modern in Los Alamos, see Hendershot.

10 Scientists and science scholars have cautioned against the misuse of scientific
metaphors to "explain" literary phenomenon, with likely the most famous
cautionary tale the "Sokal hoax" of 1996 (see Sokal; Sokal and Bricmont) and
the debate that ensued (see Derrida, "Sokal and Bricmont Aren't Serious";
Hilgartner; Ross). In this book, I try to heed some of those warnings; at the
same time, scientific metaphors do have certain explanatory powers. Taylor,
for instance, notes that in some accounts of Los Alamos fission as a scientific
process becomes a metaphor for understanding the organizational structures
and patterns of the lab itself ("Politics of the Nuclear Text"). This fascinating
argument illustrates how scientific principles influence the thinking done
within and about social structures, political organization, and even art.

11 The early-twentieth-century physics that led to the bomb was full of what
Malley calls "eternal conundrums": the convertibility of matter and energy,
the wave-particle duality of light, the uncertainty principle (206–207).

12 See, for instance, Boyer; Chaloupka; Easlea; Gusterson; Hales; Henrikson; Mariner and Piehler; Ruthven; Scott and Geist; Jeff Smith; Sprod; Weart; Winkler; Zeman and Amundson. Slightly further in the background of this study is work done on the bomb from more specifically Japanese perspectives (see Gerster, "Hiroshima No More"; Hein and Selden; Treat; Yoneyama; and considerable scholarly work published in Japanese with which I cannot claim familiarity) and from post–Cold War perspectives (see Blouin, Shipley, and Taylor; Masco). I am also indebted to Haynes for a broader but highly influential study of the figure of the scientist.

13 For psychological approaches, see Chernus; Lifton and Mitchell; Lifton and Falk. The literature on the politics of the atomic bomb is extensive. See, for instance, Schell; Titus, *Bombs in the Backyard.*

14 For rhetorical analysis, see Chilton; Schwenger; Solomon. Often cited in this type of analysis is Derrida, "No Apocalypse, Not Now," which argues controversially for the "fabulously textual" (23) nature of nuclear war. For book-length studies of literary representations of nuclear culture, see Bartter; Brians; Canaday; Cordle; Dowling; Mannix; Nadel; Scheibach; Stone.

15 For nuclear culture in the media, see Aubrey. For photography and visual culture, see Del Tredici; Goin. For film, see Broderick; Evans; Perrine; Shaheen; Shapiro. Although most book-length treatments of nuclear museums concern the Smithsonian Institution's *Enola Gay* controversy (see Bird and Lifschultz; Dubin; Harwit; Linenthal and Engelhardt; Nobile), I will also cite some shorter but useful analyses of museums focused specifically on nuclear history. I am also indebted to museum studies as a discipline in general.

16 Such works include Arbab; Day; Hecht; Hijiya; Kaiser; Taylor, "The Politics of the Nuclear Text"; Thorpe and Shapin.

17 Hecht's book offers clear and penetrating insight into some of the rhetorical devices and narrative strategies used to depict Oppenheimer in official documents, government reports, newspaper journalism, legal monographs, and other mostly contemporaneous documents. In the last chapter of *Storytelling and Science*, Hecht traces, in helpful if brief ways, how Oppenheimer has been appropriated more recently in select films, novels, and plays.

18 This summary of such contradictory views of scientists is indebted to Boyer 270.

19 This process is also evident in the omnipresence of euphemism in nuclear culture. An early example of such euphemism is the Manhattan Project physicists' use of the word "gadget" to describe the bomb. The word reduces what was at the time the deadliest object anyone had ever known into a quaint little contraption, a gizmo as harmless as a slide rule.

20 Other scholars acknowledge the necessity of an interdisciplinary approach. See, for instance, Taylor, "Nuclear Pictures" 79 n. 1.

PART I

1   For a discussion of the importance of Oppenheimer's correspondence to nuclear culture, see Taylor, "The Politics of the Nuclear Text" 431.
2   Like "text," the word "discursive" is used quite broadly in this book. It refers to myriad cultural productions through which the discourse of nuclear culture circulates: books, film, television, museum installations, and other forms.

CHAPTER 1

This chapter contains revised and expanded material from my article "The Biographies of J. Robert Oppenheimer: Desert Saint or Destroyer of Worlds," which originally appeared in *Biography* 35.3 (2012): 492–515, and which is used gratefully with permission.

1   Cognizant of Schlaeger's contention that "there is no meaningful talk about a 'life' beyond interpretation" (58), this distinction between the terms "life" and "life-text" is my attempt to maintain the distinction between the actual, historical facts of a figure's life—facts that must remain contingent and potentially unknowable—and the textual interpretation of those facts in the form of the biography. My focus in this chapter will be on the "life-text."
2   On the conservative dimensions of biography as a genre, see Batchelor.
3   This number does not include several children's books about Oppenheimer, such as Toney Allman's *J. Robert Oppenheimer: Theoretical Physicist, Atomic Pioneer* (2005) or Glenn Scherer and Marty Fletcher's *J. Robert Oppenheimer: The Brain Behind the Bomb* (2008), most of which seem to be in the "Great Man of Science" vein. Allman's book, for instance, is part of a series titled "Giants of Science," while Scherer and Fletcher's is part of a series called "Inventors Who Changed the World."
4   For modern biography's origins in the eighteenth century, see Holmes 25.
5   On the role of supposition in biography, see Ellmann 18.
6   Such similarities are discussed in Young 203.
7   Although it is a trenchant study of Oppenheimer's downfall and rehabilitation, Priscilla McMillan's *The Ruin of J. Robert Oppenheimer and the Birth of the Modern Arms Race* (2005) will not figure into this analysis because its focus on the last decade or so of his life makes it the most limited in scope of the four biographies. Her focus does, however, emphasize Powers's point that the work done in Los Alamos is but "the middle chapter" in Oppenheimer's life. Powers, "An American Tragedy," *New York Review of Books*,

September 22, 2005, http://www.nybooks.com/articles/archives/2005
/sep/22/an-american-tragedy/.

8   Hunner makes a similar although more broadly conceived argument in
    an article (and, later, a book) about how Los Alamos and the region con-
    stitute the political and technological wellspring of more than sixty years
    of nuclear culture. He, too, discusses ways Oppenheimer's redefinition of
    physics occurred specifically in the context of the American West but does
    not analyze the conceptual and representational operations of the desert in
    detail. See Hunner, "Reinventing Los Alamos" and *J. Robert Oppenheimer*
    46.

9   In comparing Oppenheimer to the figure of the Romantic artist I must empha-
    size the opposition between the Romantic artist and the Romantic scientist.
    Deeply indebted to the critical portrait offered in Mary Shelley's *Frankenstein*
    (1818), the Romantic scientist is distinctly *un*emotional, having removed him-
    self from human relations and stifled all feeling. His irresponsible shirking
    of social and ethical obligations constitutes a deeply critical portrait of the
    scientist (Haynes 3). Such a portrait is of course common in cultural percep-
    tions of American science, including perceptions of Oppenheimer, so it sits
    uneasily next to portraits of the physicist as Romantic artist.

10 For a discussion of the desert's conceptual extremes, see Schüll, 379.

11 Pike's discussion of the Burning Man Festival argues that the desert functions
    as a blank space upon which to project the elaborate aesthetic for which the
    gathering is known. Graulund makes a similar, if more grandiose point: the
    "desert landscape is, by definition, an empty landscape" (145) and an "essen-
    tially incommunicable" (146) one, but in its saturation with light, it is also a
    generative one: "It has, after all, at different times been claimed as the origin
    of monotheism, language and even of mankind" (156).

12 Titus claims that the mushroom cloud "was almost immediately recognized
    as a symbol of U.S. power" and was, moreover, quickly romanticized in
    popular culture to create "a sentimentalized myth about this period in his-
    tory" ("The Mushroom Cloud as Kitsch" 102) that helps conceal the bomb's
    destructive potential. Although this argument has merit, I find problematic
    the suggestion that popular culture is inherently sentimental. As my anal-
    ysis of these biographies and other texts about Oppenheimer implies, the
    rhetorical strategies used to represent atomic bombs are not necessarily or
    consistently kitschy, nostalgic ones.

13 The phrase comes from the title of Río's article, "The Desert as a National
    Sacrifice Zone: The Nuclear Controversy in Nevada Fiction."

14 Rosenthal makes this point in her analysis of the power of the mushroom
    cloud as a national image.

15 The term "spectator democracy" comes from the title of Kirsch's article

"Watching the Bombs Go Off: Photography, Nuclear Landscapes, and Spectator Democracy."

16 For a discussion of how biography can reproduce archetypal American values, see Rob Wilson, "Producing American Selves" 169.

17 For a discussion of the role of the pastoral in biography, see Epstein, *Recognizing Biography* 53.

18 One of Bird and Sherwin's most important original contributions to the biography of Robert Oppenheimer involves unearthing new documents relating to his leftist activities in the 1930s, documents that, they argue, prove once and for all that he was never directly associated with the Communist Party, that Strauss likely knew this, and that Strauss's vendetta was personal.

19 The mushroom, as ethnomycologist R. Gordon Wasson has noted in an extensive body of work, can function as a highly malleable metaphor in its simultaneous association with decay and toxicity, on the one hand, and food and renewal, on the other. See Wasson; Wasson and Wasson.

20 There are other examples of this sort of replacement of nature metaphors with cultural ones in physics. In 1938, when Lise Meitner and Otto Frisch discovered how to separate atoms by bombarding them with neutrons (a precursor of the process used in atomic bombs) they borrowed a term from cellular biology, from "nature," and called the process "fission." In the 1950s, however, and within a more American context, this process became better known as "splitting the atom," which as Fiege points out, "called to mind not organic reproduction, but mechanical destruction—an ax cleaving firewood, or a steel wedge, driven by a sledgehammer, cracking apart a boulder" (592).

21 As the granddaughter of James B. Conant, former president of Harvard University and chair of the National Defense Research Committee and the Office of Scientific Research and Development from 1941 to 1946, Jennet Conant has an indirect but resonant biographical connection to the work that was done at Los Alamos in the 1940s. Such a connection echoes somewhat in the approach she takes in her biography.

22 Such a trope appears in many Oppenheimer biographies and extends beyond the part of the narrative set in New Mexico. For instance, Conant is not alone among biographers in describing Oppenheimer and wife Kitty's home in the Berkeley hills after they had moved to California: "Their house was a handsome, Spanish-style ranch, perched on a steep incline high above the city, with lush gardens and a sweeping view of San Francisco Bay below" (52). The all-encompassing view, provided both by the house in Berkeley and later by Los Alamos itself, calls to mind the purported power, prominence, and omniscience of the scientist.

23 More than many Oppenheimer biographers, Conant allows glimpses of the indigenous history of New Mexico. In providing the mountain's nickname,

"Sentinel of the Navajo Land," she suggests the presence (tempered as it may be by the more prominent positioning of "Mt. Taylor," the mountain's English-language name) of epistemologies outside the purview of rationalist science. This presence, alluded to but rarely identified in other biographies, reminds us of the many things that may escape the all-knowing scientific gaze but that nonetheless lie close to the surface of conventional Western modes.

24 For a discussion of the role of these intersecting contingencies in biography, see Caine 124.

25 Charles Thorpe's 2006 "intellectual biography," which could be read alongside the 2005 biographies discussed here, takes Oppenheimer's multiplicity and his intangibility as its primary organizing principles. For instance, Thorpe quotes Oppenheimer's friend Haakon Chevalier, who claimed the physicist "could be Christ-like and Mephistophelean by turns" (15).

26 My remarks about the nature of scientific biography in this paragraph are informed by two important edited collections of essays on scientific biography: Shortland and Yeo; Söderqvist.

CHAPTER 2

1 Many scholars allude to the history-destroying potential of nuclear weapons. For a particularly good discussion of this potential in the context of postmodern American fiction, see Grausam.

2 For detailed accounts of the field of historiography, see, for example, Elizabeth Clark; Kellner; Hayden White. Some historians of historiography (for instance, Cheng) convincingly dispel the myth that the discipline of history, as it began to emerge in the United States in the late nineteenth century, was naively convinced it could access objective truth. Likewise, the histories of the Manhattan Project do not display any such naivety (although they do exhibit varying degrees of confidence in the role of science in discerning factual reality).

3 For Cmiel, objectivity is replaced with more diverse historiographic practices: "the literary theory of White, Kellner, and LaCapra will have to jostle for attention with quantifying positivism, Geertzian cultural anthropology, Gramscian Marxism, a lot of traditional archive-digging, the study of *mentalités*, various neo-objectivisms, and whatever else happens to come down the road" (171).

4 For a discussion of the role of narrative in historiography, see Munslow 14.

5 Technically, the heliotrope is a more appropriate metaphor for the hydrogen bomb, which uses a fusion process similar to what actually goes on in the sun. A fission weapon, such as that which "dawned" in the New Mexico desert in

1945, employs a rather different process. Nevertheless, the sun is a persistent explanatory metaphor in both cases.

6   For a foundational discussion of the moral questions of the nuclear age, see Schweber.

7   Absolving human beings—whether the scientists who created atomic bombs, the politicians who ostensibly control them, or the military personnel who deploy them—of responsibility is common in fictional and cinematic representations of nuclear weapons. As Hunter points out, films such as *Fail-Safe* (1962) and *Colossus* (1970), and the novels on which they are based, depict the technology of nuclear weapons systems as a force subjugating the authority of those (embodied in the figure of the U.S. president) nominally in charge of atomic weapons. Ceding control to technology—and blaming its "mechanical glitches" (213)—remains a persistent element in the fantasy of absolution.

8   An example of the normalizing function of the solar metaphor appears in the title of Ruth H. Howe and Caroline L. Herzenberg's account of the women who worked on the atomic bomb. Their book, in which Oppenheimer rightly plays only a small role, is a valuable corrective to the masculinist historical record of the atomic bomb, but its title, *Their Day in the Sun*, draws on conventional Enlightenment associations between the sun and knowledge to "illuminate" the presence of women in the Manhattan Project. In addition, their book opens when "the light of the first nuclear explosion stabbed through the New Mexico predawn darkness" (1), which lends the illuminating power of the sun a violent and penetrative function consistent with conventional representations of learning about nature. For an example (again sans Oppenheimer) of a less conventional use of the heliotrope, see Jane Dibblin's *Day of Two Suns* (1988). A harrowing account of the effects of 1950s bomb testing on Pacific Islanders, Dibblin's book employs the heliotrope as a marker of the uncanniness of the nuclear weapon. She describes the 1954 Bravo test, the largest bomb ever detonated by the United States, as "a strange sun dawning in the west" (24) and notes that the residents of the Marshall Islands, who were heavily dosed with fallout, call the predawn test the "day of two suns" (25). The strangeness of a day marked by two sunrises, one in the west and one in the east, functions (as in Szasz's *The Day the Sun Rose Twice*) as the title metaphor for the extraordinary effects the bomb has on the landscapes in which it is used and for the horrific physical toll on human beings taken by a weapon whose strangeness is one of its chief characteristics. In Dibblin's book, the sun does *not* in fact naturalize the atomic bomb. It is instead a perverse sun rising in the wrong place and underscoring how, in this case, hydrogen bomb testing in the South Pacific constituted an apostatic transgression of the physical world.

9   A number of texts lie outside the scope of this chapter. First, there are the

so-called official histories. These often bureaucratic or technical books have not reached much of a general audience and usually do not use solar metaphors in very prominent ways. Such works include Hawkins, Truslow, and Smith's *Project Y*, which Trenn characterizes as an "internal account [that] records technical, administrative, and policy-making activities" (672) of the Manhattan Project; and Hoddeson et al., which as one review notes is "more likely to be consulted than read" (Hacker 256). The U.S. Department of Energy maintains a "Manhattan Project Historical Resources" webpage (https://www.osti.gov/opennet/manhattan-project-history/index.htm) containing a number of historical accounts in several different media; although these are rightly billed as being "for the most part non-technical, highly readable accounts . . . geared toward the general reader," they are excluded from discussion as a way of keeping the scope of this chapter manageable and focused largely on textual accounts. Also beyond the scope of this chapter are texts about nuclear history more generally. Ronald W. Clark's *The Greatest Power on Earth*, for instance, covers a vast history of nuclear science up to 1980 but does not focus much on Oppenheimer. As with biographies and fiction, there is a healthy trade in children's books about the history of the atomic bomb. Among the best is Steve Sheinkin's *Bomb*, which provides a broad social history and has won a number of awards.

10 The ideology of attributing "refreshing" qualities to destruction has been most famously analyzed in Slotkin's discussion of "regeneration through violence."

11 Peter H. Wyden's *Day One: Before Hiroshima and After* (1984), a later although less well-known history of the Manhattan Project, employs a similar measurement trope and a similar evocation of a "dawning of a new day" in its title, but many of the ambiguities and negations introduced by Laurence's use of "zero" are avoided by Wyden's use of "one." The choice is representative of his book, which, in my opinion, strives for a more empirical and less lyrical representation of history and in the process skirts much of the conceptual paradoxes of the bomb's development and legacies.

12 Hales notes that Laurence's book was "constructed as much out of government desire as individual consciousness" ("The Atomic Sublime" 12).

13 Masco, for instance, calls Laurence's writing "hyperbolic" (339 n. 2).

14 Such biological metaphors constitute another important trope for domesticating the atomic bomb, a process Cohn, Easlea, Masco, and others discuss at length (and that I discuss in more detail in chapter 5). They appear again in Laurence's work when he describes dropping the bombs on Hiroshima and Nagasaki. As Captain "Deke" Parsons finishes the assembly of the bomb on board the *Enola Gay*, for instance, Laurence proclaims: "The bomb is now alive" (184).

15   For a discussion of the relationship between supernatural tropes and respon-
     sibility, see Taylor, *"Reminiscences"* 406.

16   This idea, like Hales's notion of the atomic sublime, is indebted to Nye's influ-
     ential analysis of the American technological sublime.

17   Among metaphors of illumination for discussing the "discoveries which
     threw light on the darkness of Nature" (71), Jungk uses the naturalizing helio-
     trope, for example, in accounts of how the idea for thermonuclear bombs
     came from the sun's mechanism for producing solar energy (28), along with
     disarming language about how a nuclear weapon is a "man-made star" (303).
     Jungk's Enlightenment discourse represents the sun as a helpful, benign
     presence rather than a disturbing one. That heliotropes can function in both
     ways in one text illustrates their rhetorical and conceptual complexity; nev-
     ertheless, I believe that Jungk's overall portrayal of the sun is one of uncanny
     strangeness.

18   Paul Vitello, "Lansing Lamont, Journalist and Historian of Atomic Bomb,
     Dies at 83," *New York Times*, September 15, 2013. http://www.nytimes
     .com/2013/09/16/business/media/lansing-lamont-journalist-and-historian-
     of-atomic-bomb-dies-at-82.html.

19   Lamont's use of religious rhetoric in *Day of Trinity* is intriguing and prob-
     lematic. Following Oppenheimer's mysterious pronouncement, Lamont
     provides an ornate meditation on the connection between religion and
     the site: "there was a hint of holiness about the vast silent valley that was
     Trinity—something in its history that touched the indomitability of man's
     questing spirit; something in its ageless and primitive beauty that suggested
     man's earliest temples of prayer" (73). Lamont is being somewhat ambiguous
     about the religiosity of the site, but his ambiguity ignores Oppenheimer's
     familiarity with the Hindu trinity (Brahma the creator, Vishnu the preserver,
     and Shiva the destroyer), which could be just as likely a source as Donne for
     the name, and it reduces the religions of the region's indigenous inhabitants
     to the Orientalist and imperialist clichés of timelessness and primitivity. This
     strategy results in a Christianized Oppenheimer and the occlusion of the
     native presence.

20   This oft-quoted phrase comes from Oppenheimer's 1954 security hearing,
     during which he tried to separate the scientific and technical work that
     he and the other physicists did on the Manhattan Project from its ethical
     implications. His comment, "when you see something that is technically
     sweet, you go ahead and do it and you argue about what to do about it only
     after you have had your technical success" (qtd. in Polenberg 46), has been
     interpreted as a coldly calculating endorsement of nuclear weapons. As I
     discuss in chapter 6, however, this phrase is also part of a more complex
     self-presentation.

21   When Rhodes warns readers in the foreword to the anniversary edition that, seventy years after its beginning, "the Manhattan Project is fading into myth" (1), he is asserting a fairly traditional role as historian, as one who sets the "facts" straight over the "myth" into which the Manhattan Project risks falling. The obscurity or nothingness equated with myth, the danger of "fading" posed to historical facts, constitutes an Enlightenment assertion of the reality of facts by virtue of their visibility. And maintaining that visibility, counteracting the effects of "fading," is, for Rhodes, the historian's job. Yet despite these assertions of traditional historiography, many of Rhodes's depictions of Oppenheimer, as I illustrate, abstract him into that very realm of mythology Rhodes seeks to avoid.

22   The *Oxford English Dictionary* notes that the word "histrionic" emerges out of the classical Latin *histriōnicus*—"of or connected with the theatre"— excessively theatrical, in the derogatory sense of the word. By comparison, the word "history," from the classical Latin *historia* (denoting "investigation, inquiry, research, account, description, written account of past events," and so on) appears unrelated to "histrionic."

23   Rhodes's account of Oppenheimer's later security hearing is filled with similar language and a similar accounting of Oppenheimer's self-sabotage.

24   Rhodes extends this function of the heliotrope in the title of his later book on thermonuclear weapons, *Dark Sun: The Making of the Hydrogen Bomb* (1996).

Chapter 3

1   On the techniques of fiction used in the genre of biography, see Ellis 13.

2   *Oppenheimer Is Watching Me*, Jeff Porter's memoir of growing up during the Cold War, is an important "transitional" or "hybrid" text in the way it imagines (and hence fictionalizes) Oppenheimer at the same time that it presents personal, national, and global histories.

3   For a sample of this body of criticism in an Anglo-American context, see Perry Anderson; Bové; Currie; Francese; Gibson; Hutcheon; Jameson; Lyotard; McHale; Parrish; Waugh.

4   Although it does not depict Oppenheimer, Thomas Pynchon's novel *Gravity's Rainbow* (1973), which for many scholars marks a watershed moment in the history of postmodern fiction, is profoundly concerned with nuclear weapons. Its title, for instance, refers in part to the parabolic trajectory of ballistic missiles.

5   McKay, in a recent analysis of Manhattan Project novels, calls such texts "remarkably resistant to reinvention" (160) and summarizes the supposed

reluctance of their authors as follows: "like a prisoner confronted by an open door, these writers appear unwilling to trust themselves or their readers" (170). As I will argue, however, novels such as Lydia Millet's *Oh Pure and Radiant Heart* (which McKay does not mention) place a great deal of trust in their readers and seek to challenge in profound ways the construction of the Manhattan Project narrative and, thus, its effects.

6   To emphasize its historical pervasiveness, I offer in chronological order a short, selective, international list of novels that deal in some way with nuclear war, disaster, or apocalypse: H. G. Wells's *The World Set Free* (1914), Harold Nicolson's *Public Faces* (1932), Fritz Leiber's *Gather, Darkness* (1943), Aldous Huxley's *Ape and Essence* (1948), Judith Merril's *Shadow on the Hearth* (1950), John Wyndham's *The Chrysalids* (1955), Nevil Shute's *On the Beach* (1957), Walter Miller Jr.'s *A Canticle for Leibowitz* (1959), Pat Frank's *Alas, Babylon* (1959), Robert Heinlein's *Farnham's Freehold* (1964), Philip K. Dick's *Do Androids Dream of Electric Sheep?* (1968), Robert C. O'Brien's *Z for Zachariah* (1974), Russell Hoban's *Riddley Walker* (1980), Bernard Malamud's *God's Grace* (1982), William Prochnau's *Trinity's Child* (1983), Kim Stanley Robinson's *The Wild Shore* (1984), David Brin's *The Postman* (1985), Denis Johnson's *Fiskadoro* (1995), and Cormac McCarthy's *The Road* (2006). For more comprehensive bibliographies, see Brians; Dowling.

7   For instance, Franklin writes: "The science and technology that mark progress, that distinguish forward from backward in time, become the means to annihilate all that humanity has created. Thus they display their potential to transform the future into the inchoate oblivion of the primeval prehuman past" (64).

8   On the relationship between subjectivity and history, see Elias 55.

9   Oppenheimer "stand-ins," sometimes created for aesthetic reasons and sometimes necessitated by security requirements and libel laws, are a fascinating example of the attempt to engage with a historical figure while simultaneously disavowing that attempt, but they will not be considered at length in this chapter. In addition to Hall and Halverson, other Oppenheimer proxies include Dr. Sebastian Block in Haakon Chevalier's *The Man Who Would Be God* (1959), Max Spielman in John Barth's *Giles Goat-Boy* (1966), Dr. Sandeman in Thomas McMahon's *Principles of American Nuclear Chemistry: A Novel* (1970), and Dr. Bamberger in Thomas Wiseman's *Savage Day* (1981).

10 Although it does not form a major object of analysis in this chapter, Smith's novel has received considerable critical attention (see, for example, Williams). I am also indebted to Toth, whose analysis of the discourse of toxicity in *Stallion Gate* taught me a great deal about that novel.

11 On fabulation in fiction, see Scholes.

12 There are many exoticizing gestures in this novel. Connolly's arrival in New Mexico, for instance, is figured as waking Santa Fe from its "timeless nap" (14); the Native Americans in and around Santa Fe and Los Alamos "never moved," forming "a stocky frieze" (253), an unchanging backdrop to the action taking place among the scientists; and his visit to a church in search of clues makes him feel as if "he had literally stepped back in time" and prompts him to remark wistfully on the "timelessly simple" (268) lives of the worshippers. It is significant that these exoticizing gestures are premised primarily on halting time, on freezing history to make it knowable. The effect, of course, consistent with Said's notion of Orientalism, is dehistoricization—a *removal* of the subject from history.

13 For a discussion of the connections between the figure of the detective and Oppenheimer as a savior, see Hendershot 481.

14 The term is drawn from Jacobs, chap. 4 ("The Speculative Self: Recombinant Fiction"); see esp. 106–107.

15 Imagining Oppenheimer in this counterfactual scenario has precedent. Canadian novelist Nicole Brossard's highly metafictional *Mauve Desert* (1987; published in English in 1990), for instance, depicts an Oppenheimer figure (called "longman" in the novel) in an Arizona motel. There, where he tries to embody scientific rationality, the "transparency" of representation, and other elements of patriarchal culture, Brossard deconstructs him through a variety of strategies that bring his identity into question as part of the novel's feminist ethos.

16 A discussion of a large-scale, social response to this threat can be found in Nadel. For a similar discussion, in a more specifically literary context, see Cordle 89–108.

17 An important discussion of the role of nostalgia in postmodern history can be found in Jameson.

18 For this potentially empowering sense of nostalgia, I am indebted to Cohen 218.

19 This assertion of historiographic metafiction's ability to problematize subjectivity is indebted to Hutcheon 84.

20 Elliott makes a similar argument about other counterfactual or alternate history novels (144).

21 In an epithet that could equally apply to Oppenheimer, Willis calls Edison "utilitarian yet theatrical, necromantic yet scientific" (292). The physicist-magician formulation appears elsewhere in fiction about nuclear history. In the sci-fi, future dystopia world of Walter M. Miller Jr.'s *A Canticle for Leibowitz* (1959), for instance, twentieth-century atomic scientists are referred to as "magi" (63).

22 One is reminded that Martin Cruz Smith's *Stallion Gate*, which I argue

belongs to the same tradition of representing Oppenheimer as Millet's novel does, does not dramatize the moment of atomic detonation either.

23   This point about ennui is indebted to Jameson 369.

PART II

1   Vision is deeply entangled in the discourse of knowledge, even if the metaphors are not always obvious. The word "ken," for instance, which means "to know" or "to understand," derives from Anglo-Saxon and Old Norse words for "sight" (*OED*).

2   A succinct summary of this process can be found in Taylor, "Our Bruised Arms" 5.

3   For a seminal discussion of the relationship between word and image in current visual studies, see Mitchell.

4   There is, of course, a long history in comics of radioactivity as a force behind superhero powers and mutated villains. This history rarely includes Oppenheimer, however, and remains quite distinct from the more recent, mostly "realistic" comics discussed in this section. Additionally, there has been much wrangling over the appropriate term for the genre that McCloud defines as "juxtaposed pictorial and other images in deliberate sequence" (9). Once widely called "comics," the form supposedly outgrew its mass, pulp roots and, as it became what Beaty calls "self-consciously aestheticized and politicized" (107), fell "under the gentrifying term 'graphic novel'" (108), a term that has itself fallen out of favor, in large part because such texts are often not fictional. Scholars such as Chute and DeKoven prefer the term "graphic narrative" for its ability to "to encompass a range of types of narrative work in comics" ("Introduction" 767), while Labio rejects that term as "equally unsatisfactory" because it "privileges . . . the literary character of comics over the visual, by assigning the status of mere qualifier to the visual dimension" (125–126) and wishes to return to the word "comics." Because many of the Oppenheimer representations I discuss originate not in highbrow literary culture but in more popular forms, I find myself convinced by Labio's assertion that the term "graphic novel" "points to a stubborn refusal [in academic circles] to accept popular works on their own terms" (126). Her preference for the term "comics" "reminds us of this vital dimension" (126). Labio also notes that studying comics requires "the adoption of a multidisciplinary perspective" (123–124), and because the general approach of this book is multidisciplinary, I will therefore use the word "comics" in this section to refer to these works.

5   Chute makes a convincing case in her work for the equal representational

power of hand-drawn images in comparison to forms such as photography and film. See, for instance, "Decoding Comics" 1017.

6   Chute and DeKoven have also made this point about the representational ability of comics collaboratively. See, for example, "Comic Books" 190.

7   A number of critics have discussed the politics and ethics of comics recently. See, for instance, Darda 32–33; Hatfield; Whitlock.

8   For this point about the power of silence in comics, I am indebted to Adler 2280.

9   Chute and DeKoven, "Introduction" 770.

10   Such restabilization is evident elsewhere in Oppenheimer comics. Jonathan Hickman and Nick Pitarra's *The Manhattan Projects* (2012–), for instance, while a thoroughly imaginative alternative history of the Manhattan Project, dispenses rather abruptly with Oppenheimer's ambiguities. In the first volume, Hickman and Pitarra postulate a twin brother, Joseph Oppenheimer, whose youthful oddities, contrasted sharply with Robert's intellectual precociousness, eventually blossom into full-fledged psychosis. On the day Robert is named leader of the Manhattan Project, Joseph escapes from his asylum, murders his brother, eats his body, and takes his place. Hickman and Pitarra maintain a strict separation between the Oppenheimers as they recount this part of the narrative, with the "good" Oppenheimer drawn primarily in blue panels and the "evil" one in red. Such a technique, through its clear visual separation of categories, simplifies the complexities that so frequently mark biographical, historical, literary, and cinematic representations of Oppenheimer. The technique problematically partitions out good from evil and unambiguously "explains" the construction of the atomic bomb as the product of unmitigated and purified malice.

11   One of the most well-known shadows is one cast by a person sitting on the stone steps of Sumitomo Bank near the hypocenter of the Hiroshima explosion. The steps were eventually donated to the Hiroshima Peace Memorial Museum. As discussed in chapter 5, a museum's popularly understood function as an institution for the preservation of the past is both affirmed and denied by such a display of absence.

CHAPTER 4

1   Perhaps the most famous film made about nuclear war, Stanley Kubrick's *Dr. Strangelove or: How I Learned to Stop Worrying and Love the Bomb* (1964), will not be discussed in this book in part because its satirical mode ensures that it is less about "bringing history to life" and more about refusing to engage with verisimilitude—by, in fact, "killing" history—in order to skewer

the discourses and tropes that made nuclear war appear to be a rational possibility in the 1950s and 1960s.

2   Of course, discussing film frequently involves talking not only about its visual
dimension but also about narrative structure, casting, music and sound
effects, and many other formal elements. Although such a comprehensive
approach to Manhattan Project films would be interesting (not to mention
ambitious), I wish to limit my discussion in this chapter primarily to the
visual strategies these films use to represent Oppenheimer. In part, my focus
on visual strategies is a means of redressing a lacuna in much criticism of
nuclear cinema: "its emphasis on narrative elements (such as the cultural
anxieties that nuclear films appear to express) over uniquely visual codes"
(Taylor, "Nuclear Pictures" 53–54).

3   This view of film and television is indebted to influential work by scholars
such as Fiske and Stam, as well as work more specifically on the construction of history in so-called historical film by scholars such as Chapman;
Landy; Ramirez; Rosen; Rosenstone. Inspired by their sophisticated work,
my aim is not to gauge the "authenticity" of these productions or to evaluate
their "accuracy"; instead, I focus on the proliferation of meaning that they
produce.

4   It is worth noting, as several scholars of atomic cinema have, that despite
a multitude of films and television productions about World War II, relatively few cover the Manhattan Project specifically, and even fewer depict the
bombing of Hiroshima and Nagasaki. This phenomenon, part of the general
"unspeakability" of nuclear weapons, means that cinematic representations
of Oppenheimer are relatively rare.

5   Chernus calls these policies a "schizoid strategy" (9), and Lifton has repeatedly
characterized this increased proliferation as a form of large-scale psychosis
(see Lifton and Falk; Lifton and Markusen; Lifton and Mitchell).

6   Both the term "sight machine" and its connection to derealization are drawn
from Virilio 1.

7   For this chapter to be manageable, there are a few television productions I
will not be discussing. One such example is the WGN America series *Manhattan*, which began in 2014 and, as of this writing, was renewed for a second
season in 2015. A heavily fictionalized account of Los Alamos in the 1940s,
Manhattan demonstrates a continuing interest in this period, its themes, and
its representational challenges.

8   For some provocative links between film, biography, and history, see Christie
284.

9   On the relationship between cinema and national memory, see Sturken 66.

10 One production, which I will not discuss in this chapter, is David Lowell
Rich's TV movie *Enola Gay: The Men, the Mission, the Atomic Bomb* (1980).

Although it stars Patrick Duffy and Billy Crystal, the film is rather obscure and not particularly compelling in its representational strategies. Robert Walden appears in a brief role as Oppenheimer. An even more obscure television production called *Race for the Bomb*, starring Tom Rack as Oppenheimer, aired in 1987. A joint production of the Canadian Broadcasting Corporation, Radiotelevisione Italiana, and French channel TF1, among others, *Race for the Bomb* is currently not available commercially.

11 Gusterson objects to *Fat Man and Little Boy* because it is "strewn with factual errors" (255 n. 9). The film does, of course, "take liberties" (not least in its use of fictional and composite characters, for example). I am, however, less interested in this chapter in cinema as mimesis than I am in the poetics of cinema, in the ways in which Oppenheimer, the bomb, technology, and other issues come together in provocative aesthetic ways. Such fictional assemblages (a term I find preferable in this case to "factual errors") can nevertheless be ideologically problematic in the way they embody and thus normalize the bomb.

12 This line echoes a well-known anxiety that Lifton identifies at the core of nuclear culture, an anxiety that can be traced back to the philosopher Martin Heidegger's suspicion, in *The Question Concerning Technology*, of the assumption that we are in control of technology, and an anxiety Gusterson summarizes as follows: "the very existence of nuclear weapons inevitably raises the question of whether the weapons are under our control or whether we are at their mercy" (157).

13 Taylor, for one, also discusses the "historical complicity of media corporations economically linked with nuclear-corporate contractors (e.g., NBC and General Electric), which reproduced orthodox nuclear narratives in their programming" ("Our Bruised Arms" 8).

14 For an extensive survey of the biopic, see Custen. For more recent critical engagements with that form, see Bingham; Brown and Vidal; Cheshire.

15 Oppenheimer's appearances on television—on, for instance, the American newsmagazine series *See It Now* (1955) or the British television documentary series *Panorama* (1960)—are, of course, still governed by representational strategies even though they feature the "real" Oppenheimer. As such, their analysis would be interesting but ultimately beyond the scope of this chapter, which focuses for the most part on fictional representations.

16 I make a similar argument about the use of stock footage in the 1983 nuclear disaster film *The Day After* in Banco, "'Hiroshima Is Peanuts.'"

17 Strathairn is, to my knowledge, the only actor to portray Oppenheimer twice: once in "The Trials of J. Robert Oppenheimer" and once in Sargent's *Day One*.

18 The DVD release of *Countdown to Zero* includes a special feature titled

"Oppenheimer: The Man behind the Bomb." The feature, which seems to consist mostly of material excised from the main documentary, suggests through its title ways in which the man becomes obscured by his technology and concealed "behind" its massive cultural prominence. In an interview with author Graham Allison at the beginning of the piece, Allison wonders, regarding the fantasy of "uninventing" the atomic bomb, whether it "is possible to go back and rewind that tape." His cinematic metaphor effects another technological displacement (one in which nuclear weapons are replaced by the absurdly more innocuous videotape) in addition to contributing to the self-reflexivity apparent in *Countdown to Zero.*

CHAPTER 5

1   For an analysis of the dichotomy between "liveness" and "mediatization," see Auslander.

2   See Carpenter for what is, essentially, a scholarly narrative of theater's failure to engage meaningfully with the bomb. For a more recent analysis, and a more general overview of theater and science, see Shepherd-Barr.

3   Thornton Wilder and Clifford Odets both found the subject unworkable and gave up on their projects in 1955 and 1961, respectively. In 1955, Upton Sinclair wrote "Doctor Fist," a play he never published, about an Oppenheimer stand-in named Walter Fist. Arthur Miller, perhaps the era's best-known American playwright, tried and failed to write a play, featuring an Oppenheimer-like figure, that explores contrition among atomic physicists (see Carpenter 77).

4   The term is drawn from Hye 129.

5   Despite such strategies, Kipphardt's play is well aware of the challenges of trying to capture the past. At points in the play, Oppenheimer's interrogators concede that "facts are very relative" (38), and that they have "come to realize the inadequacy of being strictly confined to facts in our modern security investigations" (20). These admissions highlight Kipphardt's notion of the importance of memory in the (re)construction of history as well as the limitations of positivist factuality (see Shepherd-Barr 76). It is also worth noting that Kipphardt's play enjoyed a surge of popularity and was staged several times in the early 2000s in light of the evolving discourses of "national security."

6   For example, a stage direction early in the play notes that one character, Lilith, derived from Jewish mythology, "lives in the walls and ceiling, crawling up and across chain-link fence, perching, seething, lunging, curling up to sleep, but never touching the floor. She is only visible to Oppenheimer" (Kreitzer 7).

7   Gordon Parsons, "Terrible Triumph of 'Man Who Became Death,'" *Morning*

Star, January 29, 2015, http://www.morningstaronline.co.uk/a-353d-Terrible-triumph-of-man-who-became-death#.Vd4x3LfCrFI.

8   See Shepherd-Barr 41–60.

9   These questions are central to current museological debates (see MacDonald; Learner).

10 One example of how a museum explains this scientific concept appears in the National Atomic Testing Museum in Las Vegas. There, looped clips from 1950s-era educational films, complete with brassy soundtracks and dated animation, play to explain fission and fusion. Such clips are historically appropriate, but as representations of science, they read as folksy and old-fashioned. Such an aesthetic diminishes science in favor of the narrative of technological progress emblematized by nuclear weapons.

11 Reynolds points out that the "man-making" activities that took place at the boys' school—outdoor pursuits meant to foster rugged individualism—anticipated the "man-making," which I discuss in this chapter, apparent in subsequent rhetorical and visual constructions of the bomb as, metaphorically, a biological entity (139).

12 In the representational strategies used at the actual Trinity site, 250 miles south of Los Alamos, Oppenheimer is conspicuous by his absence. The site, in a desert basin called Jornada del Muerto ("Journey of the Dead Man") is marked by absence and lack in general: the scrub desert shows few distinguishing marks, and aside from a giant steel container—nicknamed "Jumbo"—that was not used at the Trinity test and that sits incongruously in the parking lot, a historical marker outside the site itself and a small obelisk at ground zero function as nearly the only concrete indicators of what happened there in 1945. The site is only open to the public two days a year. Ironically, one of the strongest "presences" at the site is the elevated (but invisible) background radiation.

13 Whether they curse its name or not, visitors to Los Alamos are expected to increase as local and national historic societies continue to preserve and commemorate the work done there and elsewhere. In 2010, the Los Alamos Historical Society convened a symposium, "Oppenheimer House Planning Symposium," wherein "scholars, historic preservationists, historic house museum experts, and community members" discussed the possibilities and the challenges of turning the house on the corner of Peach Street and Bathtub Row, Oppenheimer's home from 1943 to 1945, into a museum. The subsequent "Historic Structure Report" document offers detailed glimpses at the interpretive possibilities of a future Oppenheimer House Museum. Although a full analysis of that report is beyond the scope of this chapter, reading it suggests that the house could become a fascinating nucleus of Oppenheimer representation within Los Alamos.

14 The space in the museum devoted to nonweapon forms of scientific research and technological development is also disproportionately large compared to how the LANL budget is allocated. According to 2013 information, 57 percent of the $2.2 billion LANL budget for fiscal year 2012 was spent on "weapons programs," while only 8 percent went toward "environmental management," 4 percent went to the disconcertingly vague "energy and other programs," and 11 percent went to the even vaguer category "work for others" (which presumably includes work such as the development of technology related to space travel but could conceivably include work done for private weapons manufacturing companies). See *Bradbury Science Museum Gallery Guide*.

15 For an analysis of the early 1990s debate between LANL and the Los Alamos Study Group, a Santa Fe–based antinuclear activist organization that has been resisting LANL's work since 1989, see Taylor, "Revis(it)ing Nuclear History." Taylor's analysis concerns how that debate manifested inside the Bradbury Science Museum.

16 Taylor makes a version of this argument in "Revis(it)ing" 122.

17 Because of its status as a technomilitary establishment town, Los Alamos itself has become an important site for nuclear protest (see Masco 259).

18 Oppenheimer's presence in Los Alamos is relatively understated. Along with the sober bronze statues of Oppenheimer and Groves outside Fuller Lodge, busts of Oppenheimer reside in the Mesa Public Library and in the research library of the Oppenheimer Study Center on the grounds of LANL, locations that both reinforce his identity as a scholar and academic and downplay his associations with war and weaponry. The modest Oppenheimer Drive running a short distance north and south through town offers another unostentatious commemoration. Although tourist trinkets such as "Atomic City" T-shirts and coffee mugs abound, and the atomic symbol of electrons in orbit around a nucleus is ubiquitous, Oppenheimer iconography is fairly scarce on the streets of Los Alamos.

19 Such reverential responses to statues and other monuments are common but conceptually incongruous in a science museum. These emotional experiences constitute one possible way to insert counterdiscourses into the cracks in the museum's rationalist hegemony.

20 For this point on the contributions bodily metaphors make to technoaestheticism, I am indebted to Masco 80.

21 For this point on the conflation of life and death, I am indebted to Taylor, "Register" 277.

22 As Cohn succinctly puts it, the "imagery that domesticates, that humanizes insentient weapons, may also serve, paradoxically, to make it all right to ignore sentient human beings" (699).

23 For this point on the fragility arising from familial and biological metaphors, I am indebted to Masco 88.

24 The term "hauntology" is Derrida's and refers to the ontological disruptions created by various types of absence, including ghosts, within a Western philosophical tradition that privileges presence (*Spectres of Marx* 9).

25 O. Juveland, personal communication, July 28, 2014.

26 In June 2015, the Bradbury announced that the chair would once again be on display, but only for one month. The temporal constriction of the chair's display ensures the continued dialectic of presence and absence.

27 See, for instance, Keller for an influential critique of the gendered language of science. Much literary criticism of Mary Shelley's *Frankenstein*, often a touchstone in the Oppenheimer narrative, also makes similar points about the gendering of science in relation to that novel.

28 The body of scholarly work on gender and science is vast, but Haraway is a good starting point. On the masculinism of nuclear culture, see Cohn; Easlea.

29 For a rather imaginative exploration of the possibilities of seeing the bomb in biological (and, ultimately, archetypal) terms, see Reynolds.

30 On the repressed gender narratives of the Manhattan Project in particular, see Taylor, "Register" 276.

31 My reading of embodiment at the Bradbury differs somewhat from that provided by the Los Alamos Study Group. According to Taylor, the "Museum appeared to them to be a sterile, lifeless and 'eerie' place where 'cold' technology was 'worshipped'" ("Revis(it)ing" 129). Without denying the legitimacy of that response to the Bradbury or the presence of the rhetorical and visual techniques that produce it, the museum's representations of fertile bodies, particularly in the ways they sometimes thwart conventional gender roles, frequently provide opportunity for counterdiscursive responses to the sterility and lifelessness the Los Alamos Study Group, among others, sense in this museum.

32 For a compelling discussion of the aesthetics and ideology of American monuments, see Savage 11.

33 On the dissonance of nuclear metaphors, see Gusterson 163.

34 For the notion of "spatial fixity," see MacDonald, "Exhibitions" 5. Such fixity also came into question as museums started to create web presences in the late twentieth century. As an adjunct to this spatial restlessness, the fluidity of virtual museums stands in sharp opposition to the rather old-fashioned notion of a museum as a specific place designated for the collective experience of material history. For a discussion of this contrast in the context of monuments, see Savage 4.

35 For the conservative function of museums, generally, see Luke.

36 For this point on the teleology of nuclear weapons displays, specifically in the context of the Albuquerque museum, I am indebted to Arnold 641.

37 Taylor advances the theory that "pregnancy potentially afforded Los Alamos women a measure of control in a world slipping out of control. . . . It was possibly a deep and instinctive female reflex to reproduce life and thus counter the organized, scientific male production of death" ("Register" 278). Such speculation relies on the essentialist assumption of an "instinctive female reflex" toward motherhood, but the postulation of eros as a counter to thanatos is a suggestive and influential one in the context of the Manhattan Project. See Freud's "Beyond the Pleasure Principle" for a discussion of the dialectic between the life-seeking expression of desire and the death-seeking manifestation of aggressive impulses. See also Cohn's "Sex and Death."

38 A specific discussion of the rhetoric of domestication in nuclear culture in general can be found in Schiappa. Overlaying the image of the nurturing father on the image of the nuclear weapons scientist is common in the history of Oppenheimer representation. As Easlea notes in his book on masculinity and nuclear culture, "it is entirely appropriate that J. Robert Oppenheimer, acclaimed as the 'father of the atomic bomb' and proud owner of the Medal of Merit awarded by President Truman, consented after Hiroshima to the honor of being appointed Father of the Year by the National Baby Institution" (115).

39 When I visited the museum in 2013, someone had inserted in pen the letter "d" after the word "sophisticate" in this text panel. Although this is likely simply an example of a "helpful" visitor with a shaky grasp of grammar attempting to correct the museum's text, it also reveals one of the effects of casting Oppenheimer in passive terms: his passivity makes him capable of embodying sophistication (that is, he can be sophisticated), but he cannot actively be a sophisticate.

40 The photograph, taken in 1947, is a particularly morose and washed-out image of Oppenheimer, which further undermines his agency in this representational instance.

41 For this juxtaposition, I am indebted to Vanderbilt 95.

42 Although the Nevada Test Site was, during these years, "quite literally the epicenter of nuclear technologies and nuclear experiences" (Wray 468), the United States conducted an additional hundred or so tests in Alaska, Colorado, Mississippi, New Mexico (near Carlsbad and near Farmington), and on the Marshall Islands. The nuclear weapons testing moratorium of 1992 put an end to testing.

43 On the versatility and mobility of nuclear fear, see Masco 30.

44 Las Vegas itself is an unstable place for this museum, with its identities as a base for scientific testing, a tourist destination, and a "national sacrifice zone" coming into tension with one another throughout the city.

45 Edward Rothstein, "A Place to Consider Apocalypse," *New York Times*,
    February 23, 2005, http://www.nytimes.com/2005/02/23/arts/design/a-
    place-to-consider-apocalypse.html.
46 A succinct summary of this ideology can be found in, for instance, Wiener
    113.
47 For instance, one panel first quotes Franklin Roosevelt's Pearl Harbor speech,
    then informs visitors that a "fundamental government function is to protect
    its citizens from enemies," before linking the Japanese attack of 1941 with
    a hypothetical "surprise nuclear attack" during the Cold War in order to
    justify the need to develop and maintain a nuclear arsenal. The panel con-
    cludes as follows: "A common assumption is that America's nuclear testing
    program was solely or even primarily intensified to increase the number or
    destructiveness of weapons. This is wrong. Early bombs were big, heavy,
    and 'dirty' (created a lot of radioactive fallout). As the Cold War progressed,
    America began to modernize its nuclear stockpile with smaller, radiologically
    cleaner, and safer weapons." Aside from its obviously high-handed tone, the
    panel evokes the discourse of progress and modernization to aestheticize
    the bomb—to "clean" it up. Painfully euphemistic language such as "safer
    weapon" is couched in the aesthetics of bureaucratic logic (the panel appears
    as a large file folder) to yoke the threat of global genocide to the process of
    deterrence in order to justify the construction of these weapons.
48 For these points on the nuclear museum's changing role in the war on terror,
    I am indebted to Wray 475.
49 In his critique of establishment nuclear culture, Wiener notes: "The Atomic
    Testing Museum, with its message that testing nuclear bombs helped bring
    American victory in the Cold War, has not been very successful" (123). Only
    about a thousand people a week visit the museum, fewer, Wiener claims,
    than were visiting the Liberace Museum before it closed in 2010.
50 For this point about the "persistence" of nuclear weapons, see Taylor, "Our
    Bruised Arms" 19.

Part III

1   Garner 100–103 is particularly helpful in understanding these dimensions of
    Foucault's thought.
2   For my understanding of this role, I am indebted to Day, "Nature of Sci-
    ence" 75.
3   Revealing the existence of Manhattan Project did not, of course, mean the
    end of nuclear secrecy. In fact, it laid the groundwork for even vaster and
    more complex secret plans. For instance, SIOP (Single Integrated Operational

Plan) was the United States' top-secret nuclear war plan, targeting hundreds of megatons of nuclear force at thousands of potential global targets for decades during the Cold War.

4   For this point, including my use of foundational documents as an example, I am indebted to Liste-Noya 1.

5   On these fantasies and languages of self-destruction and their origins in repression, see Melley, *The Covert Sphere* 217.

6   Dyer calls the celebrity's multiplicity "structured polysemy" (3), a helpful term for understanding how Oppenheimer can mean so many different things within relatively restricted contexts.

7   The relationship between the private and the public is a frequently discussed topic among scholars of celebrity. See, for instance, Rojek 11. Liste-Noya also discusses this relationship when he points to the opposition "between the expected transparency of public disclosure," a "self-evidence" characteristic of celebrity, and "the insistence on a realm of the personally undisclosable" (4) as a way of securing individual subjectivity.

8   In articulating my view of Oppenheimer as a celebrity, I aim to draw more on theorists such as Morin and Dyer than on ones such as Adorno and Horkheimer (particularly their essay "The Culture Industry: Enlightenment as Mass Deception") and Boorstin, who view celebrities as mere mouthpieces for the capitalist manipulation of the masses. Morin's and Dyer's theories seem better able to account for the multiple and interanimating forces and sets of agency that construct celebrities in the postwar period that Oppenheimer (in some ways) inaugurates. Other recent theorists of celebrity who have influenced my thinking include Braudy; Gamson; Inglis; Marshall; Schickel.

9   "Heavenly bodies" is Dyer's term.

10 On the crucial role of distancing in the production of celebrity, see Rojek 12.

11 The term "self-fashioning" is probably most closely associated with Greenblatt, and like "ethopoiesis" and its use of writing and reading, it focuses on the aesthetics and social standards through which an individual constructs identity.

CHAPTER 6

1   For my understanding of this role, I am indebted to Day, "Nature of Science" 73.

2   See ibid., 104.

3   On Oppenheimer's tendency to assert secrecy, see Walsh 103–104. For Walsh, Oppenheimer's access to secrets served to ensconce him in a privileged role

as a cultural prophet (a role supposedly at odds with his rational scientific identity).

4   The term "intimate strangers" is drawn from the title of Schickel's study of the culture of celebrity.

5   For a brief overview of Oppenheimer's scientific writing, see Day, "Nature of Science" 75.

6   Smith and Weiner's collection begins with the premise that Oppenheimer "maintained an air of privacy, suggesting an inner self withheld from public view" (v), and they go on to explain that his letters "revealed a relatively unknown Oppenheimer and explained much about the public figure who emerged after 1945" (vii).

7   Taylor's article "The Politics of the Nuclear Text" on Smith and Weiner's collection is a good one, although more work on the letters could certainly be done.

8   For a brief overview of the composition and general subject matter of these books, see Day 76.

9   On the importance of "the visual presentation of personality" to the identity of a celebrity, see Schumway 87.

10 Unlike the project's military commander, Leslie Groves, who wrote the operatively titled *Now It Can Be Told: The Story of the Manhattan Project* (1962), Oppenheimer never published an autobiography or an account of the Manhattan Project. The closest he came to writing an autobiography was the long letter he provided in response to the Atomic Energy Commission's accusations. For a detailed discussion of that document, see Hecht, *Storytelling and Science* 43–52.

11 As a number of scholars of autobiography point out, the "private self" is, rather than a purely autonomous entity, subject to the social contexts in which it exists and that structure its existence. See, for instance, Rak. On autobiography specifically in a nuclear context, see Taylor, *"Reminiscences."*

12 On the value of open-mindedness, broadly conceived, during the Cold War, see Cohen-Cole 254.

13 Oppenheimer's comment about the technical sweetness of the bomb is often taken as evidence of his single-minded technocratic determinism. As he noted at his security hearing, however, he was not in fact omniscient, and the dangerous legacy of nuclear weapons could not have been foreseen. His commitment to community and his commitment to technical instrumentalism are thus not mutually exclusive.

14 This observation about the iconological role of photographs in modern celebrity is indebted to Howells 113.

15 Building on the work of Lejeune and Marcus, Rak uses the term "paratext" (25)—expanded beyond the usual use of the word in reference to book covers,

editorial apparatus, and so on—to characterize the larger world outside of the text to which autobiography refers and which strongly influences the circulation, reception, and meaning of autobiographical texts.

Conclusion

1   Haynes's *From Faust to Strangelove* remains the most comprehensive discussion of the figure of the scientist in Western culture.
2   On terrorism in the (neo)liberal era, see Berman.
3   For these points about forgetting and remembering the infrastructure of the nuclear past, I am indebted to Taylor, "Our Bruised Arms" 17–18.

BIBLIOGRAPHY

Abbey, Edward. *Desert Solitaire: A Season in the Wilderness*. New York: Ballantine, 1971.

Adler, Silvia. "Silence in the Graphic Novel." *Journal of Pragmatics* 43.9 (2011): 2278–2285.

Allman, Toney. *J. Robert Oppenheimer: Theoretical Physicist, Atomic Pioneer*. San Diego: Blackbirch, 2005.

Amrine, Michael. *Secret*. Boston: Houghton Mifflin, 1950.

Anderson, Oscar E., Jr. Review of *Brighter than a Thousand Suns*, by Robert Jungk. *Isis* 51.1 (1960): 117–119.

Anderson, Perry. *The Origins of Postmodernity*. New York: Verso, 1998.

Arbab, John. "Oppenheimer and Ethical Responsibility." *Synthesis: The University Journal in the History and Philosophy of Science* 5 (1982): 22–43.

Arnold, Kenneth. "The National Atomic Museum, Albuquerque, New Mexico: Where 'Weapon Shapes' Are Not Enough." *Technology and Culture* 30.3 (1989): 640–642.

Aubrey, Crispin, ed. *Nukespeak: The Media and the Bomb*. London: Comedia, 1982.

Auslander, Philip. *Liveness: Performance in a Mediatized Culture*. London: Routledge, 1999.

Bachelard, Gaston. *The Poetics of Space*. Trans. Maria Jolas. Boston: Beacon, 1969.

Banco, Lindsey Michael. "'Hiroshima Is Peanuts': The Strange Landscape of *The Day After*." *Arizona Quarterly* 71.1 (2015): 101–128.

Barth, John. *Giles Goat-Boy*. New York: Doubleday, 1966.

Barthes, Roland. *Camera Lucida: Reflections on Photography.* Trans. Richard Howard. New York: Hill and Wang, 1981.

———. "The Death of the Author." In *Image/Music/Text.* Ed. and trans. Steven Heath. London: Fontana, 1977. 142–148.

———. "The Discourse of History." In *The Rustle of Language.* Trans. Richard Howard. Oxford: Blackwell, 1986. 127–141.

———. *Mythologies.* 1957. Trans. Annette Lavers. New York: Hill and Wang, 1972.

Bartter, Martha. *The Way to Ground Zero: The Atomic Bomb in American Science Fiction.* Santa Barbara, CA: Praeger, 1988.

Batchelor, John. Introduction to *The Art of Literary Biography.* Ed. John Batchelor. Oxford: Clarendon, 1995. 1–11.

Baudrillard, Jean. *America.* Trans. Chris Turner. New York: Verso, 1988.

Beaty, Bart. "Introduction." *Cinema Journal* 50.3 (2011): 106–110.

Beck, John. *Dirty Wars: Landscape, Power, and Waste in Western American Literature.* Lincoln: University of Nebraska Press, 2009.

The Beginning or the End. Directed by Norman Taurog. MGM, 1947.

Benjamin, Walter. "Theses on the Philosophy of History." In *Illuminations.* Ed. Hannah Arendt. Trans. Harry Zohn. New York: Schocken, 1969. 253–264.

Berlatsky, Eric L. *The Real, the True, and the Told: Postmodern Historical Narrative and the Ethics of Representation.* Columbus: Ohio State University Press, 2011.

Berman, Paul. *Terror and Liberalism.* New York: Norton, 2003.

Bethe, Hans. Review of *Brighter than a Thousand Suns,* by Robert Jungk. *Bulletin of the Atomic Scientists* 14.10 (1958): 426–428.

Bingham, Dennis. *Whose Lives Are They Anyway? The Biopic as Contemporary Film Genre.* New Brunswick, NJ: Rutgers University Press, 2010.

Bird, Kai, and Lawrence Lifschultz, eds. *Hiroshima's Shadow: Writings on the Denial of History and the Smithsonian Controversy.* Stony Creek, CN: Pamphleteer's Press, 1998.

Bird, Kai, and Martin J. Sherwin. *American Prometheus: The Triumph and Tragedy of J. Robert Oppenheimer.* New York: Knopf, 2005.

Blouin, Michael, Morgan Shipley, and Jack Taylor, eds. *The Silence of Fallout: Nuclear Criticism in a Post-Cold War World.* Newcastle upon Tyne: Cambridge Scholars, 2013.

Bock, Dennis. *The Ash Garden.* New York: Knopf, 2001.

Bogard, Larry. *Los Alamos Light.* New York: Farrar, Straus and Giroux, 1983.

Bok, Sissela. *Secrets: On the Ethics of Concealment and Revelation.* New York: Pantheon, 1983.

Boone, Joseph A., and Nancy J. Vickers. "Introduction: Celebrity Rites." *PMLA* 126.4 (2011): 900–911.

Boorstin, Daniel. *The Image: Or, What Happened to the American Dream.* New York: Atheneum, 1962.

Bové, Paul, ed. *Early Postmodernism: Foundational Essays.* Durham, NC: Duke University Press, 1995.

Boyer, Paul. *By the Bomb's Early Light: American Thought and Culture at the Dawn of the Atomic Age.* Chapel Hill: University of North Carolina Press, 1985.

Bradbury Science Museum Gallery Guide. Los Alamos, NM: Los Alamos National Laboratory, 2013.

Braudy, Leo. *The Frenzy of Renown: Fame and Its History.* New York: Oxford University Press, 1986.

Brians, Paul. *Nuclear Holocausts: Atomic War in Fiction, 1895–1984.* Kent, OH: Kent State University Press, 1987.

Broderick, Mick. *Nuclear Movies.* Jefferson, NC: McFarland, 1991.

Brossard, Nicole. *Mauve Desert.* 1987. Trans. Susanne de Lotbinière-Harwood. Toronto: Coach House, 1990.

Brown, Tom, and Belén Vidal. *The Biopic in Contemporary Film Culture.* New York: Routledge, 2014.

Buck, Pearl S. *Command the Morning.* New York: John Day, 1959.

Butler, Robert Olen. *Countrymen of Bones.* New York: Horizon, 1983.

Caine, Barbara. *Biography and History.* Houndmills, UK: Palgrave Macmillan, 2010.

Canaday, John. *The Nuclear Muse: Literature, Physics, and the First Atomic Bomb.* Madison: University of Wisconsin Press, 2000.

Carpenter, Charles A. *Dramatists and the Bomb: American and British Playwrights Confront the Nuclear Age, 1945–1964.* Westport, CT: Greenwood, 1999.

Carson, Tom. *Gilligan's Wake.* New York: Picador, 2003.

Cassidy, David C. *J. Robert Oppenheimer and the American Century.* New York: Pi, 2005.

Casti, John L. *The One True Platonic Heaven.* Washington, DC: Joseph Henry, 2003.

"Challenge of the Sixties." *Panorama.* Produced by Michael Peacock. British Broadcasting Corporation, 1960.

Chaloupka, William. *Knowing Nukes: The Politics and Culture of the Atom.* Minneapolis: University of Minnesota Press, 1992.

Chapman, James. *Film and History.* New York: Palgrave Macmillan, 2013.

Cheng, Eileen Ka-May. "Exceptional Historiography? The Origins of Historiography in the United States." *History and Theory* 47.2 (2008): 200–228.

Chernus, Ira. *Nuclear Madness: Religion and the Psychology of the Nuclear Age.* Albany: State University of New York Press, 1991.

Cheshire, Ellen. *Bio-Pics: A Life in Pictures*. New York: Wallflower, 2015.

Chevalier, Haakon. *The Man Who Would Be God*. New York: Putnam, 1959.

Chilton, Paul, ed. *Language and the Nuclear Arms Debate: Nukespeak Today*. London: Pinter, 1985.

Chow, Rey. *The Age of the World Target: Self-Referentiality in War, Theory, and Comparative Work*. Durham, NC: Duke University Press, 2006.

Christie, Ian. "A Life on Film." In *Mapping Lives: The Uses of Biography*. Ed. Peter France and William St. Clair. Oxford: Oxford University Press, 2002. 283–301.

Chute, Hillary. "Comics Form and Narrating Lives." *Profession* (2011): 107–117.

———. "Decoding Comics." *Modern Fiction Studies* 52.4 (2006): 1014–1027.

Chute, Hillary, and Marianne DeKoven. "Introduction: Graphic Narrative." *Modern Fiction Studies* 52.4 (2006): 767–782.

———. "Comic Books and Graphic Novels." In *The Cambridge Companion to Popular Fiction*. Ed. David Glover and Scott McCracken. Cambridge: Cambridge University Press, 2012. 175–195.

Clark, Elizabeth A. *History, Theory, Text: Historians and the Linguistic Turn*. Cambridge, MA: Harvard University Press, 2004.

Clark, Ronald W. *The Greatest Power on Earth: The Story of Nuclear Fission*. London: Sidgwick and Jackson, 1980.

Cmiel, Kenneth. "After Objectivity: What Comes Next?" *American Literary History* 2.1 (1990): 170–181.

Cohen, Samuel. "Fables of American Collectivity Circa 2005: Chris Bachelder's *U.S.!*, Lydia Millet's *Oh Pure and Radiant Heart*, and George Saunders's *Brief and Frightening Reign of Phil*." *Amerikastudien/American Studies* 57.2 (2012): 207–220.

Cohen-Cole, Jamie. *The Open Mind: Cold War Politics and the Science of Human Nature*. Chicago: University of Chicago Press, 2014.

Cohn, Carol. "Sex and Death in the Rational World of Defense Intellectuals." *Signs* 12.4 (1987): 687–718.

Conant, Jennet. *109 East Palace: Robert Oppenheimer and the Secret City of Los Alamos*. New York: Simon and Schuster, 2005.

Condon, E. U. Review of *Brighter than a Thousand Sun*, by Robert Jungk. *Science* 128 (1958): 1619–1620.

"A Conversation with J. Robert Oppenheimer." *See It Now*. Written by Edward R. Murrow. CBS, 1955.

Cordle, Daniel. *States of Suspense: The Nuclear Age, Postmodernism and United States Fiction and Prose*. Manchester, UK: Manchester University Press, 2008.

Countdown to Zero. Directed by Lucy Walker. Lawrence Bender Productions, 2010.

Cowart, David. *History and the Contemporary Novel.* Carbondale: Southern Illinois University Press, 1989.

Currie, Mark. *Postmodern Narrative Theory.* London: Palgrave Macmillan, 1998.

Custen, George F. *Bio/Pics: How Hollywood Constructed Public History.* New Brunswick, NJ: Rutgers University Press, 1992.

Darda, Joseph. "Graphic Ethics: Theorizing the Face in Marjane Satrapi's *Persepolis.*" *College Literature* 40.2 (2013): 31–51.

The Day after Trinity. Directed by Jon Else. KTEH, 1981.

Day, Michael A. "Oppenheimer and Rabi: American Cold War Physicists as Public Intellectuals." In *The Atomic Bomb and American Society: New Perspectives.* Ed. Rosemary B. Mariner and G. Kurt Piehler. Knoxville: University of Tennessee Press, 2009. 307–328.

———. "Oppenheimer on the Nature of Science." *Centaurus* 43.2 (2001): 73–112.

Day One. Directed by Joseph Sargent. Spelling Entertainment, 1989.

Dean, Jodi. *Aliens in America: Conspiracy Culture from Outerspace to Cyberspace.* Ithaca: Cornell University Press, 1998.

DeGroot, Gerard D. *The Bomb: A Life.* Cambridge: Harvard University Press, 2005.

DeLillo, Don. *Underworld.* New York: Scribner, 1997.

DeLoughrey, Elizabeth. "Heliotropes: Solar Ecologies and Pacific Radiations." In *Postcolonial Ecologies.* Ed. Elizabeth DeLoughrey and George B. Handley. Oxford: Oxford University Press, 2011. 235–253.

———. "Radiation Ecologies and the Wars of Light." *Modern Fiction Studies* 55.3 (2009): 468–498.

Del Tredici, Robert. *At Work in the Fields of the Bomb.* New York: Perennial, 1987.

Derrida, Jacques. "How to Avoid Speaking: Denials." Trans. Ken Frieden. In *Languages of the Unsayable.* Ed. Sanford Budick and Wolfgang Iser. New York: Columbia University Press, 1989. 3–70.

———. "No Apocalypse, Not Now (Full Speed Ahead, Seven Missiles, Seven Missives)." Trans. Catherine Porter and Philip Lewis. *Diacritics* 14.2 (1984): 20–31.

———. "Sokal and Bricmont Aren't Serious." In *Paper Machine.* Trans. Rachel Bowlby. Stanford, CA: Stanford University Press, 2005. 70–72.

———. *Specters of Marx.* Trans. Peggy Kamuf. New York: Routledge, 1994.

Dibblin, Jane. *Day of Two Suns: US Nuclear Testing and the Pacific Islanders.* London: Virago, 1988.

Doctor Atomic. Composed by John Adams. Libretto by Peter Sellars. New York: Herndon Music, 2005.

Dorsey, John T. "The Responsibility of the Scientist in Atomic Bomb Literature." *Comparative Literature Studies* 24.3 (1987): 277–290.

Dowling, David. *Fictions of Nuclear Disaster*. Iowa City: University of Iowa Press, 1987.

Dubin, Steven C. *Displays of Power: Controversy in the American Museum from the "Enola Gay" to "Sensation."* New York: New York University Press, 1999.

Dyer, Richard. *Stars*. 1980. London: British Film Institute, 1998.

Easlea, Brian. *Fathering the Unthinkable: Masculinity, Scientists and the Nuclear Arms Race*. London: Pluto, 1983.

Elias, Amy J. *Sublime Desire: History and Post-1960s Fiction*. Baltimore: Johns Hopkins University Press, 2001.

Eliot, T. S. "Hamlet and His Problems." In *The Sacred Wood: Essays on Poetry and Criticism*. London: Methuen, 1960. 95–103.

Elliott, Michael A. "Strangely Interested: The Work of Historical Fantasy." *American Literature* 87.1 (2015): 137–157.

Ellis, David. *Literary Lives: Biography and the Search for Understanding*. Edinburgh: Edinburgh University Press, 2000.

Ellmann, Richard. *Literary Biography*. Oxford: Clarendon, 1971.

Enola Gay: The Men, the Mission, the Atomic Bomb. Directed by David Lowell Rich. Viacom, 1980.

Epstein, William H. *Recognizing Biography*. Philadelphia: University of Pennsylvania Press, 1987.

Estrin, Marc. *Insect Dreams: The Half-Life of Gregor Samsa*. New York: BlueHen, 2002.

Evans, Joyce A. *Celluloid Mushroom Clouds: Hollywood and the Atomic Bomb*. Boulder, CO: Westview, 1998.

Fat Man and Little Boy. Directed by Roland Joffé. Paramount, 1989.

Fenster, Mark. *Conspiracy Theories: Secrecy and Power in American Life*. Minneapolis: University of Minnesota Press, 2008.

Ferguson, Niall. "Introduction: Virtual History: Towards a 'Chaotic' Theory of the Past." In *Virtual History: Alternatives and Counterfactuals*. London: Picador, 1997. 1–90.

Fetter-Vorm, Jonathan. *Trinity: A Graphic History of the First Atomic Bomb*. New York: Hill and Wang, 2012.

Fiege, Mark. "The Atomic Scientists, the Sense of Wonder, and the Bomb." *Environmental History* 12.3 (2007): 578–613.

Fiske, John. *Television Culture*. New York: Methuen, 1987.

Fortey, Richard. *Dry Store Room No. 1: The Secret Life of the Natural History Museum*. New York: Knopf, 2008.

Foucault, Michel. *The Hermeneutics of the Subject: Lecture at the College de France, 1981–1982*. Trans. Graham Burchell. Ed. Frederic Gros. New York: Picador, 2005.

Francese, Joseph. *Narrating Postmodern Time and Space*. Albany: State University of New York Press, 1997.

Franklin, H. Bruce. *War Stars: The Superweapon and the American Imagination.* Rev. ed. Amherst: University of Massachusetts Press, 2008.

Freud, Sigmund. "Beyond the Pleasure Principle." 1920. In *The Standard Edition of the Complete Psychological Works of Sigmund Freud.* Vol. 18. Ed. and trans. James Strachey. London: Hogarth, 1955. 7–64.

Fukuyama, Francis. *The End of History and the Last Man.* New York: Free Press, 1992.

Gamson, Joshua. *Claims to Fame: Celebrity in Contemporary America.* Berkeley: University of California Press, 1994.

Garner, Richard A. "From Sovereignty to Ethopoiesis: Literature, Aesthetics, and New Forms of Life." *Comparatist* 36.1 (2012): 86–106.

Gerster, Robin. "The Bomb in the Museum: Nuclear Technology and the Human Element." *Museum and Society* 11.3 (2013): 207–218.

———. "Hiroshima No More: Forgetting 'the Bomb.'" *War and Society* 22.1 (2004): 59–68.

Gibson, Andrew. *Postmodernity, Ethics, and the Novel.* London: Routledge, 1999.

———. *Towards a Postmodern Theory of Narrative.* Edinburgh: Edinburgh University Press, 1996.

Goin, Peter. "Magical Realism: The West as Spiritual Playground." In *Western Places, American Myths: How We Think about the West.* Ed. Gary J. Hausladen. Reno: University of Nevada Press, 2003. 253–272.

———. *Nuclear Landscapes.* Baltimore: Johns Hopkins University Press, 1991.

Goodchild, Peter. *J. Robert Oppenheimer: Shatterer of Worlds.* Boston: Houghton Mifflin, 1980.

Graulund, Rune. "Travelling the Desert: Desert Travel Writing as Indicator Species." *Studies in Travel Writing* 10.2 (2006): 141–159.

Grausam, Daniel. *On Endings: American Postmodern Fiction and the Cold War.* Charlottesville: University of Virginia Press, 2011.

Greenblatt, Stephen. *Renaissance Self-Fashioning: From More to Shakespeare.* Chicago: University of Chicago Press, 1980.

Groves, Leslie R. *Now It Can Be Told: The Story of the Manhattan Project.* New York: Harper, 1962.

Gusterson, Hugh. *Nuclear Rites: A Weapons Laboratory at the End of the Cold War.* Berkeley: University of California Press, 1998.

Hacker, Barton C. Review of *Critical Assembly: A Technical History of Los Alamos during the Oppenheimer Years, 1943–1945,* by Lillian Hoddeson, Paul W. Henriksen, Roger A. Meade, and Catherine L. Westfall. *The American Historical Review* 100.1 (1995): 256–257.

Hales, Peter B. *Atomic Spaces: Living on the Manhattan Project.* Urbana: University of Illinois Press, 1997.

———. "The Atomic Sublime." *American Studies* 32.1 (1991): 5–31.

Haraway, Donna. *Simians, Cyborgs, and Women: The Reinvention of Nature.* New York: Routledge, 1991.

Harwit, Martin. *An Exhibit Denied: Lobbying the History of the "Enola Gay."* New York: Copernicus, 1996.

Hatfield, Charles. *Alternative Comics: An Emerging Literature.* Jackson: University Press of Mississippi, 2005.

Hawkins, David, Edith C. Truslow, and Ralph Carlisle Smith. *Project Y: The Los Alamos Story.* Los Angeles: Tomash, 1983.

Hawthorne, Nathaniel. "The Birthmark." In *The Centenary Edition of the Works of Nathaniel Hawthorne.* Vol. 10. Ed. William Charvat, Roy Harvey Pearce, Claude M. Simpson, and J. Donald Crowley. Columbus: Ohio State University Press, 1962–1985. 36–56.

Haynes, Roslynn D. *From Faust to Strangelove: Representations of the Scientist in Western Literature.* Baltimore: Johns Hopkins University Press, 1994.

Hecht, David K. "The Atomic Hero: Robert Oppenheimer and the Making of Scientific Icons in the Early Cold War." *Technology and Culture* 49.4 (2008): 943–966.

———. "Imagining the Bomb: Robert Oppenheimer, Nuclear Weapons, and the Assimilation of Technological Innovation." In *The Dark Side of Creativity.* Ed. David H. Cropley, Arthur J. Cropley, James C. Kaufman, and Mark A. Runco. Cambridge: Cambridge University Press, 2010. 72–90.

———. "A Nuclear Narrative: Robert Oppenheimer, Autobiography, and Public Authority." *Biography* 33.1 (2010): 167–184.

———. *Storytelling and Science: Rewriting Oppenheimer in the Nuclear Age.* Amherst: University of Massachusetts Press, 2015.

Heidegger, Martin. *The Question Concerning Technology, and Other Essays.* Trans. William Lovitt. New York: Garland, 1977.

Hein, Laura, and Mark Selden, eds. *Living with the Bomb: American and Japanese Cultural Conflicts in the Nuclear Age.* Armonk, NY: Sharpe, 1997.

Hendershot, Cyndy. "Mythical and Modern: Representations of Los Alamos." *Journal of the Southwest* 41.4 (1999): 477–485.

Henderson, Malcolm C. Review of *The Flying Trapeze: Three Crises for Physicists,* by J. Robert Oppenheimer. *Science* 148 (1965): 811.

Henrikson, Margot. *Dr. Strangelove's America: Society and Culture in the Atomic Age.* Berkeley: University of California Press, 1997.

Hickman, Jonathan, and Nick Pitarra. *The Manhattan Projects.* Vols. 1–5. Berkeley: Image Comics, 2015.

Hijiya, James A. "The Gita of J. Robert Oppenheimer." *Proceedings of the American Philological Society* 144.2 (2000): 123–167.

Hilgartner, Stephen. "The Sokal Affair in Context." *Science, Technology and Human Values* 22.4 (1997): 506–522.

Hoddeson, Lillian, Paul W. Henriksen, Roger A. Meade, and Catherine L. Westfall. *Critical Assembly: A Technical History of Los Alamos during the Oppenheimer Years, 1943–1945.* Cambridge: Cambridge University Press, 1993.

Holmes, Richard. "Biography: Inventing the Truth." In *The Art of Literary Biography.* Ed. John Batchelor. Oxford: Clarendon, 1995. 15–25.

Horkheimer, Max, and Theodor W. Adorno. *The Dialectic of Enlightenment.* 1947. London: Verso, 1979.

Howe, Ruth H., and Caroline L. Herzenberg. *Their Day in the Sun: Women of the Manhattan Project.* Philadelphia: Temple University Press, 1999.

Howells, Richard. "Heroes, Saints and Celebrities: The Photograph as Holy Relic." *Celebrity Studies* 2.2 (2011): 112–130.

Hughes, Jeff. *The Manhattan Project: Big Science and the Atom Bomb.* New York: Columbia University Press, 2002.

Hunner, Jon. *J. Robert Oppenheimer, the Cold War, and the Atomic West.* Norman: University of Oklahoma Press, 2009.

———. "Reinventing Los Alamos: Code Switching and Suburbia at America's Atomic City." In *Atomic Culture: How We Learned to Stop Worrying and Love the Bomb.* Ed. Scott C. Zeman and Michael A. Amundson. Boulder: University Press of Colorado, 2004. 33–48.

Hunter, Robert E. "Who's In Charge Here? Technology and the Presidency in *Fail-Safe* (1964) and *Colossus* (1970)." In *Hollywood's White House: The American Presidency in Film and History.* Ed. Peter C. Rollins and John E. O'Connor. Lexington: University Press of Kentucky, 2003. 206–222.

Hutcheon, Linda. *A Poetics of Postmodernism: History, Theory, Fiction.* New York: Routledge, 1988.

Hye, Allen E. *The Moral Dilemma of the Scientist in Modern Drama.* Lewiston, NY: Mellen, 1996.

Inglis, Fred. *A Short History of Celebrity.* Princeton, NJ: Princeton University Press, 2010.

Jacobs, Naomi. *The Character of Truth: Historical Figures in Contemporary Fiction.* Carbondale: Southern Illinois University Press, 1990.

Jameson, Fredric. *Postmodernism, or, The Cultural Logic of Late Capitalism.* Durham, NC: Duke University Press, 1991.

Jonasson, Jonas. *The 100-Year-Old Man Who Climbed Out the Window and Disappeared.* New York: Hyperion, 2012.

Jungk, Robert. *Brighter than a Thousand Suns: A Personal History of the Atomic Scientists.* 1956. Trans. James Cleugh. New York: Harcourt Brace Jovanovich, 1958.

Kaiser, David. "The Atomic Secret in Red Hands? American Suspicions of Theoretical Physicists during the Early Cold War." *Representations* 90 (2005): 28–60.

Kanon, Joseph. *Los Alamos*. New York: Dell, 1997.

———. "A Novel Idea of Oppenheimer." In *Oppenheimer and the Manhattan Project: Insights into J. Robert Oppenheimer, "Father of the Atomic Bomb."* Ed. Cynthia Kelly. Hackensack, NJ: World Scientific, 2006. 24–31.

Kaplan, Robert. *An Empire Wilderness: Travels into America's Future*. New York: Vintage, 1999.

Keller, Evelyn Fox. *Secrets of Life, Secrets of Death*. New York: Routledge, 1992.

Kellner, Hans. *Language and Historical Representation: Getting the Story Crooked*. Madison: University of Wisconsin Press, 1989.

Kipphardt, Heinar. *In the Matter of J. Robert Oppenheimer*. 1964. Trans. Ruth Speirs. New York: Hill and Wang, 1968.

Kirsch, Scott. "Watching the Bombs Go Off: Photography, Nuclear Landscapes, and Spectator Democracy." *Antipode* 29.3 (1997): 227–255.

Klages, Ellen. *The Green Glass Sea*. New York: Viking, 2006.

Knight, Peter. *Conspiracy Culture: From Kennedy to "The X-Files."* New York: Routledge, 2000.

Kreitzer, Carson. *The Love Song of J. Robert Oppenheimer*. Woodstock, IL: Dramatic, 2006.

Kunetka, James W. *Parting Shot*. New York: St. Martin's, 1991.

Labio, Catherine. "What's in a Name? The Academic Study of Comics and the 'Graphic Novel.'" *Cinema Journal* 50.3 (2011): 123–126.

Lamont, Lansing. *Day of Trinity*. New York: Atheneum, 1965.

Landy, Marcia. *Cinematic Uses of the Past*. Minneapolis: University of Minnesota Press, 1996.

Latour, Bruno. *We Have Never Been Modern*. Trans. Catherine Porter. Cambridge, MA: Harvard University Press, 1993.

Latour, Bruno, and Steve Woolgar. *Laboratory Life: The Social Construction of Scientific Facts*. Beverly Hills: Sage, 1979.

Laucht, Christoph. "An Extraordinary Achievement of the 'American Way'": Hollywood and the Americanization of the Making of the Atom Bomb in *Fat Man and Little Boy*." *European Journal of American Culture* 28.1 (2009): 41–56.

Laurence, William L. *Dawn over Zero*. New York: Knopf, 1946.

Lawton, John. *A Lily of the Field*. New York: Atlantic Monthly Press, 2010.

Learner, Howard. *White Paper on Science Museums*. Washington, DC: Center for Science in the Public Interest, 1979.

Lee, Martha F. *Conspiracy Rising: Conspiracy Thinking and American Public Life*. Santa Barbara, CA: Praeger, 2011.

Lejeune, Philippe. *On Autobiography*. Ed. Paul John Eakin. Trans. Katherine Leavy. Minneapolis: University of Minnesota Press, 1989.

Lifton, Robert Jay, and Richard Falk. *Indefensible Weapons*. New York: Basic, 1982.

Lifton, Robert Jay, and Eric Markusen. *The Genocidal Mentality: Nazi Holocaust and Nuclear Threat.* New York: Basic, 1990.

Lifton, Robert Jay, and Greg Mitchell. *Hiroshima in America: Fifty Years of Denial.* New York: Avon, 1995.

Linenthal, Edward, and Tom Engelhardt, eds. *History Wars: The "Enola Gay" and Other Battles for the American Past.* New York: Holt, 1996.

Lippit, Akira Mizuta. *Atomic Light (Shadow Optics).* Minneapolis: University of Minnesota Press, 2005.

Liste-Noya, José. "Introduction: America the Secret." In *American Secrets: The Politics and Poetics of Secrecy in the Literature and Culture of the United States.* Ed. Eduardo Barros-Grela and José Liste-Noya. Madison: Fairleigh Dickinson University Press, 2011. 1–13.

Los Alamos Historical Society. "Executive Summary of the Oppenheimer House Planning Symposium, Sept. 23–24, 2010." 2010.

———. "Historic Structure Report for the J. Robert Oppenheimer House." 2011.

Lukács, György. *The Historical Novel.* Trans. Hannah Mitchell and Stanley Mitchell. Lincoln: University of Nebraska Press, 1983.

Luke, Timothy W. *Museum Politics: Power Plays at the Exhibition.* Minneapolis: University of Minnesota Press, 2002.

Lyotard, Jean-François. *The Postmodern Condition: A Report on Knowledge.* 1979. Trans. Geoff Bennington and Brian Massumi. Manchester, UK: Manchester University Press, 1984.

Macdonald, Sharon. "Afterword: From War to Debate?" In *The Politics of Display: Museums, Science, Culture.* Ed. Sharon Macdonald. New York: Routledge, 1998. 229–235.

———. "Exhibitions of Power and Powers of Exhibition: An Introduction to the Politics of Display." In *The Politics of Display: Museums, Science, Culture.* Ed. Sharon Macdonald. New York: Routledge, 1998. 1–24.

———. Preface to *The Politics of Display: Museums, Science, Culture.* Ed. Sharon Macdonald. London and New York: Routledge, 1998. xi–xiii.

Malley, Marjorie C. *Radioactivity.* Oxford: Oxford University Press, 2011.

Mannix, Patrick. *The Rhetoric of Antinuclear Fiction: Persuasive Strategies in Novels and Films.* Lewisburg, PA: Bucknell University Press, 1992.

Marcus, Laura. *Auto/Biographical Discourses: Theory, Criticism, Practice.* Manchester, UK: Manchester University Press, 1994.

Mariner, Rosemary, and G. Kurt Piehler, eds. *The Atomic Bomb and American Society.* Knoxville: University of Tennessee Press, 2009.

Marshall, P. David. *Celebrity and Power: Fame in Contemporary Culture.* Rev. ed. Minneapolis: University of Minnesota Press, 2014.

Masco, Joseph. *The Nuclear Borderlands: The Manhattan Project in Post-Cold War New Mexico.* Princeton, NJ: Princeton University Press, 2006.

Masters, Dexter. *The Accident*. New York: Knopf, 1955.

Mayer, Robert. *The Search*. Garden City, NY: Doubleday, 1986.

McCloud, Scott. *Understanding Comics*. Northampton, MA: Kitchen Sink, 1993.

McHale, Brian. *Constructing Postmodernism*. New York: Routledge, 1992.

———. *Postmodernist Fiction*. New York: Methuen, 1987.

McKay, Daniel. "Tick-Tock, Tick-Tock, Tick-…: The Fizzles, Misfires, and Time Delays of Manhattan Project Novels." *Comparative American Studies* 12.3 (2014): 159–172.

McMahon, Thomas. *Principles of American Nuclear Chemistry: A Novel*. 1970. Chicago: University of Chicago Press, 2003.

McMillan, Priscilla. *The Ruin of J. Robert Oppenheimer and the Birth of the Modern Arms Race*. New York: Penguin, 2005.

Melley, Timothy. *The Covert Sphere: Secrecy, Fiction, and the National Security State*. Ithaca, NY: Cornell University Press, 2012.

———. *Empire of Conspiracy: The Culture of Paranoia in Postwar America*. Ithaca, NY: Cornell University Press, 2000.

Millar, Peter. *Stealing Thunder*. New York: Bloomsbury, 1999.

Miller, Walter M., Jr. *A Canticle for Leibowitz*. Philadelphia: Lippincott, 1959.

Millet, Lydia. *Oh Pure and Radiant Heart*. New York: Soft Skull, 2005.

Mitchell, W. J. T. "Word and Image." In *Critical Terms for Art History*. Ed. Robert S. Nelson and Richard Schiff. Chicago: University of Chicago Press, 1996. 47–57.

Monk, Ray. *Robert Oppenheimer: A Life inside the Center*. New York: Doubleday, 2012.

Morin, Edgar. *The Stars*. 1957. Trans. Richard Howard. Minneapolis: University of Minnesota Press, 2005.

Morrow, Bradford. *Trinity Fields*. New York: Viking, 1995.

Munslow, Alun. *Narrative and History*. New York: Palgrave Macmillan, 2007.

Munz, Peter. "The Historical Narrative." In *Companion to Historiography*. Ed. Michael Bentley. New York: Routledge, 1997. 851–872.

Nadel, Alan. *Containment Culture: American Narratives, Postmodernism, and the Atomic Age*. Durham, NC: Duke University Press, 1995.

Nelson, Joyce. *The Perfect Machine: TV in the Nuclear Age*. Toronto: Between the Lines, 1987.

Niven, Larry, and Jerry Pournelle. *Escape from Hell*. New York: Tor, 2009.

Nobile, Philip, ed. *Judgment at the Smithsonian: The Bombing of Hiroshima and Nagasaki*. New York: Marlowe, 1995.

Nye, David. *American Technological Sublime*. Cambridge, MA: MIT Press, 1994.

O'Donnell, Patrick. *Latent Destinies: Cultural Paranoia and Contemporary U.S. Narrative*. Durham, NC: Duke University Press, 2000.

Oppenheimer. Directed by Barry Davis. BBC, 1980.

Oppenheimer. By Tom Morton-Smith. Directed by Angus Jackson. Royal Shakespeare Company, Stratford-upon-Avon. January 15–March 7, 2015.

Oppenheimer, J. Robert. *Atom and Void.* Princeton, NJ: Princeton University Press, 1989.

———. *The Flying Trapeze: Three Crises for Physicists.* London: Oxford University Press, 1964.

———. *The Open Mind.* New York: Simon and Schuster, 1955.

———. *Science and the Common Understanding.* London: Oxford University Press, 1954.

———. *Uncommon Sense.* Ed. N. Metropolis, Gian-Carlo Rota, and David Sharp. Boston: Birkhäuser, 1984.

Ottaviani, Jim, Janine Johnston, Steve Lieber, Vince Locke, Bernie Mireault, and Jeff Parker. *Fallout: J. Robert Oppenheimer, Leo Szilard, and the Political Science of the Atomic Bomb.* Ann Arbor: G.T. Labs, 2001.

Paglen, Trevor. *Blank Spots on the Map: The Dark Geography of the Pentagon's Secret World.* New York: Dutton, 2009.

Parrish, Timothy. *From the Civil War to the Apocalypse: Postmodern History and American Fiction.* Amherst: University of Massachusetts Press, 2008.

Perrine, Toni A. *Film and the Nuclear Age: Representing Cultural Anxiety.* New York: Garland, 1998.

Pike, Sarah H. "Desert Goddesses and Apocalyptic Art: Making Sacred Space at the Burning Man Festival." In *God in the Details: American Religion in Popular Culture.* 2nd ed. Ed. Eric Michael Mazur and Kate McCarthy. New York: Routledge, 2010. 154–173.

Polenberg, Richard, ed. *In the Matter of J. Robert Oppenheimer: The Security Clearance Hearing.* Ithaca, NY: Cornell University Press, 2002.

Poole, Robert. *Earthrise: How Man First Saw the Earth.* New Haven: Yale University Press, 2008.

Porter, Jeff. *Oppenheimer Is Watching Me: A Memoir.* Iowa City: University of Iowa Press, 2007.

Preston, M. A. Preface to *The Flying Trapeze: Three Crises for Physicists* by J. Robert Oppenheimer. London: Oxford University Press, 1964. vii–viii.

Pynchon, Thomas. *Gravity's Rainbow.* New York: Viking, 1973.

Race for the Bomb. Directed by Jean-François Delassus. Intercontinental, 1987.

Rak, Julie. *Boom! Manufacturing Memoir for the Popular Market.* Waterloo, ON: Wilfrid Laurier University Press, 2013.

Ramirez, Bruno. *Inside the Historical Film.* Montreal: McGill-Queen's University Press, 2014.

Reeder, Carolyn. *The Secret Project Notebook.* Los Alamos, NM: Los Alamos Historical Society, 2005.

"Reith at 60." *The Archive Hour*, episode 1. Presented by Laurie Taylor. British Broadcasting Corporation. May 24, 2008.

Reynolds, Peter C. *Stealing Fire: The Atomic Bomb as Symbolic Body*. Palo Alto, CA: Iconic Anthropology, 1991.

Rhodes, Richard. *Dark Sun: The Making of the Hydrogen Bomb*. New York: Simon and Schuster, 1996.

———. *The Making of the Atomic Bomb*. 1986. New York: Simon and Schuster, 2012.

Río, David. "The Desert as a National Sacrifice Zone: The Nuclear Controversy in Nevada Fiction." In *American Secrets: The Politics and Poetics of Secrecy in the Literature and Culture of the United States*. Ed. Eduardo Barros-Grela and José Liste-Noya. Madison, NJ: Fairleigh Dickinson University Press, 2011. 61–72.

Rojek, Chris. *Celebrity*. London: Reaktion, 2001.

Rosen, Philip. *Change Mummified: Cinema, Historicity, Theory*. Minneapolis: University of Minnesota Press, 2001.

Rosenstone, Robert A., ed. *Revisioning History: Film and the Construction of a New Past*. Princeton, NJ: Princeton University Press, 1995.

Rosenthal, Peggy. "The Nuclear Mushroom Cloud as Cultural Image." *American Literary History* 3.1 (1991): 63–92.

Ross, Andrew, ed. *Science Wars*. Durham, NC: Duke University Press, 1996.

Ruthven, Ken K. *Nuclear Criticism*. Carlton: Melbourne University Press, 1993.

Said, Edward. *Orientalism*. New York: Vintage, 1978.

Salmon, E. T. Foreword to *The Flying Trapeze: Three Crises for Physicists* by J. Robert Oppenheimer. London: Oxford University Press, 1964. v–vi.

Savage, Kirk. *Monument Wars: Washington, D.C., The National Mall, and the Transformation of the Memorial Landscape*. Berkeley: University of California Press, 2009.

Scheibach, Michael. *Atomic Narrative and American Youth: Coming of Age with the Atom, 1945–1955*. Jefferson, NC: McFarland, 2003.

Schell, Jonathan. *The Seventh Decade: The New Shape of Nuclear Danger*. New York: Metropolitan, 2007.

Scherer, Glenn, and Marty Fletcher. *J. Robert Oppenheimer: The Brain Behind the Bomb*. Berkeley Heights, NJ: MyReportLinks.com, 2007.

Schiappa, Edward. "The Rhetoric of Nukespeak." *Communication Monographs* 56 (1989): 253–272.

Schickel, Richard. *Intimate Strangers: The Culture of Celebrity*. Garden City, NY: Doubleday, 1985.

Schlaeger, Jürgen. "Biography: Cult as Culture." In *The Art of Literary Biography*. Ed. John Batchelor. Oxford: Clarendon, 1995. 57–71.

Schlosser, Eric. *Command and Control: Nuclear Weapons, the Damascus Accident, and the Illusion of Safety*. New York: Penguin, 2013.

Scholes, Robert. *The Fabulators*. New York: Oxford University Press, 1967.

Schüll, Natasha Dow. "Oasis/Mirage: Fantasies of Nature in Las Vegas." In *From Virgin Land to Disney World: Nature and Its Discontents in the USA of Yesterday and Today*. Ed. Bernd Herzogenrath. Amsterdam: Rodopi, 2001. 377–402.

Schumway, David R. "The Star System in Literary Studies." *PMLA* 112.1 (1997): 85–100.

Schweber, Silvan S. *In the Shadow of the Bomb: Bethe, Oppenheimer, and the Moral Responsibility of the Scientist*. Princeton, NJ: Princeton University Press, 2000.

Schwenger, Peter. *Letter Bomb: Nuclear Holocaust and the Exploding Word*. Baltimore: Johns Hopkins University Press, 1992.

Scott, Alison M., and Christopher D. Geist, eds. *The Writing on the Cloud: American Culture Confronts the Atomic Bomb*. Lanham, MD: University Press of America, 1997.

Seidel, Robert. "Books on the Bomb." *Isis* 81.3 (1990): 519–537.

Serber, Robert, and Robert Crease. *Peace and War: Reminiscences of a Life on the Frontiers of Science*. New York: Columbia University Press, 1998.

Shaheen, Jack, ed. *Nuclear War Films*. Carbondale: Southern Illinois University Press, 1978.

Shapiro, Jerome. *Atomic Bomb Cinema*. New York: Routledge, 2001.

Sheinkin, Steve. *Bomb: The Race to Build and Steal the World's Most Dangerous Weapon*. New York: Roaring Brook, 2012.

Shelley, Mary. *Frankenstein*. Ed. J. Paul Hunter. 2nd ed. New York: Norton, 1996.

Shepherd-Barr, Kirsten. *Science on Stage: From "Doctor Faustus" to "Copenhagen."* Princeton, NJ: Princeton University Press, 2006.

Sherman, Michael. "Oppenheimer: What a Trouble-Maker!" *The Public Historian* 4.4 (1982): 97–117.

Shortland, Michael, and Richard R. Yeo, eds. *Telling Lives: Essays on Scientific Biography*. Cambridge: Cambridge University Press, 1996.

Silman, Roberta. *Beginning the World Again*. New York: Viking, 1990.

Sinclair, Andrew. "Vivat alius ergo sum." In *The Troubled Face of Biography*. Ed. Eric Homberger and John Charmeley. New York: St. Martin's, 1988. 123–130.

Slotkin, Richard. *Regeneration through Violence*. Middletown, CT: Wesleyan University Press, 1973.

Smith, Alice Kimball, and Charles Weiner, eds. *Robert Oppenheimer: Letters and Recollections*. Cambridge, MA: Harvard University Press, 1980.

Smith, Jeff. *Unthinking the Unthinkable: Nuclear Weapons and Western Culture*. Bloomington: Indiana University Press, 1989.

Smith, Martin Cruz. *Stallion Gate*. New York: Random House, 1986.

Snow, C. P. *The Two Cultures: And a Second Look*. Cambridge: Cambridge University Press, 1963.

Söderqvist, Thomas. *The History and Poetics of Scientific Biography*. Aldershot, UK: Ashgate, 2007.

Sokal, Alan D. "Transgressing the Boundaries: Towards a Transformative Hermeneutics of Quantum Gravity." *Social Text* 46/47 (1996): 217–252.

Sokal, Alan D., and Jean Bricmont. *Fashionable Nonsense: Postmodern Intellectuals' Abuse of Science*. New York: Picador, 1998.

Solomon, J. Fisher. *Discourse and Reference in the Nuclear Age*. Norman: University of Oklahoma Press, 1988.

Sprod, Liam. *Nuclear Futurism: The Work of Art in the Age of Remainderless Destruction*. Alresford, UK: Zero, 2012.

Stam, Robert. *Subversive Pleasures: Bakhtin, Cultural Criticism and Film*. Baltimore: Johns Hopkins University Press, 1989.

Steenberg, N. R. F. Review of *The Flying Trapeze: Three Crises for Physicists*, by J. Robert Oppenheimer. *International Journal* 20.2 (1965): 285.

Stone, Albert E. *Literary Aftershocks: American Writers, Readers, and the Bomb*. New York: Twayne, 1994.

Sturken, Marita. "Reenactment, Fantasy, and the Paranoia of History: Oliver Stone's Documentaries." *Spectator* 20.1 (2000): 23–38.

Szasz. Ferenc Morton. *The Day the Sun Rose Twice: The Story of the Trinity Site Nuclear Explosion, July 16, 1945*. Albuquerque: University of New Mexico Press, 1984.

Taylor, Bryan C. "'Fat Man and Little Boy': The Cinematic Representation of Interests in Nuclear Weapons Organization." *Critical Studies in Mass Communication* 10.4 (1993): 367–394.

———. "Nuclear Pictures and Metapictures." In *National Imaginaries, American Identities: The Cultural Work of American Iconography*. Ed. Larry J. Reynolds and Gordon Hutner. Princeton, NJ: Princeton University Press, 2000. 52–82.

———. "'Our Bruised Arms Hung Up as Monuments': Nuclear Iconography in Post-Cold War Culture." *Critical Studies in Media Communications* 20.1 (2003): 1–34.

———. "The Politics of the Nuclear Text: Reading Robert Oppenheimer's *Letters and Recollections*." *Quarterly Journal of Speech* 78.4 (1992): 429–449.

———. "Register of the Repressed: Women's Voice and Body in the Nuclear Weapons Organization." *Quarterly Journal of Speech* 79.3 (1993): 267–285.

———. "*Reminiscences of Los Alamos*: Narrative, Critical Theory, and the Organizational Subject." *Western Journal of Speech and Communication* 54.3 (1990): 395–419.

———. "Revis(it)ing Nuclear History: Narrative Conflict at the Bradbury Science Museum." *Studies in Cultures, Organizations and Societies* 3.1 (1997): 119–145.

Tennyson, Alfred, Lord. "Lucretius." In *The Poems of Tennyson*. Ed. Christopher Ricks. Vol. 2. Berkeley: University of California Press, 1987. 707–721.

Thackara, James. *America's Children*. London: Chatto and Windus, 1984.

Thorpe, Charles. *Oppenheimer: The Tragic Intellect*. Chicago: University of Chicago Press, 2006.

———. "Violence and the Scientific Vocation." *Theory, Culture, and Society* 21.3 (2004): 59–84.

Thorpe, Charles, and Steven Shapin, "Who Was J. Robert Oppenheimer? Charisma and Complex Organization." *Social Studies of Science* 30 (2000): 545–90.

Titus, A. Constandina. *Bombs in the Backyard: Atomic Testing and American Politics*. 1986. 2nd ed. Reno: University of Nevada Press, 2001.

———. "The Mushroom Cloud as Kitsch." In *Atomic Culture: How We Learned to Stop Worrying and Love the Bomb*. Ed. Scott C. Zeman and Michael A. Amundson. Boulder: University Press of Colorado, 2004. 101–123.

Toth, Bill D. "Commercial Fiction as Toxic Discourse Matrix: Martin Cruz Smith's *Stallion Gate*." Conference presentation, University of Kansas. Lawrence, KS. May 31, 2013.

Treat, John Whittier. *Writing Ground Zero: Japanese Literature and the Atomic Bomb*. Chicago: University of Chicago Press, 1995.

Trenn, Thaddeus J. Review of *Project Y: The Los Alamos Story*, by David Hawkins, Edith C. Truslow, and Ralph C. Smith. *Technology and Culture* 26.3 (1985): 672–674.

"The Trials of J. Robert Oppenheimer." *American Experience*. Directed by David Grubin. PBS, 2009.

Vanderbilt, Tom. *Survival City: Adventures among the Ruins of Atomic America*. New York: Princeton Architectural Press, 2002.

Vidal, Gore. *The Smithsonian Institution*. New York: Random House, 1998.

Virilio, Paul. *War and Cinema: The Logistics of Perception*. 1984. Trans. Patrick Camiller. New York: Verso, 1989.

Walsh, Lynda. *Scientists as Prophets: A Rhetorical Genealogy*. Oxford: Oxford University Press, 2013.

Wasson, R. Gordon. *The Wondrous Mushroom: Mycolatry in Mesoamerica*. New York: McGraw-Hill, 1980.

Wasson, R. Gordon, and Valentina Pavlovna Wasson. *Mushrooms, Russia and History*. New York: Pantheon, 1957.

Waters, Frank. *The Woman at Otowi Crossing*. 1966. Rev. ed. Athens, OH: Swallow, 1987.

Waugh, Patricia. *Metafiction: The Theory and Practice of Self-Conscious Fiction*. New York: Routledge, 1984.

Weart, Spencer R. *Nuclear Fear: A History of Images*. Cambridge, MA: Harvard University Press, 2012.

White, E .B. *The Wild Flag: Editorials from the "New Yorker" on Federal World Government and Other Matters*. Boston: Houghton Mifflin, 1946.

White, Hayden. *The Content of the Form*. Baltimore: Johns Hopkins University Press, 1987.

———. *Metahistory: The Historical Imagination in Nineteenth-Century Europe*. Baltimore: Johns Hopkins University Press, 1973.

Whitlock, Gillian. "Autographies: The Seeing 'I' of the Comics." *Modern Fiction Studies* 52.4 (2006): 965–979.

Wiener, Jon. *How We Forgot the Cold War: A Historical Journey across America*. Berkeley: University of California Press, 2012.

Williams, Paul. *Race, Ethnicity and Nuclear War: Representations of Nuclear Weapons and Post-Apocalyptic Worlds*. Liverpool: Liverpool University Press, 2011.

Willis, Martin T. "Edison as Time Traveler: H. G. Wells's Inspiration for His First Scientific Character." *Science Fiction Studies* 26.2 (1999): 284–294.

Wilson, Rob. "Producing American Selves: The Form of American Biography." *Contesting the Subject: Essays in the Postmodern Theory and Practice of Biography and Biographical Criticism*. Ed. William H. Epstein. West Lafayette, IN: Purdue University Press, 1991. 167–192.

Wilson, Robert R. Review of *Brighter than a Thousand Suns*, by Robert Jungk. *Scientific American* 199.6 (1958): 145–146, 148–149.

Winkler, Allan M. *Life under a Cloud: American Anxiety about the Atom*. Urbana: University of Illinois Press, 1999.

Wiseman, Thomas. *Savage Day*. New York: Delacorte, 1981.

Wray, Matt. "A Blast from the Past: Preserving and Interpreting the Atomic Age." *American Quarterly* 58.2 (2006): 467–483.

Wyden, Peter H. *Day One: Hiroshima and After*. New York: Simon and Schuster, 1984.

Yoneyama, Lisa. *Hiroshima Traces: Time, Space, and the Dialectics of Memory*. Berkeley: University of California Press, 1999.

Young, Robert M. "Darwin and the Genre of Biography." *One Culture: Essays in Science and Literature*. Ed. George Levine. Madison: University of Wisconsin Press, 1987. 203–224.

Zeman, Scott C., and Michael A. Amundson, eds. *Atomic Culture: How We Learned to Stop Worrying and Love the Bomb*. Boulder: University Press of Colorado, 2004.

Zindel, Paul. *The Gadget*. New York: HarperCollins, 2001.

INDEX